THE RESILIENCE OF INDIGENOUS RELIGION

The Resilience of Indigenous Religion

A STRUGGLE FOR SURVIVAL OF TINGKAO RAGWANG CHAPRIAK IN MANIPUR

KAMEI SAMSON

MANOHAR
2022

First published 2022

ISBN 978-93-94262-44-7

Published by
Ajay Jain *for*
Manohar Publishers & Distributors
4753/23 Ansari Road, Daryaganj
New Delhi 110002

Typeset by
Ravi Shanker
Delhi 110095

Printed at
Replika Press Pvt. Ltd.

Contents

Acknowledgements

This book could see the light of publication primarily because of the Indian Council of Social Science Research (New Delhi). The conception of this book, though it happened sometime in 2016, was on the day I was awarded a postdoctoral fellowship for this work by the ICSSR, New Delhi for the period 2017-19. I acknowledge and thank the ICSSR for its invaluable support rendered to me for the production of this work. I also express my sincere gratitude to Manipur University that provided me with the invaluable opportunity to pursue my postdoctoral work under its esteemed Department of Anthropology. My heartfelt gratitude to Prof MC Arun of the Department of Anthropology who helped me towards the successful completion of the work despite his many responsibilities as the Head of the Department.

I cannot thank Dr Hanjabam Sukhdeba Sharma, Faculty in the Department of Social Work, IGNTU (Manipur Campus), enough for his invaluable advice.

I also thank all those elders and youth who tolerated my half-baked knowledge about Tingkao Ragwang Chapriak and helped me gain some more from each of them. I admire and also thank the eloquence of Mr Chaoba Kamson, General-Secretary of Tingkao Ragwang Chapriak (Assam, Manipur & Nagaland). His perennial willingness to talk about Tingkao Ragwang Chapriak displayed his confidence in his faith and identity and made our conversations meaningful. Mr Khomeimacha Kamson was invariably ready to quench my thirst for knowledge about the Rongmei people. His insight into village traditional institutions and religion helped me learn and unlearn many aspects of human society in general. I also thank my friend John Gaingamlung Gangmei, Faculty in the Department of Social Work, Rajiv Gandhi University, Itanagar whose invariable prompt willingness to drag me along with him for his PhD data collection always unfolded a priceless opportunity in the field for me to learn about my people.

My family never failed to energise the human side of my being. They always helped me to remain connected with my personal life from where I drew immense moral strength to continue with my academic endeavour.

Prayagraj, Uttar Pradesh KAMEI SAMSON
30 May 2022

Preface

The book is a sociological study of the resilience of Tingkao Ragwang Chapriak (TRC)—the indigenous religion of the Rongmei people of Manipur. It examines the underlying factors contributing towards the ability of the adherents of Tingkao Ragwang Chapriak to continue with their religion despite stigmatisation, conversion and persecution by sections of Christians. The Tingkao Ragwang Chapriak among the Rongmei people in Manipur valley presents a plethora of opportunities for a sociological study of religion. The social and political functions of religion, especially in the context of a high degree of pluralism in society, are illuminated in this study. The book is intended to serve the academic interests of researchers working on indigenous religions. The readership can also include researchers and teachers working within an interdisciplinary domain as besides qualitative and quantitative methods both sociological and social-psychological theories are being used in this work.

The art of not writing is closely linked among the Rongmei people with the art of oral traditions rooted in their belief systems. The art of oral traditions infuses a greater degree of legitimacy in the domain of religion as writing is invariably the art of mankind and not divine. Nevertheless, contemporary accounts of the Rongmei people, including their belief systems are beginning to witness comfort with scripts. The Bengali script used by the neighbouring Meetei group proffers itself as a convenient means towards what may be called textual belief. This journey from oral beliefs to textual beliefs is not without the narratives of conflict and assimilation at various levels of their interactions. The quantitative and qualitative changes across eras that the Rongmei people underwent in their beliefs and practices, underscore the social, historical and political dimensions of religions. This raises a question on the issue of the pristine state of religion. For how long can religion be guarded against any external influence? Does change in belief system tantamount to dwindling credibility of its divinity?

Methodologically speaking, the emphasis is on theoretical and methodological triangulation. Both social change theory and social identity theory are used to understand the resilience of the indigenous faith of the Rongmei people amidst dominant Hindus and tribal Christians. It is observed that the idea of change is indispensable in understanding the resilience of an indigenous faith despite the commonly held belief in the essentiality of primordiality in religion. The socio-political and economic changes influence the religion of the indigenous people. Changes are witnessed even in their beliefs apart from changes in ritualistic practices.

The Rongmei people belong to the Zeliangrong group who are settled in the contiguous area of Assam, Manipur and Nagaland. Religious reformations have been witnessed since the days of Jadonang Malangmei who fought against the British in the 1920s. Since the days of the British when Christian missionaries were actively engaged in proselytisation in tribal areas, the indigenous faith of the Rongmei people has constantly been under attacks, especially by the Christians and occasionally by the Hindus. The reformations in religion were a strategy adopted by both Jadonang Malangmei and Rani Gaidinliu during the colonial days to effectively organise the people against the colonial force. This book also reflects the contemporary relevance of the legacies of their religious movements. Thus, the book is also an examination of the continuity between the past and the present religious movements with complex underlying factors contributing to the resilience of an indigenous religion. The complexity of the phenomenon consequently demands an interdisciplinary approach to capture the underlying dynamics of religion.

Reformations continued even after independence to rejuvenate the indigenous faith against the onslaught of condemnation and proselytisation. In this process of reformations, the prevalent oral traditions and oral histories on their collective identity played a crucial role in fomenting a collective memory of the past and a collective vision. Such memories with contemporary lived experiences marked by shared cultural commonalities allow for collective identification. The Rongmei people engage in the social identification process in the context of their collective memories about their collective identity. Certain internal and external factors build the resilience of Tingkao Ragwang Chapriak and makc it appealing to their emerging youths and also respectable to the outsiders–both friends and foes.

The reformations within the belief systems of Rongmei people that influenced partially even the dynamics of the village polity are discussed. Customs and traditions are often intended to be retained in their pristine form. The strength of the claim of the elders to the originality of the traditional institutions and their associated practices reinforces the credibility of such institutions and practices. However, change is the only constant reality in society. Also, change is very much a reality of social systems. The impacts of TRC's reformation upon the traditional village institutions, especially in the realms of beliefs and religious practices, are areas of continued sociological research. The believers of TRC wish to convey a message to their fellow believers and others who are not within TRC that every belief and practice of TRC is primordial. The atavistic impression is well managed among the TRC groups. There is a sense of pride among the followers of TRC for being able to continue to follow their ancestral paths of beliefs and practices. Despite the contested and supposedly a new name of even their God; new ways of worship; disowning of certain old rituals; endeavour towards the religious text; idols (not idolatry) and many other organised strategies of mobilisation that cut across the traditional village frontiers TRC continues to claim to be primordial in the sense of being the same as their ancestral beliefs and practices.

The Rongmei people following Tingkao Ragwang Chapriak, a reformed religion, are seen to be not shying away from changes in their religious beliefs and practices. Interestingly, however, despite all the reformations consciously heralded by the Rongmei people of Tingkao Ragwang Chapriak the idea of primordiality in the sense of unchanging is a sincere atavism. This brings in scope for furthering discourse on the concept of primordiality within the domain of religion. The author discusses the concept of primordiality by deviating from the conventional conception of it as something always in existence without any change. The idea of change and primordiality are interrelated to theorise the claim of primordiality with an element of a reformation in a discourse on religion. Thus, primordiality agrees with the phenomenon of reformation or change in this work. This possibility of harmony between primordiality and reformation within religion is analysed within the theoretical framework of social change. Their identification with their ancestral religion is seen to be crucial in their claim of primordiality of their reformed religion. Such identification with their ancestral religion is closely interlinked with identification with their collective ancestral identity. This is illuminated with the help of social identity theory.

Such a complex phenomenon witnessed among a small community of Manipur engendered a keen interest in one to examine both as an outsider in term of religious affiliation and as an insider in term of the cultural sameness, I share with the followers of Tingkao Ragwang Chapriak. As a researcher, it is my insatiable thirst for knowledge on identity that propelled my endeavour towards this little initiative towards understanding the Rongmei people and their religion within an interdisciplinary paradigm.

Prayagraj, Uttar Pradesh KAMEI SAMSON
30 May 2022

CHAPTER 1

Introduction

Understanding religions may be considered a pre-requisite task towards understanding any society. This may be said because of the prominence that religions occupied in the distant past and even in contemporary societies. True, there is unsettled speculation about whether religion preceded society or society engendered religion. This is so because there is also a belief in God—the epicentre of religion according to this book—as the cause of everything, including religion and society. In this sense, society may be perceived as having conceived in the womb of religion. Anthropologists claim the origin of religion to be coinciding with the emergence of anatomically modern humans during the Upper Paleolithic (Peoples, Duda and Marlowe 2016: 262). And the origin of anatomically modern humans is traced to 43,000–42,000 calendar years before the present (Higham et al. 2011: 521). Therefore, religion cannot be the cause of human society. The Homo Sapiens or the Neanderthals who came much before the anatomically modern humans were very much social and had their societies. When religion is taken to be essentially a result of human interactions and thus a sub-set of society or culture as witnessed in the definition of culture given by Edward B. Tylor (1958: 1) the causative factor of religion may be logically traced to human society. Such a debate is beside the contentious debate on the indispensability and expendability of Gods entity within the phenomenon and institution of religion. Tylor prefers to present the 'minimum definition of Religion' as 'the belief in Spiritual Beings' (1871: 424). A greater debate is on God's existence itself.

Religion has generally been seen as a boon to human society. However, Bernard Bosanquet speaks of religion as the 'knot, the centre, of all human difficulties' (1920: vi). Despite the prominence of religion in personal and social lives, the study of religion has not been met with equal enthusiasm across eras and disciplines. It has been observed during the socialist era that the study of religion was difficult and sometimes even impossible to be carried out (Rogers 2005: 5). Nevertheless, 'science of religion' or 'religiology' (Kishimoto 1967: 81), is gradually assuming prominence in academics. Religion is widespread in social norms, morals, customary practices, social institutions, modern governance, business, medicines and even among rocket scientists. However, its scientific study is not as proliferating as its omnipresence. Perhaps because of its little prospects in conventional job markets, study of religion has been and is not likely to be as prominent as other themes. A study of religion for a job is, however, not rudimentary. A trend is observed in which some students and scholars of religion flock to religious institutions with a moderately promising source of livelihood. The mushrooming Christian theological colleges and institutions even in a Hindu dominant India bear proof of this cursory casual observation.

Religion, according to Gavin Flood's conception, is '. . . of fundamental public concern . . . central to global politics, cultural or identity politics, ethics, and the socio-economic processes of late modernity' (1999, cited in Levene 2006: 60). This statement captures the omnipresence of the significant influence of religions despite the marvellous advances in science and technology and positivism in social sciences. It also illuminates the relevance of religions beyond personal affairs and extending even to socio-economic and political realms. Such conception of religion allows for an interdisciplinary approach to its study.

Samuel P. Huntington is of the view that the conflicts in the future would be based on the clash of cultures of diverse civilisations and they will be neither economic nor ideological (1997, cited in Rockmore 2006: 117). Huntington's postulation on the clash of civilisations places the study of religions in a crucial position because an understanding of a culture without delving into its corresponding religion would be shallow. Contemporary developments in geopolitics also reflect the elements of religion as underlying currents in both flash and sustained conflicts across nations and cultures. Be it in politics, economy, developmental discourse, governmentality, health services, education, food habits, etc., we witness the gyrating influences of religion that impact the lives of the people.

Despite the sweeping influence of religion, a study of the same was seen to decline in the early parts of the nineteenth century, primarily due to works of Sigmund Freud, Friedrich Nietzsche, Karl Marx, and Charles Darwin, who systematically cast doubts on the understanding of reality from a religious point of view (Schmalzbauer and Mahoney 2008: 16). Such influence even led to a clamour for a separation of religion and state. Secularism is conventionally viewed as a separation of state and religion. However, the United States of America, despite its historical trajectory of a struggle for independence with an effort to separate religion and politics, is now proud of a Constitution which is influenced by Christianity (Rockmore 2006: 121). On 30 July 1956, President Dwight D. Eisenhower appended his signature on the law with a declaration of 'In God We Trust' as the official motto of the United States and its currency also bears the words 'In God we trust'.[1] This impeccably points to a belief in God or the centrality of religion in a nation or a state despite the conventional understanding of secularism in the sense of the separation of state and religion. The kind of secularism conventionally understood in India, according to Shashi Tharoor, is a state in which the state equally and positively attends to the welfare of all the religions in India (2018).

Besides some social scientists such as Lester Ward, academic organisations like the American Sociological Society, and philanthropists like Andrew Carnegie played their roles in pushing religion far from the frontiers of the academic domain (Schmalzbauer and Mahoney 2008: 17). But sometime in the 1990s, there was a resurgence of interests in a study of religion with diverse backgrounds such as 'believers and skeptics, insiders and outsiders, those who integrate faith and scholarship, and those who emphasise the separation of religious values from academic research' and they studied religion 'purely as an object of study' (ibid.: 17). The pace of growth of the study of religion in academics is thus inconsistent and it was attempted by theists, atheists and agnostics with varying intentions and interests. Religions may not be the heart and soul for atheists or agnostics but religion as a domain of academic pursuit is dear to them too.

The study of religion is context-specific. Besides language and religion, the political environment influences the course of academic activities across the globe (Antes, Geertz and Warne 2004: 3). What has already been obsolete in the western countries suddenly became popular in the former communist countries after the downfall of the communist regime in Europe (ibid.: 2). The modern states also determine the course of religions in their favour. Studies of religions may also be influenced by conceptual limitations. Scholars are bound to face certain conceptual dilemmas while studying certain religions on account of the diverse beliefs and practices, and varying socio-economic and political establishments with political ideologies that do not agree with the religious ideologies. Theological terms which were necessities in Christendom were found to be insufficient in understanding other faiths (Martineau 1888: 2). Often heaven and hell are like two sides of the same coin in many belief systems. However, some belief systems do not have a concept of hell. The concept of hell is absent among the Champa group of Tingkao Ragwang Kariak (TRK) and in the belief system of Tingkao Ragwang Chapriak (TRC) of the Zeliangrong people (Gangmei 2014: 6). Nevertheless, the existence of a human being is sometimes explained meaningfully around these concepts. Similarly, the idea of God which is supposedly the most essential in almost every belief system, is absent in Buddhism which is, though a belief system, not considered to be a religion but 'nearly resembling psychotherapy' (Watts 1959, cited in Aich 2013). Every religion is a belief system but every belief system is not a religion. Interestingly, even Hinduism may be and may not be a religion (Tharoor 2018: 9-10). The idea of God is also absent in certain variants of Hinduism! (ibid.: 9). The concept of trinity and the reverence towards the divine motherhood of Mary within the Catholic Church sometimes barricades a scope for confraternity among various Christian denominations. This requires one to adopt different approaches even to understand Christianity with diverse theologies around the same God and for the same destiny of the souls.

Religious studies by European scholars on the religions of India may be said to have begun on wrong footings. Many of them initially ventured into the field of Indo-European philology and in their endeavour to study Sanskrit they encountered the religious philosophies as most of the Sanskrit literature is on religions (Kumar 2004: 136). The studies of religions in India by Europeans were, therefore, an offshoot of the philology of Sanskrit. Studies on religions of India were immensely supplemented by the translation of Sanskrit texts into English by Max Muller, witnessed during the beginning of the nineteenth century (ibid.: 136). It must also be noted that the works of Indo-European philologists were to achieve the goals of educating the Christian missionaries about the religions and cultures of the people and also to inform the colonial administrators and thus facilitate the process of colonisation (ibid.: 137). Thus, it may be concluded that philology led the European scholars to encounter religions in India and this forms the basis of Indology and 'religiology'. The study of Indian societies was deeply rooted in the analysis of religious beliefs and practices and inter-religion relationships. One can certainly doubt the methodological preparedness of European scholars to study religions in India.

In India, the academic pursuit of religion is still moderate. Most universities in India are yet to open their doors to 'religiology'. Religions are studied in a very sectarian manner. Pratap Kumar presents a glimpse of a limited scope of religious studies in the Indian context (2004: 128). It is observed that some prominent religions are studied in places where their are adherents in a majority. Thus, according to Kumar, we find Hinduism being studied in Benares Hindu University and few other universities; Islamic studies sustain well in Aligarh Muslim University and Osmania University; Patiala University houses the Sikhism studies and Christianity is studied in many seminaries and theological institutions with an exception of a chair in Christianity in Mysore University. Most Indian universities, according to Pratap Kumar, are found to study religions as philosophy and logic and not as a religion per se. Pratap Kumar contends that some religions of the tribal people are now beginning to be studied by their intelligentsia primarily confined within the discipline of social/cultural anthropology (ibid.: 128). In India, interests in religion are growing and religious studies penetrate other fields of studies such as journalism, economics, business administration, political science, literature, media and even film studies (ibid.: 128). This is a positive growth in the studies of religions.

It must be acknowledged that there remains a certain degree of difference between western scholars and south Asian scholars when it comes to religious studies. Unlike western scholars, as observed by Pratap Kumar, south Asian scholars are not able to sustain a secular outlook towards religion in religious studies (2004: 133). This certainly renders the methodological basis of the Asian religious scholars tenuous. South Asian scholars, according to Kumar, get very personal with religion and their religious backgrounds influence the academic discourse on religion. The scope for bias is ample within south Asian religious studies.

For Indian social scientists, religion is a 'way of life' (ibid.: 133). Even one of the greatest scientists of the world C.V. Raman is known to be not an atheist. C.V. Raman once wrote,

> it is my earnest desire to bring into existence a centre of scientific research worthy of our ancient country where the keenest intellects of our land can probe into the mysteries of the Universe and by so doing help us to appreciate the transcendent Power that guides its activities. This aim can only be achieved if by His Divine Grace, all lovers of our Country see their way to help the cause (Pisharoty 1982: 59).

A man of such stature for whom scientific research has been a part of his life acknowledging and invoking the divine intervention of 'His Divine Grace' proves the deeply seated transcendent power of religion even within its widely acclaimed greatest foe, science.

The relevance of religion is seen even in the efforts of leaders wielding immense political power. A Union Minister of the Government of India proposed *Bhagwat Gita*, one of the religious texts of Hinduism, to be made 'Rashtriya Granth' (national scripture).[2] A Chief Minister of one of the Indian states claimed the superiority of the *Bhagwat Gita* over the Indian Constitution.[3] Interestingly, even scientific institutions such as the Archaeological Survey of India and the Geological Survey of India were reportedly found to be influenced by a dream of a seer who saw gold hidden under the earth and they reportedly went to the extent of digging the earth in search of the dream-gold.[4] The significance and relevance of religion among space scientists, if not space science in itself, is not a far-fetched example. The scientists in the Indian Space Research Organisation reportedly invoked the blessing of *Lord Balaji* at Tirupati in Andhra Pradesh before every space mission and its former chief unequivocally stated that one could not take chance with God and poison (*Times of India* 2013).[5] In India, the idea of secularism which is conventionally understood as the separation of religion and state is, according to Shashi Tharoor, a 'state that was equally indulgent of all religious groups, and favoured none' (2018: 200). Thus, India is free from any religion being the state religion but administratively and dutifully help minority religious institutions.

Another instance of the contemporary relevance of religion is the Karnataka political scenario in the aftermath of the 2018 General Assembly Elections. The leader of one of the parties that emerged as the single largest party reportedly consulted an astrologer to ascertain the auspicious time for the swearing-in ceremony.[6] Such is the extent of the significance of religion in the lives of people, irrespective of their intellectual attainment. Any issue on religion is so sensitive and relates with a personal conscience that even studies of religions in the Indian context are found to be deprived of critical nature and most of them are 'merely (good) descriptive studies' (Kumar 2004: 138). Many of the traditional dogmas and religious sanctions are still firm and continue to exercise control over individual minds and societies.

Religion has existed since time immemorial[7] in different forms and through different eras withstanding the ever-growing forces of science and technology and the market-driven economy. Many belief systems of small communities have continued to exist despite the forces of science and technology, globalisation, proselytisation, Sanskritisation, Hinduisation and even persecution. However, many belief systems of small groups continue to face criticism from the supposedly dominant belief systems. A hierarchy is being created for different belief systems in which the belief systems of the numerically dominant groups are invariably made to be viewed as superior. The belief system of a particular group numerically dominant in a certain place may be pushed to a level lower than the belief system of a numerically lesser group if the religion of the latter group represents a major religion in a larger national or global context. The belief systems of smaller groups and especially of the tribal people are relegated as mere superstitious practices or at the most categorised as a sub-group of the dominant religious group. Often their belief systems are disrespectfully categorised as cult or animism. Nevertheless, they persist against all odds.

Religions are also graded according to the degree of 'simplicity and austerity' and the higher the level of austerity and simplicity, the higher or better the position of the religion (Bousset 1907: 27). This methodology of the gradation of religions seems irrelevant given the contemporary religious groups with growing wealth in their possession. The budgets of Venkatachalapathi temple in Tirumalai at Tirupati at $392 million for 2015-16 and the Vatican of Rome at $274 million for the same year (Tharoor 2018: 41) should have put them far behind several known and even unknown religions or stigmatised cults. One knows where they stand. If one were to arrange the hierarchy of religions by this methodology of austerity and simplicity, the belief systems of the tribal people may be adjudicated to higher positions with greater reverence. But looking at the bare facts of conversion among the tribal people and severe criticism against their religions one may infer the demeaned position of the tribal belief systems despite their 'simplicity and austerity' which according to Bousset must raise the status of a religion.

Often, the tribal people following their ancestral belief systems, are stigmatised even by their fellow tribal people who are into other globally known religions. Tribal people, because of their stigmatised belief systems, are often contemptuously considered to be troglodytes who are not even aware of whom to worship and pray. Their belief systems are also attacked as superstitious and scathingly condemned. Narratives of killing and sacrifices of blood of animals and even human beings have been the essential fodder in any attack against tribal belief systems. Thus, according to Bousset, 'The highest law of the tribe is blood-revenge' and '[i]t is considered the absolute and unconditional duty of the tribe to answer for the life of the individual, and to avenge the injured and murdered man' under '... the law of "an eye for an eye, a tooth for a tooth, a life for a life"' (1907: 57). In the context of several attacks against tribal belief systems, it has become exigent to analyse the relevance and credibility of their belief systems by accounting for their lived experiences without being tainted by a blindfolded and bulldozing objectivity.

In India, both the Hindus and the Christians who are the closest neighbours of the tribal people, do not seem to accept the belief systems of the tribals as distinct religions by and large. While some Hindus either condemn or accept tribal belief systems as sub-groups of Hinduism to the extent of calling the tribals 'backward Hindus' (Ghurye 1963) many Christians sweepingly condemn every tribal belief system and preach them to abandon their beliefs. Soihiamlung Dangmei observed that Heraka, one of the belief systems of Zeliangrong people, is seen as preserving the Sanatana Dharma and considered as part of Hinduism (2013: 28). There is also a trend in which several of the 'local animist and tribal faiths' of various non-Hindu groups are assimilated within Hinduism (Tharoor 2018: 22). The presence of several local temples in the Himalayan hill regions with local female deities with suffixed names 'Maa' or 'Mata' is spectacular. The existence of tribal faiths independent of any major religions seems anathema to both assimilationists and, for lack of an appropriate term, *condemnists*. A critic can contribute to positive growth but not a condemnist.

Tribal belief systems are seen to be mundane and lacking intellectual and supernatural characteristics. Such perception is witnessed even among their adherents strongly appealed to by the glitter of populous and popular religions. This reflects the observation made by Henri Tajfel and John C. Turner that 'certain forms of political, economic and social subordination of a social group tend to eliminate or even reverse its ethnocentrism' (1979: 37). The sustained stigmatisation of religions of the relatively smaller or weaker groups may lead to the admiration of the religions of the relatively stronger or larger groups by members of the smaller or weaker groups. And Peter Berger observed that religions are at the risk of losing plausibility if they appear ordinary, mundane and lack supernatural aura in daily life and to sustain this plausibility, religion requires a community that would endorse the religious norms and doctrines rather than doubting them (1967, cited in Ecklund and Park 2009: 279). We see ever-growing activities of religious groups in the contemporary period endeavouring to keep their religions relevant. Some have entrenched even into electoral politics and even in medicines. Many religious groups act as pressure groups to ensure their agenda being given a rightful place even in several national debates on wide ranging issues. The separation of religion and state is an ideal illusion.

With expanding significance that religion assumes in human societies, there are diverse perspectives held about religion. While religion can even influence one's personal life including health issues (Prest, Russelb and D'Souza 1999: 69; Malone and Dadswell 2018) it is also viewed not exclusively as something spiritual or personal but social as well (Durkheim 1965: 169). Moreover, A.A. Goldenweiser says, '*the reality underlying religion is society*' [italics original] (1917: 121). However, I will very briefly examine the sociological approach to the study of religion to adhere to the scope of this book.

Sociological Study of Religion

A sociological investigation into religion is concerned with the behaviour of individuals influenced by religious teachings and doctrines. It studies individual or group behaviour as a result of belief in religious tenets. A sociological study of religion delves into the belief system, practices such as rituals and patterns of organisations of a religious group and the interactions between all these and social institutions and structures. Some of the classical works on the sociology of religion are Harriet Martineau's Eastern Life: Present and Past (1848), The Elementary Forms of the Religious Life (Durkheim 1965, 1912), The Protestant Ethic and the Spirit of Capitalism (Weber 1930, 1904) and Religious Groups (Weber 1978). Among others, Religion and Society Among the Coorgs of South India (Srinivas 1952) is another crucial work on the sociology of religion.

Sociological approaches to religion may be examined within the three broad sociological perspectives: functionalism, conflict and symbolic interactionism. Functionalist perspectives on religion hold the view that religions perform various functions in society such as controlling the behaviour of the people and bringing about positive changes. Religions, according to the conflict perspective, breed inequality and conflict and result in social tensions due to religious differences. Symbolic interactionism studies how people interpret their religious experiences. It studies how people ascribe sacredness to religious symbols, teachings and practices in daily lives.

In a sociological study of religion—history—having something 'to do with the origin and development of social customs, of moral ideas, and of government' (McCorkle, n.d.: 4), needs to be taken into account. Such an approach is seen in the much-acclaimed work of M.N. Srinivas: *Religion and Society Among the Coorgs of South India* (1952). To comprehend the interface between society and religion, history of the people of the society concerned is indispensable. Given the significance of history in the understanding of Sociology of the contemporary period, the latter has even been termed as 'history of the present' (Seale 1998: 3). This underscores the need for an interdisciplinary approach towards a study on religion within the discipline of Sociology.

A historical dimension of religion that looks into the past events helps in the argument concerning the supposed existence of God and revelation. Depending on historical chronology accounted in the text, sociological view on the existence of God asserts as:

> The Christian revelation assumes the existence of God as the necessary basis of all being . . . . Further, it declares the fact of a divine revelation in the infancy of the human race, and a progressive revelation through prophets during the ages afterward, until that revelation culminated in the birth, character, life, teachings, miracles, death, resurrection and ascension of Christ (McCorkle n.d.: 4).

To approach such a historical account of God one must cease to be a sceptic and be sympathetic towards Christian revelation (McCorkle n.d.: 4). One cannot probably approach religion as an infidel and with a 'stimuli of Ingersollism' (ibid.: 4). Does this mean that one must be a follower of a religion? Does one need to change one's religion every time one studies new religion? McCorkle is probably suggesting a broad outlook on every religion. One must not be critical towards religion to demolish the foundations of its beliefs and practices. Religion is a crucial component of human society without which the social norms and values that maintain social order would be meaningless. Studying religion and its influence on society is also not to create a hierarchy of religions or prescribe any form of a supposedly ideal society. It is an attempt to understand the belief system as perceived and experienced by the believers or non-believers. What I did in this study is understanding the sociological significance of religion by adopting an interdisciplinary approach. I probed into the interface between religion and various structures of society to understand the resilience of the religion under study. I distanced my religious affiliation from the one I studied. I approached the religion under study as an outsider.

The American approach to religion has been reductionist and lacks the seriousness which religion demands (Smith et al. 2013: 1). Smith et al. assessed the tenuous state of religion in American sociology from a historical point of view. According to Smith and others, American sociology was conceived as an attempt of the Protestant churches to inspire a religiously inspired social reform. Such an evangelical Protestantism was later begun to be viewed as less scientific and illegitimate given the secularised university-based sociology considered to be a legitimate profession. Thus, in America, the sociological approach to religion was not friendly.

The new Sociology of universities had to ward off the traditional Christian authoritative control over knowledge about society. The academics in America were jolted by the religion-related events across the globe from their sense of complacency with their earlier 'secularization-theory model' (Smith et al. 2013: 5). They had to necessarily examine religion(s) if they had to remain relevant in the changing social environment. They were compelled by the global events in the form of religious fundamentalism, communalism, the Iranian revolution, terror attacks of 11 September 2001, renewed religious fervour in China, efforts of Pope John Paul II against communism and so on. However, the American sociologists were not intellectually prepared to meet such growing significance of religion of their time. And some faced the realities with 'begrudging resistance' (ibid.: 5). Another reason for poor acceptance of religion in American sociology is the intense vigour of the American sociologists challenging and refuting the structural-functionalism of Talcott Parsons of the mid-twentieth century with alternative theories such as phenomenology, symbolic interactionism, dramaturgy, ethnomethodology, 'rational choice' theory, versions of neo-Marxist, state-centred theories, etc., that could not address the problem of religion theoretically. Though they realise in the 1970s, the relevance of culture, belief, ideology, non-rational behaviour, ritual, and 'superstition' still extant in society they were caught off guard to meet such challenges. They had invested faith in the ability of modernisation to absorb all religious beliefs, however, it failed to do so. The secularisation of culture did not help in bringing religion within the field of cultural sociology that emerged in America in the 1980s. Religion was viewed as a subcomponent of culture and as culture was secularised, religion was not attended to in cultural studies.

Methodologically speaking, Smith et al. (2013) observed that American sociology was preoccupied with pre-defined concepts that attempted to capture the views of the people within the so defined and limited concepts and limited response options of the survey thus limiting a comprehensive understanding of religion and its impacts on the lives of people. Such a positivist approach seriously undermined the study of society and religion in particular. The survey, nevertheless, has its advantage as one can 'make claims about populations, map the prominence of various phenomena, and spot trends whose importance could be assessed over time' (ibid.: 925) . Smith et al. assert that 'inductively driven by significant qualitative field research—would have a big payoff in revealing the intricate and subtle ways that religion actually influences people's lives and the social world' (ibid.: 910). Smith et al. espouse an interdisciplinary approach to studies of religion by sociologists as much of the best religious studies have been done outside of sociology (ibid: 918) and no single discipline can single-handedly address the emerging contemporary issues around religion (ibid. 2013: 919) comprehensively.

Indian sociologists questioned the Orientalist approach that equated Indology with religion and further challenged the interpretation of Indian society as a manifestation of a simple religious truth into complex social relations (Robinson and Clarke 2007: 4). Indian society is much more than daily ritualistic life. It has many economic, social, secularised cultures and political realities that cannot be captured within the parlance of Indology or oriental religious discourse alone. For Indian sociologists, religiosity is not the defining characteristic of Indian society.

In this context of a discussion on the sociological approach to religion, it is exigent to discuss the views of Andre Beteille who in his article 'Religion as a Subject for Sociology' (1992) elaborated the methodological concerns in this area of study. Andre Beteille, from a methodological point of view, finds linkage between the sociological study of religion and studies of caste, gender, politics and nation. This speaks volumes about the significance of the study of religion from a sociological standpoint. However, some sociologists, like those emphasising a materialist interpretation of history, according to Beteille, may sideline religion until it has impact on society in the form of communalism. Methodologically speaking, Beteille does not want to see a sharp contrast between different approaches to religion. Rather he sees the possibility of an interdisciplinary approach with a clear idea about the points of departure of the approaches. A sociological approach to religion, according to Beteille, is concerned with the tasks of observation, description, interpretation and explanation of the religious beliefs and practices operating in the society.

Beteille outlined two approaches that are common to sociology and anthropology: comparative and investigative. Stressing the significance of the comparative approach, Emile Durkheim termed comparative study as sociology and not just one of the approaches of sociology. Radcliffe-Brown viewed social anthropology as comparative sociology. Such acquiescence shared among anthropologists and sociologists throws open doors for an interdisciplinary approach to the study of religion as further espoused by Andre Beteille. The comparative method, according to Beteille, facilitates bringing onto the same platform all religions with equal considerations without any prejudice, though it is already refuted in theology. Such an approach may be difficult and some may even think of it to be impossible from a theological point of view. However, to ensure fairness to every religion and minimise value attachment of the researcher, comparative method stands as an effective approach to a study of religion in which value neutrality is, for some, inconceivable.

Value-neutrality is explained by Beteille as 'to understand religious institutions, religious beliefs and religious practices from the outside, without becoming personally committed to the values by which they are sustained within a given religious faith' (1992: 1868). Such a position is hard to be achieved. Emile Durkheim, according to Beteille, failed to ensure fairness to every religion despite the use of the comparative method in the study of religions. This is so because Durkheim came along with the baggage of attachment to the theory of evolution in which some belief systems are inferior to others due to a lower degree of rationalisation. Durkheim placed Protestant Christianity at one end and the belief systems of the so-called primitive societies at the other end. Sociologists, according to Beteille, study religions from outside without failing to understand the deeply seated meanings of beliefs and practices.

The second sociological approach to religion is the investigative approach towards the relationship between religion and society. The relationship between various social institutions, according to Beteille, is the domain of sociology. And among them, a relationship with religion is one. And religion, despite its manifest nature cannot be understood without viewing it in the context of the various social institutions. Beteille is emphasising the view that religion cannot be understood in itself as a social fact without any reference to other social institutions. And once again stressing the importance of an interdisciplinary approach, Beteille invokes the view of Pastor Naumann who believed that religious reform in Germany could not be successful without a reformation in politics. This re-emphasises the need to do away with the exclusivist outlook of any discipline. In this second approach, sociologists may go for a longitudinal study of literature on populations, observe the people's lives in the community, study the religious phenomena or the religious groups or institutions may be studied.

Striking again a note of the similarity between sociological and social anthropological approaches to religion, Beteille maintained that both try 'to observe and describe how people act as well as to understand and interpret the meanings they assign to their acts' (1992: 1867). Here another methodological concern is raised. Should one observe the behaviours first and understand the meanings later? Or, can the behaviours be understood if one first acquires the meanings of the actions of the people? Emile Durkheim and Radcliffe Brown (as stated in the Foreword to *Religion and Society among the Coorgs of South India*) prefer to observe the behaviours first as a preliminary requirement to understanding the meanings of the actions of the people. However, Max Weber always stressed the need to first understand the meanings of the actions.

Noting a point of departure between theological and sociological approaches to religion, Beteille observed that for sociologists religion is important not because of its accepted truth but because of its utility in society. Theologians stick to the accepted truth of religion they follow and study. Beteille made sure of the position of sociology on religion as being focussed on utility and not on accepted truth in the words: 'The sociology of religion always, and perhaps necessarily, comes to grief when it moves beyond its proper empirical concerns under the urge to decide on the truth or otherwise of a religious doctrine' [sic] (1992: 1867). This is also a caution against the deeply religious scholars who would embark on a study of religion from a sociological standpoint to be wary about being biased in favour of one's belief system. One cannot compromise the academic rigour in favour of one's position before a religious leader as done by Evans-Pritchard who attacked sociology of religion fiercely as he did not desire to invite the ire of Bishop of Gloucester. It is observed earlier that Beteille noted the impossibility of complete objectivity in a study of religion and he addressed this issue with a notion of 'fairness'. And speaking of the academic rigour he stated that '. . . as in dealing with human beings generally, we have to be governed by considerations not merely of intellectual rigour but also of fairness' (ibid.: 1869). One needs to look out for any sign of bias against any religious group to which one is not affiliated. And in adopting a comparative approach to the study of religion, one must ensure a fair degree of critical analysis. One needs to avert analysing a belief system in the context of the beliefs and practices of other religions.

Henri Bois, in *A Sociological View of Religion*, had long maintained the truth value of religion and stated, '. . . for it is a sociological law that no institution based on falsehood and error can survive. Religion has thus its roots in reality and corresponds to a human need' (1916: 1). Bois endorses a sociological approach in which one studies a subject matter in its simplest form before engaging oneself with the more complex one. And this is offered by Bois as an explanation for the choice of Durkheim studying the primitive religion in its simplest form which, Bois believes, carries the evidence of its origin.

A serious loophole in the approach to a tribal belief system is embodied in that of G.S. Ghurye's examination of the tribal belief systems. This is not to attack the whole of sociological approaches to a study of tribal religions. G.S. Ghurye made a debilitating observation on tribes through a methodologically impaired selective and partial observation of the comments of the Census Commissioners of the period ranging from 1891 to 1931 (Xaxa 2009: 32-3). In it, Ghurye conjectured several features of tribal belief systems and the Hindu religion as indistinguishable. Methodologically, Ghurye, according to Virginius Xaxa, failed to corroborate his observations of the comments of the Census Commissioners on tribal belief systems with fieldwork data which he should have collected as an impartial and diligent sociologist. Based on his unrealised flawed methodology, he called the tribals 'backward Hindus' in his work *The Aborigines "So-called" and Their Future which is Now Known as the Scheduled Tribes*. Such an approach resulted in enduring social turbulence in which contemporary politicians, academicians and fundamentalists scuffle to appropriate the tribals within the Hindu group.

From the error of G.S. Ghurye, one has to learn the indispensability of fieldwork. Armchair research, as Ghurye is seen to have done in the case of the tribal belief system, must be averted. Methodologically speaking, even research that depends only on secondary data needs a visit in the field. There may be abundant literature produced by the people as believers on their belief system that may not be as scientific as the scholars' work. And several of the earlier findings could have been drastically changed.

As seen above, Sociological approach to religion delves into the significance and relevance of religion in society. One may illuminate this further by briefly examining the work of M.N. Srinivas among the Coorgs of South India. Srinivas's work *Religion and Society among the Coorgs of South India* (1952) represents an interdisciplinary approach by a sociologist which I intend to do in this book. This work may be seen as an account of the relationship between social structure and various religious beliefs and practices. According to A.R. Radcliffe-Brown, in the Foreword, the work is a descriptive analysis of the religious practices of the Coorgs. Radcliffe-Brown claimed comparative descriptive analysis of many beliefs as the 'only method' to answer the question: 'how does religion contribute to the existence of society as an ordered and continuing system of relationships amongst human beings?' (ibid.: vii).

It is interesting to note that even a renowned anthropologist Radcliffe-Brown called Srinivas 'a trained anthropologist' (ibid.: vii). This speaks of the interdisciplinary approach of M.N. Srinivas. It must also be noted that Srinivas sometimes even used unverifiable source of data such as folk songs and folklores. He used this while illuminating the nature of the position of women in Coorg society and feuds between the nads or group of villages. According to folksongs, even women killed tigers and serenaded men. However, elsewhere Srinivas questioned one of the folksongs that presented to him an account of the administrative system of the Coorgs due to its orderings and he feared accuracy being rendered expendable to favour impeccability of the account (1952: 59-60).

In his work among the Coorgs, M.N. Srinivas displayed his calibre as an anthropologist, besides as a sociologist and a historian. Presenting a descriptive picture of the Coorgs he presented the Coorgs from the ninth century AD to the modern era. Such a historical background of the peasant people certainly forms a preamble to an understanding of the complex nature of their contemporary society. Through the use of historical materials, Srinivas was able to enlighten the nature of relationships between the Coorgs and rulers who ruled them and this consequently illuminated the nature of the Coorgs society and their relations with other groups.

His understanding of the caste system enabled him to elicit the complex social relations between different caste groups bound by Hindu belief systems. His effort to illuminate the sustenance of the social structures based on the caste system is indeed commendable. The caste system, according to Radcliffe-Brown, is a religious group in essence with specific religious obligations. Srinivas showed how the Coorgs of different castes share solidarity with their autonomy and obligations. A feature that made the work of Srinivas one of the best to rely on to understand Hinduism, is the assimilation of Coorg deities as gods and goddesses of the Hindu pantheon based on which he coined the much-acclaimed term 'Sanskritization'.

He showed how the Hinduism of the *Vedas*, the *Upanishads* and the *Puranas* slowly formed certain parts of the local belief systems. Srinivas adopted a factual study of the process of the interplay between Hinduism and the local belief systems in which he analysed the ritual idioms of the Coorgs and Hindu forms of expressions. It is because of his emphasis on the processes that he was able to coin a theoretical concept such as Sanskritization that involves a process of so-called lower castes imitating the ways of life of the so-called higher castes. He simplified the religious terms using the most relevant and extant terms. Through the illumination of the interplay between Hinduism and local belief systems, he was able to disprove the rigidity of social systems of the caste as generally held by western scholars.

Also, it is interesting to note the two types of structures illuminated by Srinivas (1952: 42-3) with an example of oracles of the Bana caste who occupy a higher position in the context of a ritual of ancestor-propitiation but always occupying a lower position in the context of social hierarchy within the community of Coorgs. This gives one a picture of the distinction between ritual structure and social structure. It is through the analysis of the caste system with its close affinity to religion that Srinivas was enlightened on the social structures of the Coorgs.

There is a possibility of weakness of the data used by Srinivas in terms of their relevance. This is so because the data he used in the book was collected from 1940 till mid-1942 which is ten years earlier than the year of publication of his work, and given the changes, though slow, Coorg society underwent, one may question the relevance of the data. Also, as mentioned in the Preface, Srinivas continued even after June 1942 to gather information (data) without his presence amongst the Coorgs. This is clear from his words of gratitude to an informant who, according to Srinivas, provided information for 'over a period of ten years' (1952: xiii). This is one of the weaknesses of his book and not necessarily a weakness of his approach to religion and society of the Coorgs. Moreover, Srinivas accepted the changes in Coorg and admitted his failure to update the book in the second print nearly twelve years after its publication. Moreover, the census data that could provide him with relatively more details were of 1931 while 1941 Census gave him just the total population of the Coorg and no information was available on the composition of the population.

A Call for an Interdisciplinary Approach

Scholars have long acknowledged the necessity of stepping beyond the confine of their disciplinary methodology and adopt interdisciplinary approaches in their attempt to study religion. Theology needs to come out of its metaphysics and engage in what is termed as 'cosmotheandrism' meaning studying the significance of God, symbols of the world and human beings and their relations (Panikkar 1993, cited in Robinson and Clarke 2007: 3). This demands a need to look into sociology and anthropology as well among others. As a part of an attempt to understand taboo and totem through psycho-analysis Freud had to bank on the works of anthropology to identify people who are described by the anthropologists 'as the most backward and miserable of savages' among whom most archaic practices are still found (2004: 2). It also means looking into an account of any group in the context of the situation during which the data was collected. Here one must take precaution not to analyse any account out of context. This necessitates understanding the historical, political and economic contexts of the time when the data was collected.

Both sociologists and theologians look into religion in the realms which are 'local, material, and integral to life' (Robinson and Clarke 2007: 5). Both disciplines deal with the aspects of daily lives of human beings and concentrate highly on aspects that concern human realities. For sociologists, religion is a social phenomenon. However, for psychologists what interests them in a study of religion is the way religion operates in the minds of the individuals. Olivera Petrovich's writing underpins the inherent psychological dimension in the historical, anthropological and sociological studies of religion. A historical study of religion requires psychology as there is a need to investigate recurring patterns of thought and timeless patterns of experience which are purely a psychological domain (Smart 1987: 571, cited in Petrovich 2007: 352). According to Petrovich, historians search for patterns in religious texts but psychologists look for the same in human thoughts and behaviour. Even in a sociological study of religion, the significance of psychology is underlined. For, although religion is a social institution whose several features can be conceptualised through the social life of individuals, religion is initially an individual mental affair without any social dimensions (Petrovich 2007: 352). A realm of psychological explanations in an anthropological study of religion is evident as Nisbet contends that anthropologists look for religion in (a) psychic states, (b) ritual acts, or (c) awe of celestial bodies and terrestrial phenomena (1987, cited in Petrovich 2007: 352). Religion is invariably conceptualised in common parlance as a personal affair. It is conceived as a matter concerning belief. However, given the evidence of religious beliefs, rituals, obligations and festivals endemic in all the aspects of individual and social lives an interdisciplinary approach is invariably a boon to studies of religion.

Religious studies over the ages have had several perspectives. Theology, supposedly the closest to religion itself, did not hold an exclusive sway over religious studies. Even atheists and agnostics contributed immensely to religious studies. While psychologists look into the feeling, thinking and will of human beings to study religion, sociologists examined the inter-relationship between religion and societies. While historians depend on treatises, poems and texts the philosophical approach have no such sources of data in a religious study. Philosophers just have to think and reason. Nevertheless, every discipline leaves scope for an interdisciplinary approach. And such an interdisciplinary approach to a study of religion is seen in the work of M.N. Srinivas among the Coorgs of South India.

Studies of religion may not be endemic but the presence and significance of religion across realms of society are deeply rooted. The growing reference to religion or God even among scientists sometimes even in the context of scientific endeavours also suffices the claim of the relevance of religion even in the highly rationalised world view. The relevance of religious studies remains extant.

Locating Tingkao Ragwang Chapriak in Religious Studies

In strife-torn parts of India, where armed conflict is erroneously a synonym for daily life, religious activities thrive for personal and social, political and economic reasons. Religion remains practically relevant in every walk of life. Tingkao Ragwang Chapriak is one such religion that interlinks every aspect of the life of its followers. There is a growing involvement of the state in the religious affairs of the people, especially in the domain of festivals by sponsoring such festivals towards the promotion of social harmony. Several of the unknown belief systems are gradually emerging seeking the attention of the state for protection. Similar to the proliferation of several denominations within Christianity there are several belief systems within a single group of people. Such proliferation of several denominational churches within a group finds its parallel within Zeliangrong groups (Zeme, Liangmai, Rongmei and Inpui) with many non-Christian belief systems. A proper sociological analysis of Tingkao Ragwang Chapriak is still hard to come by despite its vigorous reformative activities since the early 1990s amidst the rising political tide of the Naga armed struggle around the same period.

Zeliangrong[8] groups who are scattered in Assam, Nagaland and Manipur have belief systems closely linked with the social, economic and political milieu of the three states. According to

Professor Meijinlung Kamson,[9] the Amang Society was the first religious sect of Zeliangrong. It was formed in 1965. Amang, a legendary figure was declared as the prophet. The Amang Society looked for a prophet and not God. This group is now hardly spoken of. The Amang Society was followed by the Champa Society in 1969. Champa, meaning the chosen or the most preferred (Gangmei 2014: 5), is a relatively smaller religious group of the Hamai[10] people. The belief system of the Champa is known as Tingkao Ragwang Kariak. Kariak means ways. Tingkao Ragwang Chapriak (TRC) is a belief system known to be practised especially by the Rongmei people. Tingkao Ragwang Chapriak is defined as 'the religion of Tingkao Ragwang, the Supreme God' (Kamson 2011: 45). Based on the 2001 Census,[11] the total devotees of TRC in Assam, Manipur and Nagaland stood at 23000 (ibid.: 45). According to Budha Kamei, the population of Tingkao Ragwang Chapriak stands at 30000 as per the 2011 Census.[12] The rise in the figure may also be interpreted as a decrease in the intensity of the vigour of proselytisation as severe sanctions were imposed upon the newly converted Christians by the village authorities after TRC became more prominent in the early part of the 1990s. Heraka is another belief system followed mostly by some Zeme people, especially in the erstwhile North-Cachar Hills in Assam. Unlike TRC, Heraka followers do not appease gods and goddesses.

The practice of construction of temples which was pioneered by Jadonang Malangmei among the Zeliangrong people (Kamson 2011: 9) is still not widespread. Many villages still do not have structured places of worship. Conversion is one religious phenomenon that ails the cordial social relations between various religious groups. *'Conversion is sin'*, *'Regain culture, regain identity'*, *'Culture and faith are inseparable, don't pollute them'*, are some of the dictums popularised among the followers of TRC. Fearing conversions of TRC followers to other religions Chaoba Kamson, the General Secretary of Tingkao Ragwang Chapriak Phom (*phom*= organisation) of Assam, Manipur and Nagaland, unequivocally stated, '. . . we should construct a place of worship[13] in every village so that our people may not convert to other religion rather our people will concentrate to our religion' (ibid.: 9). Despite this deep-seated fear, the TRC community is seen to be resilient in maintaining its claimed primordial religious identity.

There is also a trend among many Christians participating in the cultural activities of the Zeliangrong community. Their participation is not seen to be extended to the realm of beliefs, rituals and prayers. However, Chaoba Kamson stated that 'All the festivals are related to the worship of Tingkao Ragwang, the Supreme God' (ibid.: 17). The significance of rites and rituals in festivals is also stressed by Larilung Kamei (ibid.: 60). Christians are beginning to be seen to be actively engaged in state endorsed festivals of the tribal people. The tribal Christians occupy a crucial position in the interface between the state and tribal cultures. This is because the number of prominent officials in the state administration is significantly Christian. Another reason is that the tribals in Manipur valley have no representatives in the Assembly who are tribals.

It is a commonly known fact that early unsophisticated Christians condemned and destroyed traditional attires, songs and certain ways of life on the ground that they belonged to Satan. The beating of the locally made animal hide drum was banned inside the church. The entity worshipped by their forefathers was condemned and called Satan. Besides other reasons, this immensely contributed to conversions to Christianity. With the presence of a vibrant Christian population, the strength of ancestral belief systems was immensely reduced. However, from the early 1990s, the Rongmei community exhibited enduring collective strength in preserving its claimed primordial belief systems and it contributed towards sustaining the collective ancestral Zeliangrong identity while negotiating with certain insurmountable social, political and cultural changes.

The primordiality of TRC is sometimes questioned by the neighbouring Christians. What Ira W. Howerth observed towards the beginning of the twentieth century still resonates in the evangelical endeavours of the Christian missionaries of the present days. 'The Evangelical controversialist', according to Howerth, '. . . for instance, seems bent on excluding by his definition what he calls the superstitions of man, or of sharply distinguishing between the so-called natural religions and revealed religion' (1903: 185).

Thus, within the parlance of informal discourse, it has become an often-repeated claim that TRC was a creation of some influential individuals and, therefore, it does not qualify as a religion. Thus, TRC is rendered as a group sans divinity. Such allegation is certainly taken as heresy by TRC followers. Refuting such allegation Chaoba Kamson—leader of TRC—passionately asserted that, 'Tingkao Ragwang already exists. He was not created by anyone' (2011: 10). Thus, Cahoba Kamson links the idea of God with the religion TRC itself. For him religion and God are inseparable and both are divine and primordial. In the context of such attacks on the credibility of TRC's religiousness, it becomes interesting to delve into the factors that sustain its belief systems, and the allegiance and commitment of its adherents. This book is a result of a research study of the factors that contribute towards the resilience of TRC to withstand the influence of other religions upon its followers and the continued existence of its belief systems and practices. The study explores both the internal and external factors that contribute to the resilience of TRC.

It was observed that the American population was organised mostly not through political parties but religious bodies and associations, or secular cults for the nonreligious people (Editor 1978: 3). But this trend is seen to be changing in recent times. Michael Hout observed that American people, according to the 2016 General Social Survey (GSS), are becoming detached from the organised religion with 22 per cent of the adult population in 2016 preferring no religion which is 13 per cent more from the 1994 GSS survey (2017: 78). Such a parallel of disinterestedness in religion is hard to be conceived among the TRC followers of Rongmei people given the recent phenomenon of religious reformation in the 1990s.

The Zeliangrong people, especially the Rongmei, reacting to the force of proselytisation of the evangelical Christians, firmly view their group identity through the prism of religion. The Rongmei Christians initiated the tradition of categorising themselves as *Ra-Ningmei* (worshipper of God) and derogatorily referred to the adherents of traditional belief systems as *Jou-Jangmei*[14] (consumer of wine). Like the Rongmei Christians, the Tingkao Ragwang Chapriak group also organises more resolutely and asserts their religious identity. They too have a category to categorise the Christians. The Christians are – humorously, not derogatorily – categorised as *'Amen nun'* meaning Amen group. This assertion of the TRC group is a response to the unfavourable categorisation of the adherents of ancestral belief systems, especially by the Christians.

The idea of resilience is analysed within the theoretical paradigm of social change. The essence of TRC beliefs may be retained while its practices may be reformed or transformed. This implies the need for a critical understanding of reformation and transformation in religion. Thus, the resilience of TRC is traced primarily in the continuance of its essence despite certain changes in practice aspects. Within the context of empirical reality, the prevalence of places of worship, documented doctrines, religious symbols, hymnal books, and gatherings are analysed. At the group level, the dynamics of ancestral collective identity play a crucial role in fomenting religious identity. The religious identity of the TRC group subsequently consolidates the ancestral collective identity prevailing beyond the frontier of their religious identity. There is a mutual identification of the group members within the domain of religion. There is also a process of distinctly identifying and categorising other groups and warding them off from the ancestral collective identity and religious identity. This is critically analysed within the theoretical framework of social identity.

In the context of the Zeliangrong people, there has been not a single study carried out on the sociological significance of Tingkao Ragwang Chapriak. The growing prominence of Tingkao Ragwang Chapriak as a reformed belief system among the Zeliangrong people is hard to ignore because of its recurrence in mundane daily lives and the public domain. Tingkao Ragwang Chapriak has withstood the onslaught of conversion by the Christian missionaries, it has resisted the attempts of Christian missionaries to convert them. Many efforts have been made by Tingkao Ragwang Chapriak to sustain its belief systems. However, we are yet to be very casual about its presence in literature. It is hardly known outside Manipur. The present book with emphasis on the intricacies of its beliefs and its significance in the village polity will be welcome among the social scientists interested in the study of little communities. The fieldwork data provided will be of immense value to the larger theoretical discourse on a study of religion.

The adherents of Tingkao Ragwang Chapriak have produced some literature on their belief systems and descriptive accounts of their belief system. However, they are primarily to account for the description of Tingkao Ragwang Chapriak. Serious sociological analysis is yet to be witnessed. The growing literature on the sociology of religion is yet to embrace much of the sociology of Tingkao Ragwang Chapriak though it represents a very small size of the population despite two great leaders of India–Jadonang Malangmei and Rani Gaidinliu–belonging to the Rongmei tribe. This book will, I believe, contribute theoretically with its interdisciplinary approach adopted, and also bring closer to the readers the unfinished project of Jadonang Malangmei and Rani Gaidinliu who struggled religiously to salvage their ancestral religion against the ever-changing shades of discrimination and proselytisation. This book is about a religious group whose survival, amidst discrimination and proselytisation, is sought to be ensured through a reformation of its ancestral belief system, even at the risk of being categorised as new and man-made, rather than dissipating violence of frustration against the architects of discrimination and proselytisation.

NOTES

1. *National Legal Foundation*. In God We Trust. Accessed 20 June 2018. http://www.nlf.net/Activities/briefings/in_god_we_trust.htm.
2. Sushma pushes for declaring *Bhagavad Gita* as national scripture. *The Hindu* (New Delhi), 7 December 2014.
3. Pragya Kaushika. Sushma Swaraj wants the *Gita* recognised as a 'national scripture'; Haryana CM says *Gita* above Constitution. *The Indian Express* (New Delhi). Updated: 8 December 2014, 4:30:58 p.m. Retrieved from http://indianexpress.com/article/india/india-others/sushma-swaraj-pushes-for-declaring-bhagawad-gita-asnational-scripture/
4. ASI begins excavation at old UP fort after sadhu dreams of buried gold. *Times of India*. (October, 2013).

5. *Times of India*. (November, 2013). Superstitions and beliefs of Indian space scientists. Retrieved from http://timesofindia.indiatimes.com/india/Superstitions-and-beliefs-of-Indian-spacescientists/articleshow/25409651.cms.
6. *India Today*. (16 May, 2018).Yeddyurappa 'consults' astrologer on auspicious time for swearing-in. https://www.indiatoday.in/india/video/political-jostling-notwithstanding-yeddyurappa-consults-astrologer-onauspicious-time-for-swearing-in-1234712-2018-05-16.
7. Here I do not necessarily claim primordiality for any religion. Time immemorial is not necessarily primordial as a claim of time immemorial could also be due to lack of knowledge about the beginning of something for which time immemorial is claimed. However, I do acknowledge that there is a thin membrane between primordiality and time immemorial. Whatever is primordial may be said to be time immemorial, but the reverse does not hold true. A sheer lack of recorded time of distant past can be clubbed under time immemorial as the point of beginning is not in memory. Thus, time immemorial is used in the context of something whose beginning is not known or recorded in any form of knowledge.
8. The name Zeliangrong is used here to refer collectively to Zeme, Liangmai, Rongmei and Inpui peoples. The author does not necessarily endorse or attempt to reinforce the popular use of the name. However, it must be admitted that there is no name so far that fairly covers the historical, political, economic trajectories and collective aspirations of these four groups besides the name Zeliangrong. Zeliangrong is used here merely for conveniences in analysis. The political significance of the name Zeliangrong is evident even in the coverage of religious activities of TRC that cover Manipur, Assam and Nagaland. These three Indian states are invariably associated with the name Zeliangrong.
9. Personal communication in August 2012.
10. Hamai refers to Zeme, Liangmai, Rongmei, Inpui, Thangal, Maram and Kharam people. Zeme, Liangmai, Rongmei and Inpui people were earlier erroneously identified collectively as Zeliangrong. Zeliangrong is a name of an organisation resulting from an imminent socio-economic and political developments post-independence of India. On 2 April 2018, the Zeliangrong Union at its Zeliangrong Assembly at Majorkhul in Imphal West, Manipur declared unanimously that the name Hamai will be used to collectively identify Zeme, Liangmai, Rongmei and Inpui. The Assembly, although not participated by Thangal, Maram and Kharam people, resolved to include Thangal,

Maram and Kharam within Hamai if they express their willingness to continue to be identified as Hamai. In Liangmai language Hamai literally means God's child. Hamai is used instead of Zeliangrong because Hamai is the only name declared as a name of people. Zeliangrong, though used to refer to people, was originally declared as an organisation which was later misinterpreted as a name for people. Thangal, Maram and Kharam who are also identified as Hamai are not identified within Zeliangrong. Therefore, the name Zeliangrong, due to absence of most appropriate collective name for Zeme, Liangmai, Rongmei and Inpui people, is continued to refer to Zeme, Liangmai, Rongmei and Inpui because of the relevance of TRC within these groups. Note that TRC has so far no relevance among Thangal, Maram and Kharam. The declaration of 2 April 2018 of the Zeliangrong Union has still not materialised.

11. This claim of Census data is not reliable as enumeration in 2001 and even that of 2011 is based on the categories Kabui and Kacha Naga. One cannot distinguish the religious identities of the Zeliangrong groups based on the two names used in the Censuses.
12. Budha Kamei. Tingkao Ragwang Chapriak. *The Sangai Express*, 11 November 2012, 12:51 a.m.
13. It must be noted here that followers of Tingkao Ragwang Chapriak do not have temple or house of God which is termed in Rongmei language as Rakai. Rather the idea of place of prayer/ worship or Kalumkai (kalum= pray; kai= house) is asserted against Rakai (Ra= God; kai= house).
14. Jou, which literally means wine, is not taken to be a simple kind of drink. It is closely associated with morality and spirituality. The consumers are morally and spiritually condemned by certain sections of Christians. Such perception towards jou and the consumer of the same is influenced and shaped by the ill-effects of drunkenness witnessed in some families and against which many—irrespective of religions—have raised their voices.

CHAPTER 2

Rongmei People

Conceptualising the 'Rongmei'

There cannot be mere identification of the Rongmei people. The Rongmei people have to be conceptualised historically, politically and sociologically based on shared identity narratives within the larger Zeliangrong collective identity rooted in shared oral traditions. The nomenclature, Rongmei, carries along with it a narrative of their migration. No Zeliangrong elder or scholar has done justice to the origin of the Rongmei people. Conflicting myths and legends are factors for a lack of systematic account of the origin of the Rongmei people.

Myths and legends are valued lesser than facts and pieces of evidence. So far, there is no absolute historical account of the Rongmei people about who they were and how they lived. There is no written historical account of the Rongmei people unaffected by the social and political milieu of the neighbouring societies. Even the one written by a well known Rongmei scholar is found to be subject to the subdued position of the Rongmei people. The history of Rongmei is conceptualised deductively from that of the dominant group. This reflects history as an invention in the present by historians 'for their own purposes' as a 'function of ideology' in which 'objectivity lies only in the conventions of common logic and evaluation of evidence by which the community of historians agree to abide' (Washbrook 1985: 94, cited in Aloysius 1998: 4). In the later part of this chapter, I am attacking such a historical account even at the cost of seeming to appear callously subjective. Nevertheless, subscription to myths and legends associated with the identity narrative of the Rongmei people always provide the much-needed sense of collective identity and a sense of who they were, who they are or how they represent themselves.

The oral traditions that store their origin narratives which are completely detached from other groups point to their desire for self-determination. Such desire for self-determination is to be found only in their myths and legends and not in the power-dictated written account of their neighbouring groups. It is in this context that Rongmei identity cannot be identified through the so-called historical accounts alone but conceptualised from their myths and legends.

Rongmei people's identity cannot be conceptualised in isolation. Their identity needs to be analysed within the domain of collective identity narratives of Zeme, Liangmai, Rongmei and Inpui. The apotheosis of identity narrative of the Zeliangrong groups seems to be a distant dream as evident from the unsettled contemporary conflicts between their narratives. Their identity narratives change, very often, partially to suit emerging socio-economic and political milieus (see Samson 2015a).

According to Chaoba Kamson, the General Secretary of TRC Phom (TRC Organisation), the population of the TRC community, as of the year 2020, stands at about thirty thousand. The exact figure of the TRC community population in Manipur valley is not known to be available. However, there are over sixty five Rongmei villages in the four valley districts of Manipur, i.e. Imphal East, Imphal West, Thoubal and Bishnupur. Some villages do not have TRC adherents.

Professor Gangmumei Kamei, in an interview in 2012, pointed out to the author that the Zeliangrong people were already settled in the southern parts of the present Manipur since the era of BC. However, he did not give even a rough figure of the Before Christ era. Gonmei Lanbilung Kabui mentioned the finding of tools in Tharon Cave located in Tamenglong district of Manipur and relate them to Hoa Bi Hian culture of Vietnam that flourished in about 7000-8000 BC (2018: 3). This suggests the probable presence of the Rongmei people in the south-western parts of Manipur hills from about 7000-8000 BC.

Zeme, Liangmai, Rongmei and Inpui have 'a patrilineal society with two Moieties or major clans namely, Pamei and Newmei' (Kamei 2009: 11; Pamei 1996). Zeliangrong people collectively believe that there were originally only Pamei and Newmei clans. It is believed that to create possibilities for continuity of the Zeliangrong people through marriages, God inspired them to further divide themselves into more clans. Thus, the Rongmei has Kamei, Golmei, Gangmei and Longmei as the major clans. Kamei and Golmei are the equivalents of the original Pamei and Newmei respectively. Officially, in Manipur, Zeme and Liangmai are also collectively known as Kacha Naga. Similarly, Rongmei and Inpui are also collectively recognised as Kabui. Ethnically and linguistically they belong to Tibeto-Burman of southern Mongoloid groups.

Rongmei in Manipur Valley

The relationship between the Rongmei people and the Meitei is romanticised and immortalised. Such romanticised stories of relationship are widely accepted by the Rongmei in the valley. However, such romanticised stories of relationship could not eliminate the other facets of the reality of the life of the Rongmei people in the valley described as 'semi-servile' (Hodson 1911: 5). Often, colonial writings are dismissed as biased and intended to create a chasm between communities. The account of TC Hodson—when juxtaposed against the Meiteis' tale of Khamba Thoibi that also contains a reference to a commendable service of Kabui Salang Maiba—stands contradictory and seems plausible to be dismissed. However, one cannot miss the etymologies of the names of some of the Rongmei villages that reveal the origin of their settlement in the valley and reflect an abjectly unpleasant state of the Rongmei people in the Meitei kingdom.

Ragailong and Namdunlong are two Rongmei villages situated to the west of Khuman Lampak Stadium located in Imphal East. These villages are collectively identified as Pandon by outsiders. Pandon is a corrupt name for *palton* which is also a corrupt form of the military unit platoon. Ragailong was initially settled by those who served the platoon. Some elders say that they were employed as sweepers in the military camp. Namdunlong was established later by a few individuals who also served the platoon stationed near Ragailong village. The erstwhile camp of the platoon near Ragailong village is now a transit camp of the Assam Rifles. Thus, the military connection with these two villages is continued and also the name Pandon.

Namthanlong is a village situated near the new Assembly building. It was earlier derogatorily known as Muchi which is a corrupt term for *mochi* (cobbler). It is said that the original villagers were tanners and cobblers who served the British. Kakhulong is a Rongmei village close to the governor's bungalow. Earlier it was popularly known as Saabang (*Saab* = officer; *bang* = servant). Unlike all these villages Majorkhul carries a favourable narrative. Majorkhul is a Rongmei village without any alternative Rongmei name popularised. It was believed to have been given by a major of a Meitei king before the colonial days. Oral tradition speaks of forced labour imposed upon the Rongmei people by the Meitei king before the colonial days for which many Rongmei people were held captive and transported to the valley from their ancestral lands in the hills. This forced labour was continued under colonial power.

The Manipur valley was divided into seven principalities: Meitei, Moirang, Khuman, Luwang, Angom, Chinglei and Ningthouja. Sanamahism is the ancestral belief system of the Meitei people. Meitei principality subdued the principalities of Moirang, Khuman, Luwang, Angom, Chinglei and Ningthouja and consolidated into a single Meitei identity. Many tribals of the hills were captured by the Meitei kings and they were assimilated within the Meitei identity through forced ascription of Meitei surnames. In the process of enhancing the prosperity and strength of the kingdom in the valley, many Meitei kings assimilated many tribals of the hills into the Meitei fold through the granting of Meitei surnames (Kabui 2018: 16-20). At the height of assimilation into the Meitei group, there was also Hinduisation of the Meitei including some tribals under the Meitei suzerainty in the valley. In November 1739, many Kabuis and Tangkhuls were Hinduised with an ascription of the Kshatriya caste with sacred water under the rule of Meitei king Pamheiba who later adopted the name Garibnawaz (ibid.: 21). According to Gonmei Lanbilung Kabui (2018), unlike the Loi people of Manipur valley who are now categorised as scheduled caste, some tribals identified as Kei were restricted from becoming Hindus and they were not accepted within the fold of Meitei clans. Kei refers to the Rongmei and Inpui people who were guarding the royal granaries in the peripheries of the valley. Kei means a granary.

The term Kei needs to be further qualified to capture a historical glimpse of a section of Kabui or Rongmei people who were neither assimilated into Meitei clans nor converted to Hinduism or Sanamahism. The term Kabui is relevant here as it covers even the Inpui people settled in the valley and who were identified as Kei along with the Rongmei people. Large sections of Kabui people were assigned the role of protecting the royal granaries located in the valley at the peripheries of the royal palace called Kangla. They were not assimilated into the Meitei clans like the earlier tribal captives. During the reign of king Meidingu from the twelfth century AD and until the eighteenth century AD many tribal captives were absorbed into the Meitei group. They were placed at a low position of social hierarchy like the Lois who refused to accept Hinduism. The genesis of Kei is traced to the rule of king Khagemba (AD 1597-1652). Some of the valley villages presently settled by the Kabui which were originally places of Kei or royal granaries are Changangei, Chaopok, Keikhu, Keinou, Keiren, Koirengei, Mongsanggei and Tamphagei. All these villages are located in rural parts of the Manipur valley. Interestingly, some of the villages were originally settled by the Inpui who now identify themselves as Rongmei. This enables the Inpui people to identify with the larger group, Rongmei people who play a relatively significant role in contemporary valley politics.

While those Meiteis who refused conversion to Hinduism were excommunicated and became Lois, these tribal people securing the Keis were denied conversion and were assigned the roles of serving the kingdom in different capacities (Kabui 2018: 21). These sections of the tribal people later formed the major inhabitants of Manipur valley Rongmei villages who retained their ancestral belief systems and cultural practices. Some Rongmei people, in the late twentieth century, however, were known to have worshipped Hindu deities and adhered to Meitei Sanamahism[1] without any experience of coercion. But this Sanamahism among the Rongmei in Manipur valley was limited to the worship of the deity Sanamahi. It precluded every rite of passage of the Rongmei people. But Hinduism and Sanamahism among the Rongmei people withered away significantly with the reformations of the Zeliangrong ancestral belief system and the emergence of Tingkao Ragwang Chapriak in the early 1990s. Nevertheless, some Rongmei people in the valley are still found to follow Sanamahism and worship Hindu deities despite following the Rongmei ancestral rites of passage. According to Chaoba Kamson,[2] a family from his village entered details in the Census survey questionnaire as a follower of Sanamahi in the 2011 Census. Another Rongmei village, Oinam, according to Chaoba Kamson, had a family that admitted to not know Tingkao Ragwang even after 2011 and claimed to worship Sanamahi.

Village System

Establishing a Rongmei village requires many specific rituals. After a site for a village is identified, a ritual known as *Daan Saanmei* is performed to know if the new site is suitable for human settlement. Usually, the one who found the site is accepted as the Nampou or owner of the land or village. According to Kalauna Pamei, the art of establishing a village was blessed by Raguang (God) through a priest named Charav Khandipu when the Rongmei people began settling in Chaguang Phwngning (Chawang Phungning) (2009: 45). Budha Kamei writes about the establishment of a new village in which he acknowledges Nampou as the owner of the village (2018: 4; also see Pamei 2009: 45). Budha does not mention Khullakpu even once in his writing on village establishment. This strongly reaffirms the foreignness of the institution of Khullak. All the villages of the Rongmei people in the valley, including the Inpui may be said to have not founded as done customarily in the hills. In the valley, the Rongmei people did not go about looking for a village as in the hills. Most of the villages in the valley were given either by the Meiteis, or the British both out of the necessity of oppression and generosity.

Gonmei Lanbilung Kabui traced the origin of Khullak to the period of subjugation of the Zeliangrong people under the Hinduised Meitei king, Garibniwaz (2018: 85). Khomeimacha Kamson[3] also pointed out the absence of a position of Khullak in the traditional Zeliangrong village polity. Khomeimacha Kamson compared Nampou with the Supreme Commander of a nation. Nampou, according to Khomeimacha, is like the President of India. Customarily, Nampou holds the final authority over all matters concerning a village. Khullak is a new institution injected by the Meitei rulers to facilitate the oppression and subjugation of the villagers in the hills. Khullakpu is more of an administrator of a bureaucratised institution as defined in the Village Authority Act of 1956 (Tiba 2006: 96). At present, the system of Khullak is also found in the hills where Christians dominate. The institution of Khullak is erroneously associated with ancestral belief systems. The coming of Chairmanship along with the election system may be viewed as a compensatory institution for the Christians in the hills where traditional institutions have been annihilated by the passion of evangelisation of the Christian missionaries. In the hills, both the institutions of Khullak and Chairmanship continue to prevail over the customary institutions. In the valley, there is no Chairmanship as the rural villages are covered under Panchayats. The enduring effect of this treacherous craft in the form of Khullak and Chairmanship is witnessed in the process of land acquisition for state projects in which the state machinery negotiates primarily with the Khullakpus and Chairmen often ignoring the Nampou, the original and customary head of a village. Tiba further illuminated the disastrous effect of the Village Authority Act of 1956[4] in the context of the Maram people. According to him, 'At Maramei Namdi, the Act of 1956 had a far-reaching effect as far as the village administration is concerned. The *sugong* [Chief or Khullakpu] till then was the executive, legislative and judicial authority. This act drastically curbs his authority' (2006: 96). The Act undermined the power and functions of Nampou and Khullakpu and empowered the Chairman elected under the provision laid down in the Act. The Chairman is not bound by any customary or moral obligation, unlike the Nampou who is both a religious and moral significant figure of a village. The Khullakpu or the Chairman have no fear of taboo even while misusing the village land and resources for personal gains.

A Chairperson may be unmarried and very young. However,

among the Rongmei people, a Khullak institution is internalised in the customary law and accordingly a Khullakpu must be married and must be someone having a wife and not a widower. Khullakpu must be the oldest man among the clan that traditionally holds the position of Khullakpu in the village. Unlike the vote-based Chairmanship of the Village Authority Act, Khullakpu's position can be hereditary and it is actualised by a ritual and not determined by the ballot box.

Traditionally, the village institution headed by Nampou is the highest and it is called *Pei*. Now, *Pei* consists of Nampou, Khullakpu, Banja and Gaanchang in descending order. After the *Pei* it is *Khangchu*. *Khangchu* is similar to a military barrack. Traditionally, it hosts the male youth and married men of a village. It is headed by married men. The responsibility of Khangchu is to enforce the decision taken by the *Pei*. It also acts as an institution assigned with the task of protection of the village. Then there is *Mathenmei*, *Lapui or Lakpui Kaibang* and finally *Luchu*. These last three institutions are of old women, married women and girls respectively. Widows may be members of either *Mathenmei* or *Lakpui Kaibang* depending on the age. *Luchu* is headed only by unmarried girls. Each of these institutions is housed in different houses in a village. Such houses are called Khangchu kaibang, Mathenmei kaibang, Lakpui kaibang and Luchu kaibang.

In the process of establishment of a village two gates are constructed where the youth of *Khangchu* stand guard to protect the village. The Nampou has to identify the water body for the village and ritually sanctify the water body by raising an iron axe[5] (locally called *tan laogai*) and invoking the blessing of Tingkao Ragwang. The water body remains religiously crucial as water has to be fetched from it on the festive day of Nanuh. The water from it continues to be used for daily consumptions and other purposes. Entry into a newfound village is also marked by a ritual performed by the Nampou. No person can enter the village before the Nampou performs the ritual. The Nampou will hold a spear tied with a necklace of cornelian beads at one of the gates. All the villagers will be sanctified as they touch the beads while entering the village. After entering the new village every family is required to get a ritualised fire made inside the village. Each family is required to make a fire in their kitchen hearth with the ritualised fire. The Nampou will also identify a place for a long jump game. The place is locally known as *Daanshangpung*. Every family after entering the new village will perform a ritual called *Napkaomei* or calling of rice or food by offering a *loidupu*, a domesticated male fowl/cock to Tingkao Ragwang. Two places for village deities which are called *Kaipi Bambu* and *Kaiba Bambu* will also be finalised by the Nampou. All these ritualistic paraphernalia are integral to the life and culture of the Rongmei people. The fertility of the soil, availability of a perennial source of water, protection from enemies and wild animals are some of the factors considered while identifying a new village. In all these, what remains most important are the rituals at different stages. However, it must be noted that the Rongmei villages in Manipur valley were not established following all the aforesaid rituals as the villages were given either by the Meitei rulers or the Britishers with a degree of compulsion for settlement.

Khullakpu rules a Rongmei village. The succession of Khullakpu is strictly confined to the clan to which the Khullak belongs. Khullakpu is assisted by a council of the village comprising the elders of the village of different clans. Unlike in Christian dominated villages with Khullakpu who is a Christian, the Khullakpu of a village who is not a Christian 'looks after both the secular and religious functions' (Rongmei and Kapoor 2005: 108). Even in villages dominated by followers of ancestral belief systems, the influence of Nampou is not seen to be as significant as those of the Khullakpu. And gradually the elected young Chiefs are seen to be more prominent. Colonel W. McCulloch observed that among the Kabuis, the Khullakpu or the Chief have lost their authority over religious affairs (1859, cited in Hodson 1911: 102). It must be noted here that the Khullakpus in valley Rongmei villages are conventionally termed as the Chiefs of the villages.

The governance of a village is based on customary law and a village administration operates in a consultative relationship between the Khullakpu and the council of elders (Rajkumari 2012). The powers of the Khullakpu are checked by the village council. The Khullakpu consults the elders in the council known as *Pei*. The issue concerning conflicts between any two individuals or groups is settled at *Pei* which is also a traditional village court. Customarily, no pronouncement of punishment amounts to capital punishment[6] in the *Pei*. The worst forms of punishment under the supervision of the *Pei* ever known is ex-communication by casting a culprit out of the village and a test of truth by immersion of a plantain leaf into river water in which the plantain leaf of the culprit is believed would be drowned. Another way of dealing with a serious complaint is the immersion of both the accused and the plaintiff into the river water and finding out who emerges first from the water. The one who emerges first will be labelled as the culprit.

It is of utmost significance to unambiguously present the difference between Nampou and Khullakpu. Khullakpu is conventionally identified as the Chief. Influenced by the autocratic power of the Meitei rulers, the authorities of the state, after independence, accepted Khullakpu as the highest and the sole authority of a tribal village. Even a Rongmei scholar such as Gangmei Jangailu in her thesis identified the first settler as the chief of a village erroneously (2013: 33). She went to the extent of calling the chief by the name Nampou (ibid.: 33). This error of identifying the chief as the Nampou puts Gangmei Jangailu's entire thesis on a shaky foundation. Customarily, Nampou is the final authority for he is the founder of the village. Khullakpu is an imperial leftover that continues to serve the interest of the modern state and not a part of the traditional customary institution. Under the influence of Meitei rulers, Rongmei villages internalised the practice of appointing a Khullakpu ritualistically by the Nampou. But the fact remains that the institution of Khullak is foreign to Rongmei traditional village polity. Being a stooge of the autocratic Meitei rulers Khullakpu enjoyed more powerful authority and sustained the legacy of a foreign rule. The sanctity of the traditional authority of Nampou is further battered with the institution of Chairmanship under the popular body known as village authority in the hills. It is further attacked with the coming of the autonomous district council in the hills that often operates against the customary laws in the best interest of the state.

Another striking difference between Nampou and Khullakpu is

concerning their life partner.[7] It is a fact that the position of Khullakpu is not customarily rooted in the belief system of the Rongmei. Nevertheless, it has been internalised and ritualised as part of their belief system. This is evident from the prevalent belief and practice in some Rongmei villages (not in all villages) in which a Khullakpu whose wife has passed away is not allowed to continue to hold the post. It is considered against the customary law and a taboo to go against this practice. So this issue is not a religious issue but a matter of adaptation for survival. However, one needs to be certain that the institution of Khullak is not inherent in the customary social system of the Rongmei and, therefore, the element of taboo in this context is an exaggeration. Nevertheless, it is a reflection of the pivotal role and reverence assigned to women in Rongmei society. A wife is believed to be the strength of a man. The wife of a man is expected to offer her views on any issue, though not in public fora but in their private space, i.e. when they are at home. It is a commonly held knowledge that some wives influence men that affect their decisions and actions in social, political and religious realms that have far-reaching implications on the people. A Khullakpu, by his duty and role, is expected to have someone who would invariably help him, not only in decision making but also in matters conventionally believed to be mundane. The wife of a Khullakpu is expected to give noble advice and help him in taking the right decision and do justice to people. Khullakpu is the one person of a village who would interact with the Meitei rulers and now with the modern state authorities.[8] He cannot be alone without any emotional, moral and physical support at his ripened age. However, the Nampou may not be expected to compulsorily have a living wife. Nampou is the owner of a village and the law of succession is not subject to the marital status of the potential successor of a dying Nampou. The law of succession is sanctified by the divine plan. The Meitei rulers did not disturb the tranquillity of such a divine institution of the Rongmei and, therefore, the authority of Nampou is left untouched within the confines of a village. The Meitei rulers associated rather freely with the Khullakpu whom they instituted to expand their influence and rule in Rongmei villages. The position of Nampou remains confined to one particular clan that established the village unless there is a collective decision of the clan to offer the authority of Nampou to another clan.

What is the stand of TRC on the status of Khullakpu? Khomeimacha Kamson vividly recalled the General Secretary of TRC Phom (Assam, Manipur and Nagaland) approving of a widower continuing with the post of Khullak. But Khomeimacha unequivocally remembered that earlier it was not accepted within the TRC community. He further said that he had told the General Secretary of TRC not to mellow in such a wavering stand on such an issue. Thus, an assessment of TRC as a reformed religion impacting a change in village polity, is not a farfetched claim. Interestingly, all the belief systems of Zeliangrong accord a certain degree of a divine essence to Khullak position despite being an externally induced autocratic instrument. Thus, Khomeimacha rightly summed up the institution of Khullak as an institution concerning the question of survival amidst foreign elements with not an iota of religious significance in the beginning.

The Rongmei villages are not strictly uniform in their social composition. Every tribe and tongue can be an inhabitant of a village after accepting any of the Rongmei clans. However, no villager is allowed to sell their land to any other non-Zeliangrong people. It was observed among the Nagas that 'No one will sell the land of one tribe to an outsider' (Ramunny 1993: 2, cited in Iyer 1994: 675). The Nampou customarily holds control over the village though each villager is the owner of his respective land and house. A similar pattern of landholding system is prevalent among the Kachins in Burma (now Myanmar). Among the Kachins, the concept of *madu* signifies the 'final authority' of the chief over everything of the village and *madu wa* explains the ownership of a house-holder or a villager's ownership of a house (Leach 2004). The practice of not selling any part of village land to others who do not belong to the Zeliangrong group speaks of the strong belief in the divine value of the land which is far removed from the commercial value of a commodity. A similar conception of land is well illuminated in the classic Letter from Chief Seattle to the President of the United States of America, Franklin Pierce. Such strong adherence to customary law concerning village land is still extant among TRC and other belief groups. With such customary law among the Rongmei, the collective identity of Zeliangrong groups is reaffirmed and strengthened. Unfortunately, such attachment to the land is gradually fading away with the predominance of the institution of Khullak. There are several instances of Rongmei village Khullakpus in the hills either selling land to Kukis or singly settling compensation amount on account of land acquisition for state-funded projects in the hills and causing immense trouble for other villagers. Amidst all these uncomfortable experiences of the Zeliangrong people, the group that still holds on to customary laws and practices, and preserves the ancestral ethos and identities of the tribe is, among few others, Tingkao Ragwang Chapriak. The belief systems of the Zeliangrong people have withstood all such inevitable changes.

The belief system of any of the groups of Zeliangrong people can be analysed in the context of any of the other remaining groups. They have the same religious origin. The Zeliangrong groups, though divided dialectically, still celebrate their collective origin. It is evident from the strength of responses from the survey that a significant number of the surveyed people still believe that the Zeliangrong people share a common origin. They believe that their ways of life, even if it is confined to the Rongmei community, nurture their common Zeliangrong identity. 64.5 per cent of the surveyed Rongmei TRC followers share a belief that their TRC belief system is a strong factor in keeping alive the collective Zeliangrong identity. Each of the four groups has clan equivalents in the other three groups. The basic structure of a village polity is the same across the four groups.

Customary Exogamy

The original Zeliangrong clans, i.e. Pamei and Newmei are further divided into several sub-clans to facilitate inter-clan marriages and forbid clan endogamy. Other clans, Gangmei and Longmei, apart from the sub-clans of Pamei and Newmei, are also created. Same clan marriage is taboo. The marriage system is strictly exogamous in some Rongmei villages in Manipur valley. In the hills due to erroneous interpretation of the Church's teachings on 'holy marriage',[9] same clan marriage is hardly tabooed. The practice of exogamy is indispensable in an understanding of village polity. The customary law concerning marriage exercises social, religious and political functions that shape the state of affairs of a Rongmei village. The institution of marriage is extremely crucial as it is the most basic factor deciding the nature of every relation known to exist between human beings and between human beings and God, gods and goddesses. Certain rituals, the law of succession, certain rights and privileges become meaningless or impossible for those who defied the customary clan exogamy.

The Zeme Council Nagaland states, '... in certain exceptional cases a man can choose his life partner from the same clan but a lineage span of not less than ten generation (Heu kerei)' (2011: 9) must separate their parents. Such a case of leniency is best understood as an influence of Christianity upon the Zeme of Nagaland, the Indian state, which claims to have 95 per cent of its population as Christians. It could also be a remnant of the occasional old practice of same clan marriage during the days of headhunting in which difficulties abounded in finding a life partner from outside the village. However, among the Rongmei in Manipur valley, the privilege of such exception is ruled out. Some of the practices among the different groups of Zeliangrong may vary though certain beliefs remain impressively uniform across the groups. According to Chaoba Kamson,[10] same clan marriage brings the curse of God upon the village. The village is cursed to have very low productivity and never to prosper as long as the same clan couple(s) dwell in the village. For this reason, such couples are immediately excommunicated and thrown out of the village. They are punished severely to the extent of burning their pieces of clothes to symbolise their deaths.

Clan exogamy is strictly associated with totemism. Sigmund Freud relates totem with taboo as: 'The most ancient and important taboo prohibitions are the two basic laws of totemism: not to kill the totem animal and to avoid sexual intercourse with members of the totem clan of the opposite sex' (2004: 37). Identifying with the same totem enables members of a clan to practise clan exogamy strictly.

Sexual intercourse between individuals sharing the same totem is firmly tabooed. There is no moral, social and religious approval of such intra-clan marriage.

Totemism may be put into a proper religious perspective from the oral tradition shared among the Kamei clan of the Rongmei people. A man named Kaamguang had a wife named Phungluanliu. They had seven sons and a daughter. The daughter was the eldest of eight siblings. The seven sons were Singongmei, Malangmei, Pamei, Phaomei, Khandangmei, Ngaomei and Kamson in descending order of their ages. The daughter was Poutaliu also known as Duithuanlu. The origin of Kamei's totem begins from one of the descendants of Kaamguang. The following story is extracted from a contribution made by Kamei Ganglaona (2008) for a Souvenir on the occasion of the Silver Jubilee of Kamei Kaikhong Kariumei of Ragailong village, Imphal, Manipur.

One fine morning a mother who was a wife of a Kamei clan was preparing to leave for their field along with her husband. They were in hurry. The mother told her daughter to cook plantain stem. Plantain stem is called *ngak* or *angak* in the Rongmei dialect. As the mother was in a hurry and she was moving away from her house, her daughter did not hear her instruction properly. The daughter heard it as *ngana* meaning a baby. The daughter tried to clarify. She asked her mother whether she meant *ngana*. The mother who had walked some distance away from her house also did not hear her daughter saying *ngana*. The mother heard it as *angak* and she replied to her daughter affirmatively. The daughter became extremely tense and helpless. She cooked the rice but she was still not sure what to do with her mother's instruction. In such a state of dilemma, she was further troubled by an evil man named Kaboutou who told her that her mother had asked her to kill and cook the *ngana*. She wondered if her mother had told her to cook the *ngana*. She took a sword and tries to kill her younger sibling. Every time she tried to kill the baby she found it smiling. She could not kill the baby. But Kaboutou came and warned her against her mother's beating if she didn't cook the *ngana*. She finally killed and cooked the *ngana*. After the *ngana* was cooked she was extremely terrified. To escape the wrath of her parents she became Ahui-na (green pigeon) and perched on a tall tree. Her parents came back and saw what their daughter had done to the *ngana*. But they loved their daughter despite what she had done. They called her to come back. The daughter refused and left for good.

It is because of this belief in the human origin of green pigeon that it is taken as the totem of the Kamei clan. The parents of the girl who became Ahui-na decided from that day that all the descendants of Kaamguang who became members of the Kamei clan would avoid eating and even touching Ahui-na. The name Kamei is derived from the name of their ancestor Kaamguang. The names of seven sons of Kaamgung became the sub-clans of the Kamei clan.

Among the Rongmei group totem points to a common ancestor, meaning a single bloodline. The aforesaid oral tradition, no matter how mythical it might be, successfully guides one to capture the shared essence of totemism that strictly regulates clan exogamy. Such is the social function of mythology and its perennial relevance in a scientific study of society.

Marriage is also one crucial domain that reflects a sense of ethics among the Rongmei people. Marriage is not merely about religious obligation towards God. It carries a strong ethical connotation that offers a perspective towards understanding the social life of the people. Among the Rongmei people if a boy and a girl elope they may share the same bed on the first night they elope. But if they get married, after going through all the customary practices the newly wedded couple are made to sleep separately for the first five days. The bride is made to sleep with her friends in the groom's house for five consecutive nights. The groom will go and sleep in the common dormitory in Khangchu for five days. After *jang pangu kokmei* meaning completion of five days, the newly wedded couple will share a bed and consummate their marriage.

In olden days, marriage often took place between a boy and a girl who might not be acquainted with each other. The decision of parents and elders was highly revered. The potential couple hardly questioned the wisdom of the elders. In such marriages as the bride and the groom were new to each other, they were given time to know each other and get cosy with each other and with other members of the family of the groom. For this purpose, five days were earmarked for the newly wedded couple to prepare emotionally to finally consummate their marriage. This is no longer a common practice.

Rationalised Identity

Zeliangrong people are known to have assimilated people who are of different ethnic groups. This is spectacular within the Rongmei people, especially in Manipur valley. There are villages in Nagaland in which some Angami villagers adopted the cultures of Zeme and now identify themselves as Zeme people. The reverse is also known to exist in Nagaland. The cause of this is traced to the practice of headhunting and prolonged feuds between the Angamis and the Zeliangrong people. Rongmei elders claim that there are Rongmei people in Mizoram who are now identified as Mizos. They were believed to have settled in the present state of Mizoram during the period of *Sangna Ri* (headhunting). They are believed to have adapted to their surroundings as a survival strategy. Due to continuous efforts to survive amidst headhunting, the Zeliangrong and the Nagas, in general, failed to develop and consolidate a rich language and script. This has resulted in the present plethora of oral traditions.

The social system of Rongmei people allows for the assimilation of any group of people within the clan system of the Rongmei. The Rongmei people have four major exogamous clans. They are Kamei, Golmei, Gangmei and Longmei. While the first three clans have their sub-clans, the Longmei does not have sub-clans. Corresponding clans among Zeme, Liangmai and Inpui also practise clan exogamy. Sometimes non-Zeliangrong people are assimilated into any of the clans after going through a ritual under the supervision of the *Pei*.

There are three ways to become Rongmei. Firstly, it is through birth. The second means is marriage. The third process is through adoption and it is controversial. Adoption is of two types. The first type of adoption is a mere adoption of a non-Rongmei by a family of any of the Rongmei clan. In this type of adoption, the new entrant does not adhere to social and cultural obligations. He is not necessarily recognised by the highest authority of a village as a member of a village. But his or her presence in a village as a member of one of the clans is acknowledged. He or she cannot be a member of the highest body of a village, *Pei*. Another type of adoption goes through a similar process as mentioned in the first case but also become a member of a *Pei*. The children will be members of Khangchu (boys' dormitory) and Luchu (girls' dormitory). A wife will also be a member of Lapui Kaibang and Mathenmei Kaibang subsequently. Depending on the clan of the adopted family, the head of the family may even become the Nampou or Khullak of a village. Therefore, the two types of adoption are classified as *Pei tin makmei* (one without membership in a *Pei*) and *Pei tinmei* (one with membership in a *Pei*) respectively.

When non-Zeliangrong people are assimilated within the Rongmei group they are mandated to be adopted by a family of one particular clan and they are bound by the practice of clan exogamy of the Rongmei people as long as they are in a Rongmei village. This applies to both types of adoption. They are part of the culture and belief systems of the Rongmei people. They become Rongmei using adoption to the effect of strictly adhering to clan exogamy irrespective of their earlier identity. This group of Rongmei people may be termed as rationalised Rongmei as they become Rongmei after a meticulous calculation of the pros and cons of such a process of indigenisation into the Rongmei group. It is seen that the adoption of Rongmei identity is crucial in identifying one's identity with the larger Rongmei group to facilitate the enjoyment of benefits reserved only for the Rongmei people in a Rongmei village. The rationalised Rongmei thus engage in social categorisation in distinctly identifying the various Rongmei clans. This process happens simultaneously along with social comparison as the to-be rationalised Rongmei differentiates between the Rongmei and his or her pre-adoption identity. Finally, he or she identifies with the Rongmei identity as he or she is assimilated into the Rongmei group.

The term rationalised Rongmei refers to those who adopt Rongmei identity to usher in social, political, economic and cultural benefits from the Rongmei group and the village in particular. This is a rationalised identity. The rationalisation of Rongmei identity is contextual. Where a village has a Christian population the rationalised Rongmei, if Christian, are detached from most of the cultural elements and enjoy the right to settle as members of the village with the right to own land and a right of inheritance of the landed properties by the progenies. The rationalised identity with a religion different from the ancestral belief system of the village is a double-edged rationalisation in which the attainment of rationalised identity wards off the complexities of the ancestral belief system of the village while availing of the social, political and economic benefits. If the rationalised Rongmei is not Christian, proximity to cultural elements is witnessed to be stronger. There are rationalised Rongmei from the second type of adoption who abandon the Rongmei surname and use the original surname which is not of the Rongmei. It is in this systematic calculation done through the adoption of a Rongmei surname initially when the benefits are endowed by the village authority and later relinquish the Rongmei surname after the benefits are firmly rooted that the concept of rationalised identity becomes more appropriate.

In one of the most influential Rongmei villages, Namgailong,[11] in Manipur valley, a Meitei family became Rongmei through the *Pei tinmei* type of adoption discussed above and enjoyed land right. The man was a Meitei and married a Rongmei woman of a Gangmei clan of Namgailong village. Later, he even became a member of Namgailong village *Pei*. His son married a Meitei girl. After his death, his son who married a Meitei girl along with his family converted to Christianity. The name of the great-grandson, who was also an inhabitant of Namgailong village, is entered under Meitei surname, 'Singh', in his school record. Note that even to this day non-Zeliangrong people or any individual with non-Zeliangrong surnames are not given the right or privilege to buy land in Rongmei villages. Some rationalised Rongmei individuals adopt Rongmei surnames and buy land. After years of settlement, they re-emerge with or assert their former non-Rongmei surnames despite identifying themselves as Rongmei. Thus, there are Rongmei with non-Zeliangrong surnames. 'Singh' in Rongmei!

Khomeimacha Kamson[12] holds a view that disagrees with the practice of clan adoption. According to him, the change of or adoption of a clan is wrong from a religious point of view. Clans, according to him, are given by God. It is God's plan to be born in a particular clan and to adhere strictly to the customary practice of clan exogamy. The clan system is misused. A very pertinent question is raised by Khomeimacha Kamson: Can a person from a Kamei clan converted to a Gangmei clan marry someone from a Kamei clan? This question thus reduces the practice of clan adoption by any of the Zeliangrong groups as farcical which is untenable religiously and genetically as well. In the context of clan adoption by non-Zeliangrong, although genetically it is tenable, clan being a divine creation, it is, according to Khomeimacha Kamson, considered to be religiously wrong.

The bathing ritual of Tingkao Ragwang Kariak (TRK) and similar ritual among TRC, and ritualised induction of outsiders as practised among Pupou Chap among the Rongmei people, open an opportunity for any outsiders to penetrate the social and cultural fabrics of Rongmei people to the extent of either strengthening or demolishing the sanctity of the beliefs and social institutions. Given the emerging trend of identity assertion among various groups, the practice of assimilation of other groups within the Rongmei group even by adopting any of the Rongmei clans is becoming a cause of uncomfortable identity dynamics. This assimilation practice stands relevant in a new identity discourse bearing the concept of rationalised identity.

The concept of rationalised identity also helps in understanding another phenomenon of uxorilocal as witnessed among the Rongmei people. It is observed that some Rongmei men go for what is locally termed as *Noumangmei* meaning matrilocality to the extent of some matronymic instances. A similar practice is illuminated by the term *zhao-xu* in the Chinese context. According to Xiaoying Qi, 'surnaming practices are family strategies of social and economic significance' (2017: 2). Qi traces the root of widespread matronymic cases in China to the state policy of population control that espoused one child. This policy led families with no male child to marry their daughters under the condition that the groom accepts matronymic. This is done to ensure what is termed by Baker as a 'continuum of descent' (Baker 1979, cited in Qi 2017: 7) of the bride's male ancestors. Besides 'enhanced sense of personal identity, liberalised values, feminist viewpoints, educational achievement, pre-marriage professional identity', 'low religiosity' is identified as the reasons for women continuing with their surnames even after their marriage (Qi 2017: 2). In the case of Rongmei's practice of noumangmei, the continuum of descent is mostly in favour of the groom's ancestors. The surname of the groom is transposed to the bride. The practice of matrilocality and matronymic, similar to the Chinese context, is also seen among the Rongmei bride's family with no male siblings to live with the bride's parents. However, a man who goes for noumangmei becomes the talk of the village and an object of mockery.

It is the belief in and practice of clan exogamy that binds the Rongmei together. This is also the case with the other three Zeliangrong groups. Besides the oral traditions and common linguistic origin what keeps together the four Zeliangrong groups is this clan exogamy. Such sameness prevailing among the four groups infuses a sense of unity. It is thus, the religious elements of their ancestral belief systems that bind them together.

Zeliangrong as Nationalism

G. Aloysius conceptualises 'nation' as 'a socio-political community in modernity' and sees nationalism 'as an ideology or a movement' (1998: 11). Therefore, nationalism, according to Aloysius, may be said to be organic in that it evolves and grows as we see an element of cognition in being 'ideology' and a growing process in being a 'movement'. This concept is appropriate in the context of Zeliangrong nationalism which is never recognised by others in terms of specific geographical boundary. The spirit of nationalism as an ideology, if not as a movement, can be claimed to be still extant amidst myriad of other nationalisms.

The Indian nationalism, the Naga nationalism, the Meitei nationalism have not completely subsumed the pan-Zeliangrong nationalistic feelings shared across the geographically and politically trifurcated Zeliangrong people. The fact that the nomenclature Zeliangrong was coined and Zeliangrong Union was formed in 1947 to systematically organise Zeme, Liangmai, Rongmei and Inpui people for socio-economic development in an independent India within the framework of the Indian state based on their shared belief in a common ancestor and thus shared culture and beliefs unambiguously, fits Zeliangrong nation as 'a socio-political community in modernity' (Aloysius 1998) bereft of politically recognised geographical boundary.

According to G. Aloysius—nation—in the sense of 'a socio-political community', precedes nationalism (1998: 11). A formal emergence of Zeliangrong nationalism may be seen as a late phenomenon. It was never seen until the formation of Zeliangrong in 1947. The constituent groups of Zeliangrong even before the formation of their modern collective identity 'Zeliangrong' in 1947 shared an implicit sense of fraternity kept alive in their folk songs, rituals, customary laws and practices. F. Fukuyama sees nationalism as a 'specifically modern phenomenon because it replaces the relationship of lordship and bondage with mutual and equal recognition' (1992: 266, cited in Aloysius, 1998: 146). Also according to B.R. Ambedkar, 'Nationality is a social feeling. It is a feeling of the corporate sentiment of oneness which makes those who are charged with it feel that they are kith and kin' (1990, Vol. III: 31, cited in Aloysious 1998: 153). Zeliangrong constituent groups, notwithstanding their primordial knowledge of fraternity, were constantly engaged in headhunting. But with the resurgence of collective feeling towards the end of colonial rule there emerged Zeliangrong nationalism undoing all the bygone differences towards building fraternity.

G. Aloysius refuted the attempt of Ranajit Guha to consolidate peasant and tribal movements. Such an attempt, according to Aloysius, would tantamount to distorting 'the specificity of tribal consciousness' which according to Aloysius, invariably carried along with them 'a territory-based identity component' (1998: 74). Despite the almost complete absence of written record the tribal had an unambiguous sense of their territory that never came in conflict with those of other groups. However, Zeliangrong nationalism will be a misplaced argument if one begins the argument based on the territorial limit of its expanse. Today Zeliangrong nationalism is contextually ideological. Zeliangrong regionalism expressed as Zeliangrong homeland was a movement since the 1980s. Zeliangrong regionalism is subsumed within Naga nationalism as 'Zeliangrong regionalism within Naga nationalism' in the unwritten words of Professor Gangmumei Kamei as told to me by Gaidon Kamei, former President of United Naga Council in 2012. Zeliangrong nationalism as an ideology was a socio-economic aspiration expressed in 1947. The transference of Zeliangrong nationalism to Zeliangrong regionalism within Naga nationalism may be understood in the context of the words of G. Aloysius: 'The mobilization of the nation's masses in nationalism takes place not merely' based on the 'certain primordial affinity in culture, as in ancient times, but on the basis of commonality of political purpose and destiny as the emergence of a socio-political community' (1998: 15). G. Aloysius further observes, 'Nationalism as self-determination for the cultural collectivity is inextricably tied to nationalism as self-determination of the individuals within that collectivity' (ibid.: 16). Zeliangrong is a part of Nagas' belief in a common ancestor. However, it is not merely under the common belief in the same ancestor and several similarities of cultural realities that Zeliangrong shares nationalism with other Naga groups. The sole desire for self-determination consolidated their past commonalities to forge future commonalities despite the many differences. This belief in the same ancestor draws the Nagas to a shared cultural pattern and they view themselves as a cultural collectivity. Zeliangrong people see the possibility of self-determination within this Naga cultural collectivity marked by stronger affinity. This Zeliangrong nationalism is contemporarily more extant in the sense of collective identity despite the conflicting hues of collective and individual nomenclatures.

It is interesting to note that so far there is no known oral tradition among the Zeliangrong people that illuminates any duel or war for land. Zeliangrong nationalism is rooted in their common origin of social, political, economic, religious and cultural realities. The dimension of territorial nationalism seems to have emerged in Zeliangrong nationalism after they sensed a threat to their land inherited from their ancestors. They seemed not to have enjoyed a sense of owning land individually. Thus, in their social system, there is a person called Nampou meaning owner of the whole village. Though Nampou is sanctioned as the symbolical owner of the land of the village he is not an owner of the village in the sense of individual ownership. But a fact remains that the individual villager does not own land that may be considered as his exclusive possession. The ownership of land enjoyed by an individual in a village extends only within the context of the Zeliangrong community. Thus, land may be sold to any of the constituent Zeliangrong groups even without the knowledge or permission of the village authority if the buyer is also from the same village. No individual is allowed to sell land to any other non-Zeliangrong groups. It is also forbidden to sell land even to fellow Zeliangrong groups from other villages if the village authority of the owner of the land is not informed about the transaction. Thus, the ownership of land ceases once Zeliangrong individuals come in contact with any non-Zeliangrong groups and even with fellow Zeliangrong groups of other villages. Identity is linked to the land. Thus any part of a village is linked with the identity of the villagers. The identity of an individual villager is associated with the village lands and the social institutions operating within the village territory. Land cannot be simply possessed without establishing a relationship with the village collective ethos and social institutions. The villagers are bound by the customary laws of the Zeliangrong and these laws are in the custody of the village authorities. Ignoring the village authorities of the traditional institutions in any matter concerning the customary laws is equivalent to a breach of the laws that leads to social and religious sanctions. Such relationship with the land is immensely disturbed with the coming of the institutions of Khullak and Village Authority under the state.

Such rich and complex social dynamics that build and nurture the collective Zeliangrong identity is based entirely on customary laws which are rooted in their beliefs. Being one of the collective guardians of Zeliangrong ancestral beliefs and various customary laws and practices, Tingkao Ragwang Chapriak may be regarded as a key player in the domain of Zeliangrong collective identity and Zeliangrong ideological nationalism.

More than their religious identities they prefer to identify themselves with their cultural elements. In the Table 2.1 it is observed that 60.5 per cent of the respondents assert their cultural identity over religious and professional identities. Their Zeliangrong and Rongmei identities are seen to be more crucial in their identity.

Table 2.1: The First Identity Preferred to be Claimed

Identity	*Per cent*
Religious	31.1
Cultural	60.5
Professional	3.0
Don't Know	5.4
Total	100.0

Source: Author's survey.

Here a distinction is made between cultural identity and religious identity by secularising the notion of culture given the Zeliangrong Christians who continue to remain Zeliangrong and Rongmei despite their conversion. It is in this context that culture is delineated completely from religious element to allow an inclusive notion of culture to include Zeliangrong and Rongmei people of other religions.

The customary laws are believed to continue to enjoy divine sanction. The age old traditions of maintaining their customary laws are to a large extent continued. Even Christians are found to adhere to some of the customary laws. Thus, even Christians are not allowed to go against clan exogamy. It is a belief in the divine sanction on all these practices that such age old traditions are still witnessed and the Zeliangrong collective identity and Zeliangrong nationalism are ritually affirmed. TRC by being the dominant religious group plays a crucial role in reaffirming the divine sanction endowed upon all the customary laws and practices. Zeliangrong nationalism is not directly connected with TRC as a religion but with the many customary laws and practices all rooted in the beliefs of TRC.

TRC is a belief system and not a political institution. It does not influence any political ideology or agendas. However, strictly within the Zeliangrong context, TRC plays a crucial role in protecting the rights of the Zeliangrong people with its adherence to many customary laws. Land rights remain protected from the land-amassing toxic spirit of capitalism. The land is still sacred and not commodified. With several villages proclaiming TRC, the village institutions are gradually dominated by TRC adherents.

It is a fact that many followers of TRC prefer to identify themselves as Kabui instead of Rongmei. Despite this, it is also a no lesser truth that the collective identity of Zeme, Liangmai, Rongmei and Inpui under the nomenclature Zeliangrong is still accepted within TRC. Thus, TRC is very much a part of the Zeliangrong Religious Council (*Zeliangrong Ra Chap-Riak Phom*). Many of the correspondence with other civil societies and government institutions are carried out under the Zeliangrong Religious Council. In the attempt of the TRC adherents to acquire land from the government of Manipur for a collective burial ground for villages located in Imphal urban areas Zeliangrong Religious Council played a pivotal role in all the correspondences with the Forest Department of Manipur Government and United Committee, Manipur (UCM), a valley-based organisation. For reasons unknown, Zeliangrong Religious Council has been rechristened as Tingkao Ragwang Chapriak Phom (Phom means organisation) (Kamei 2009: i). However, writings on TRC (Kamson 2011a; Kamson 2014) continue to use the name Zeliangrong even after the change of the name.

Notwithstanding the usage of the name 'Zeliangrong', a section of Rongmei people in Manipur valley religiously fight for the name Kabui. The origin of the name Kabui as a name of people is mysterious and there is no indisputable evidential conclusion on the origin of this name used to identify a people. All Zeliangrong Students Union (Assam, Manipur & Nagaland) claims Kabui[13] to be originally used by the Meitei to refer to the so-called Kabui. The author endorses this assessment of the Students Union. The assessment of the author is based on the historical material drawn from the reading of the work of Gangmumei Kamei (2015).

There is a reference to a man named Loitongbam Kabui sent as Cheithaba in 1478 (Akoijam 2004: 26). This account of Cheithaba given by Akoijam is doubtful. According to Gangmumei Kamei, Cheitharol meaning sending of a person to announce the end of a year by symbolically releasing a stick, began in 1484 AD (2015: 40-1). According to Gangmumei Kamei, Cheithaba was a state ceremony and the person sent as Cheithaba is made a 'scapegoat for the evil burdens of the king and the country for the coming year' (ibid.: 41). Nevertheless, it is noted here that the name Kabui is already in use by the Meitei in the fifteenth century much before the coming of the British in the name Loitongbam Kabui. But interestingly, Loitongbam is a Meitei name and not a Rongmei / Kabui name.

There is also a suggestion that the name Kabui was already in use even before the fifteenth century AD. This is based on the name Kabui Salang Maiba in the Khamba-Thoibi epic. According to the epic, when Khamba was seized and produced before the Kabui Salang Maiba the former said, 'Wherefore have thy men seized me and taken my load straps from me? I am come hither to see my Father's friend the Salang Maiba [*sic*]' (Hodson 1908: 145). According to Gangmumei Kamei, based on his understanding from the Moiranglon, king Chingkhu Telheiba '[p]erhaps' ruled in the twelfth century and the beginning of the thirteenth century (Kamei 2015: 220). Based on Moirang Kangleiron, the Khamba-Thoibi epic emerged during Telheiba's reign (K. Sobita Devi 1985: 64, cited in Kamei 2015: 219). Based on chronology prepared by K. Matum in his *Moirang Kangla* and M. Nodiachand's *Moirang Salai*, there are six rulers from Chingkhu Telheiba, whose reign is not dated, to Sanahongba whose reign is dated as AD 1381-1432 (Kamei 2015: 203). The preceding rulers before the reign of Chingkhu Telheiba are also not dated though the numbers of years of their rule are given. The reigns of the four rulers between them are also not dated. Chronologically, Chingkhu Telheiba ruled for 55 years, Punshiba for 72 years, Khongjamba for 53 years, Yoirenba for 49 years and Punshi Khurelchanba for 69 years. Summing up the years of rule from Chingkhu Telheiba to Punshi Khurelchanba one gets 298 years. Subtracting 298 years from 1381, the year that began the reign of Sanahongba whose reign is dated one gets the year 1083 which is the beginning of the reign of Chingkhu Telheiba. Thus, the reign of Chingkhu Telheiba is AD 1083-1138. Therefore, Gangmumei Kamei's assessment of the reign of Chingkhu Telheiba ending towards the beginning of the thirteenth century is erroneous. One may safely conclude that the epic of Khamba-Thoibi, that mentions Kabui Salang Maiba, prevailed during the eleventh and twelfth century. This also affirms a conclusion that the name Kabui meaning a Mithun in Liangmai dialect was a name used to identify the so-called

Kabui by the Meitei much before the arrival of the colonisers or western anthropologists.

However, one is not sure why the Meitei would have used the name Kabui to identify the people so far called Kabui. Did Salang Maiba acccpt thc 'Kabui' in his name which meant Mithun in his language? Did the name Kabui for Salang Maiba attach any religious significance to his role in the royal court given the ritualistic significance of Mithun in the Zeliangrong belief system? These are questions one needs to attach to a study of Zeliangrong identity. However, the most important question is, did Salang Maiba give his name to the Meitei as Kabui Salang Maiba? Another question is, was the reference to Kabui Salang Maiba the first reference to the name Kabui? The possibility of the so-called Kabui having adopted this name is not to be ruled out given the sacredness of the animal Mithun or Kabui.

Despite the limitations in the nomenclature 'Zeliangrong', it is still exigent in several discourses concerning various Zeliangrong belief systems. Zeliangrong is a fulcrum that exerts a centripetal force upon all the various religious, cultural, economic and political experiences of the groups. The name Zeliangrong thrives alongside political aspiration. Thus, it is said, 'No other future but the political future is the real future of Zeliangrong'.[14]

NOTES

1. The mother of the author who is a tribal Christian since her childhood recollected an incident in the 1970s in which she was asked by her mother-in-law to arrange the offerings for Sanamahi deity. Her husband's family belonged to Pupou Chap. She clearly remembered bringing fried pulses from tea hotel. Her husband's aunty had a riot-laughter on learning fried pulses being bought for offering to Sanamahi. The author also, as a child, witnessed in the 1980s and 1990s, many of his Rongmei neighbours having a place for Sanamahi inside their houses in one of the corners of a main bedroom. The author belongs to a Rongmei tribe scheduled as Kabui.
2. He mentioned this while speaking on the occasion of TRC Youth Conference 13-14 October 2018.

3. Khomeimacha Kamson is a retired Assistant Conservator of Forest in the forest department of Manipur state government. He is a Khangbon in Ragailong Khangchu and Ganchang in the *Pei*. Ganchang is the first entry level in a *Pei* and Khangbon is the highest level at Khangchu.
4. There is another disastrous impact of the Village Authority Act of 1956 in the context of Zeliangrong people. The Act has been deeply internalised especially by the tribal people in the hills as the positions injected by the very Act translate into certain powers and benefits to the elected tribal leaders. Tharon village under Tamenglong district, quite interestingly, terms the practice of election under the Village Authority Act of 1956 as tradition of the village since time immemorial while rejecting the institutions of Khunbuship or Nampou and Khullak. The village recognises 'chairmanship', elected under the Village Authority Act, as 'village tradition since time immemorial' (see the appendix for the newspaper clipping). Khunbu is a Meitei translation for Nampou which is a traditional institution of Zeliangrong people. Interestingly, this has been derecognised in the interest of 'chairmanship'. During the military operations in the hills during the heydays of Naga struggle against India, several villagers were tortured and maimed. The village leaders, especially the Khullakpu, were the first targets. The Khullakpu was called out in dark and forced to summon all the villagers. Often the Khullakpu bear the brunt of the rage of the military personnel. It immensely discouraged village elders from assuming the post of Khullak despite the traditionalised powers conferred upon it. However, after the coming of peace in the hills and the institution of Village Authority Act, 1956 many villages began to eye for the post of Chairmanship because of its lucrative powers and functions. As the posts of Nampou and Khullakpu are hereditary and officially not conferred any power or role in a village administration, the elected post, Chairmanship, which is lucrative and tempting, came to be viewed as an integral part of a village polity and thus erroneously termed as a 'tradition since time immemorial'.
5. Some people callously refer to hoe instead of axe. Note that it is an axe which is used as a *tan laogai* and not hoe. A hoe is a long-handled metal blade while an axe may be defined as a metal tool for chopping. *Tan-laogai* must be an axe and not a hoe.
6. Among the Zeliangrong people no form of punishment imposed by a *Pei* can amount to capital punishment. The punishment system of the Zeliangrong people is primarily deterrent in nature to the extent

of imposing heavy fines upon the culprit when proven guilty. In view of the nature of livelihood marked primarily by hunting and farming with some domesticated animals, the kind of punishment imposed conventionally in the form of pig and sometimes even a fully grown mithun often took a heavy toll on the daily life of the family of the culprit. Seeing such heavy toll on the normal functioning of daily life due to heavy fine imposed many are often deterred from committing similar wrongs. Sometimes punishments are in the form of severe excommunication in which the culprit, sometimes other family members too, is chased away from the village for good. Another form of excommunication is termed locally as *singlup khaimei*. Singlup khaimei is discontinuation of membership of the family of the culprit in which the family is forbidden from meeting and talking with any individual of the village within the village, this includes even the closest relatives of the excommunicated family. They are forbidden from drawing water from the village pond. No one from the village will enter the house even if someone dies in the family. No ritual will be performed and they will not participate in village festivals and other secular activities. Save for the permission to settle in the village they are considered to be non-existing in the village. Such a severe form of excommunication served the purpose of deterring the villagers from doing any wrong. Considering the degree of severity of deterrent measures reformative theory of punishment may be said to be not widely extant. Also retributive theory of punishment is meaningless in Zeliangrong groups.

7. This observation and analysis is attributed to Khomeimacha Kamson who was interviewed on 9 October 2018.
8. Even in the present days the Khullakpus of Rongmei villages in Manipur valley are used as mediums to compel the Rongmei people in the valley by the valley based organisations vigorously fighting against the aspirations of the Nagas for 'Nagalim'. A valley based organisation, United Club of Manipur organised a rally on 31 October 2018 with an aim to save Manipur. On this day the village *Pei* of Ragailong again made an announcement that the villagers are to participate with a traditional muffler in the rally compulsorily and failure to participate would lead to an imposition of monetary fine. This is not the first time. Such 'compulsory' attendance of Rongmei people in the valley in rallies organised by All Manipur United Club Organisation (AMUCO) and UCM was common in the year 2001 when a ceasefire agreement between the Government of India and National Socialist Council of

Nagalim (Isak-Muivah) popularly known as NSCN-IM was extended without territorial limit. The village *Peis* strictly ordered the villagers to attend the rallies wearing traditional attires of the Rongmei.

9. Fuamling Latdan Charuk is the six commandments of the Church. This six commandments form a part of Morning Prayer in local Catholic Church. One of the six commandments says Catholic members must not allow marriage of a couple who are related within three generations. This means that the great grandfathers from the same family line must be different. Their great grandfathers may have the same father. However, the most important part of this commandment is its subjectivity to the social norms of a community. Thus, if the social norms of a community forbids same clan marriage the commandment of the Catholic Church must not be entertained. It has been wrongly interpreted and there are already many same clan marriages.
10. He was responding to a question raised by a participant in the TRC youth conference on 14 October 2018 at Ragailong, Imphal (Manipur).
11. Namgailong is a dummy name of the village used here to respect the identity of the rationalised Rongmei family. The name of the great grandson is retrieved from the school attendance record. It is not displayed in this book as the names of other students written close to his name in the attendance record can lead to identifying the said great grandson. The principle of 'the best interest of the child' in the UNCRC is respected here.
12. In an interview on 9 October 2018.
13. Despite being condemned for being used as a name of people Kabui is well appropriated by the Inpui who wish to exclude Rongmei in the nomenclature Kabui. Many Inpui expressed that Kabui should be used to identify only the Inpui and must not include the Rongmei. Interestingly, the Inpui, on the contrary, do not wish to use the name Kabui as a name of their group for Kabui, according to Inpui, is derogatory. Kabui is also known as mithun and Bos frontalis is its scientific name. It is a domesticated free-range bovine species which has been domesticated for over 8000 years (National Research Centre on mithun). The term Kabui is most unlikely to be originally of Inpui as an older group Liangmai has it as their term. According to *Liangmai-Hindi-English Dictionary*, kabui is also given as a Liangmai word. The Liangmai translation for the Hindi word for cow has been given as 'Metam, kabui' (Kumar 1971: 7).

14. This was said by Benjamin Gangmei while speaking on the eighty fourth commemoration day of Zeliangrong Solidarity Day (*Chuksumei*) on 1 April 2018 at Chingmeirong organised by Zeliangrong Baudi. Chuksumei is a ritual which is "community's oath taking ceremony" known as *Chuksumei* (Kamei 2004: 11). *Chuksumei* ritual was conducted on 1 April 1934 at Tamenglong district of Manipur in the presence of representatives from Zeme, Liangmai, Rongmei, Inpui and even Maram (Kamei 2004). The ritual was performed to forgive the past misdeeds and end past animosities caused as a result of head hunting. The 1934 ritual declared 'solidarity and common brotherhood' (ibid.: 11). Essentially it was a ritual based on the belief in common ancestor of Zeliangrong groups and Maram people. However, such ritual is now commemorated with Christians' participation. At the commemoration of Chuksumei organised by Zeliangrong Baudi at Chingmeirong the General Secretary of TRC Phuam was present and seated as a dignitary on the dais along with many Christians who spoke profoundly on the significance of Chuksumei and it's contemporary relevance. Therefore, TRC cannot be viewed as a reality isolated from the collective Zeliangrong identity and the feeling of Zeliangrong nationalism. The reciprocal effect of customary laws on the Zeliangrong people even upon the Christians due to the religious effort to make customary laws relevant across religious groups among the Zeliangrong groups by the TRC group also cannot be ruled out.

CHAPTER 3

Belief Systems of Rongmei

As mentioned earlier, the ancestral belief system of any of the Zeliangrong groups may be analysed by referring to the belief systems of any of the other three groups. Despite the minor cultural variations between Zeme, Liangmai, Rongmei and Inpui, it is still possible to resort to referential understanding. Variations abound even within a group. Thus, according to Zeme Council Nagaland, 'there could be some slight variation in usage and application of the customary laws from village to village [but] that doesn't mean discord' they have been 'streamlined systematically with the majority' (2011: 3). Therefore, it is pertinent to look into the collective belief system of the Zeliangrong people and also recognise the variations across time and space.

The relation between the tribal people and the supernatural power they worship is marked by a principle of 'natural relationship-blood relationship' in which the supernatural power is believed to be the giver of life and either a father or mother (Bousset 1907: 62). According to Gangmumei Kamei, Zeliangrong religion is essentially characterised by polytheism with an element of henotheism and there is a practice of worshipping one supreme God picked from multiple gods (2006: 65). When Gangmumei Kamei claimed that Zeliangrong belief system is marked by polytheism with an element of henotheism he, unconsciously, admitted theoretical ambiguity. Is this the most appropriate understanding of henotheism?[1] Henotheism is the worship of many gods in which the power and jurisdiction of each god are defined and there is no overlapping of their power and authority. According to Max Mueller, it is, essentially, worship of God in different forms of God, manifested in gods. In the Zeliangrong belief system, there is no such manifestations of God or Tingkao Ragwang. There is no belief in the incarnation or *avatars* of Tingkao Ragwang. He is one and in one formless entity. Henotheism simply does not fit into any of the Zeliangrong belief systems. So, no belief system may be said to have the features of both polytheism and henotheism simultaneously. Henotheism understood in the line of Max Mueller's (1881) conception, seems to have no relevance in Zeliangorng belief systems. They are either monotheistic or polytheistic with an exception of the nature of TRK. Polytheism applies to Pupou Chap and Tingkao Ragwang Chapriak. Heraka is controversially polytheistic. Tingkao Ragwang Kariak is debatably monotheistic.[2]

The supreme God the Zeliangrong people worship is believed to be 'the creator of the universe, dispenser of good and prosperity and who lived in heaven' (Kamei 2004: 148). Three groups of deities known to be worshipped by Zeliangrong people are the Universal God and the gods of the lower realm, the deities presiding over the villages and the family's ancestors (Kamei 2004). Wine is used as an indispensable part of life from cradle to the grave. It is truly an elixir of the religious life of the Zeliangrong or the Rongmei people. However, the ferocious attack by the foot soldiers of Christian evangelisation against the belief systems and customary practices of the Rongmei people hinges immensely on local wine and this demands an analysis of the local wine.

The Wine in Perspective

Before engaging oneself in a cursory glance over the various belief systems of the Zeliangrong people, it is crucial to know how their belief systems have been viewed in general, especially by the Christians. The Christians view of the ancestral belief systems of the Rongmei people is closely tied to the local wine called *jou*.

Jou jangmei chap is the conventional derogatory epithet used by the Rongmei Christians to refer to all the Zeliangrong belief systems. *Jou jangmei* is a name used for all the followers of *jou jangmei chap*. It simply means the religion of the wine drinker. *Jou jangmei* means wine drinking or wine drinker. The followers of traditional belief systems are sweepingly identified as *jou jangmei* not just because of the use of wine in religious rituals.

Wine is an indispensable part of the religious life of the Zeliangrong people. But it is never known to have been an indispensable part of their economic activities until the Kabui (Rongmei and Inpui) settled in the valley. Wine was produced primarily for religious purposes and for basic consumption. It is used in various rites of passage of the Zeliangrong people. With growing needs and aspirations infused by their ways of valley life and with no effective alternative sources of livelihood and no political representative from among them to address their valley-tribal specific grievances, producing wine on a commercial scale became gradually phenomenal in valley Kabui villages. The religious significance of wine readily served as a protective shield against blanket condemnation against surplus commercial production.

Making wine requires a large volume of water. The topography of their new habitat in the valley ensured these needs. Some of the major rivers in Manipur valley that serve to sustain the livelihood of the Rongmei people are the Imphal river, Thoubal river, Iril river and Nambol river. These four rivers and many other water bodies with the easy valley based means of transportation immensely helped the Rongmei in the valley to produce wine on a commercial scale. Some families earn in terms of thousands in a day. The high density of population in a small valley compared to the sparsely populated hills also proves to be a perennial source of customers. This large production of wine in several villages also led to their villagers easily procuring wine for daily consumption. Many youths and young fathers lost their lives due to mindless drinking. Huge financial loss on costly medical treatments, domestic violence and many young widows are other bitter effects of the production of wine on a commercial scale. These effects are keenly observed by the neighbouring Christians and they are consequently called *jou jangmei* and their belief system condemned, unfavourably compared with Protestant Christianity and categorised as *jou jangmei chap*. It is this valley based life that gave rise to what may be termed as valley culture in which their way of life depends immensely on their daily economic activities that sustain their lives and that suit the valley topography. While in the hills with terrace farming and forest goods and wild animals, there is a forest culture in which daily commercial activities are highly restrained. This variation in the daily economic activities to sustain their lives shaped their world view and their religious life. It also shapes and nurtures their relationship with the neighbouring communities especially the Meetei Hindus and Meetei traditionalists.

Variants of Belief Systems

Zeliangrong people believe in a God who was and is known by different names. Traditionally, many gods and goddesses were also worshipped. Several spirits were appeased with elaborate sacrifices. They also worshipped the natural forces which they either feared or were in awe of. All these features are most prominent among the *Pupou Chap* with a diminishing of such features in other religious groups of the Zeliangrong people.

The beliefs were shared and heresies were strictly checked. The Zeliangrong people in Manipur valley migrated from the surrounding Manipur hills. Migration into the valley began even before the coming of Christianity in the hills. Thus, many brought along with them their ancestral belief systems as they came to Manipur valley. It may be noted here that when the Rongmei people began settling in the valley they followed only one belief system which had no name but was popularly known as *Pupou Chap* meaning ancestral belief systems. Note that *pupou chap* is not a name of any religion like *Heraka*, *Tingkao Ragwang Kariak* or *Tingkao Ragwang Chapriak*. The propensity of not addressing an older or powerful entity with a name is explicit here.

The belief systems of Zeliangrong people may be categorised into *Pupou Chap*, *Heraka*, *Tingkao Ragwang Kariak* and *Tingkao Ragwang Chapriak*. This classification may be viewed as variations in the degree of reformations except in *Pupou Chap*. But this classification based on the degree of reformations does not reflect stratification in any sense. Reformation means changes in some aspects to a certain degree. Reformation does not at all connote maintaining the status quo. Results of reformation are always placed against the status quo and primordial state. And Gangmumei Kamei defined 'Primordial religion' as 'religion with a primordial existence; existing since the beginning of time' (2006: 15). In the context of the connotations of the terms 'reformation' and 'primordial' one may safely claim that *Pupou Chap* or ancestral belief system may be considered to have been in existence since time immemorial with no changes in beliefs and practices and thus primordial. *Heraka*, *Tingkao Ragwang Kariak* and *Tingkao Ragwang Chapriak*, however, carry several reformed features and, therefore, their claim of primordiality needs further critical examination. This may not be callously interpreted into an outright dismissal of their claim of primordiality. The idea of the primordiality of religion can be interpreted in different ways.

Assertively defending the primordiality of TRC its former youth wing Secretary,[3] in the context of Zeliangrong belief systems, claimed that every religion is *pupou chap* but one needs to give a name to one's belief system and thus TRC is a *pupou chap* and *Tingkao Ragwang Chapriak* is its name. *Pupou* sometimes refers even to one's father and one's grandfather. In the Zeliangrong context, *Pupou Chap* conventionally means the primordial religion because *Pupou* also conventionally means ancestors that include even the first human being based on their oral tradition and mythology. Therefore, the term *Pupou* is another way of conveying the notion of primordiality.

Another analysis of the primordial nature of *Tingkao Ragwang Chapriak* was given by Chaoba Kamson.[4] According to him, *Tingkao Ragwang Chapriak* is a primordial religion. *Tingkao Ragwang* existed with no marked beginning. A debate on the beginning of His existence is absurd for He existed all the time. However, He was known by different names.[34] He was imagined and acknowledged by human beings in different ways and, therefore. He had different names indicating several qualities giving rise to the misconception of *Tingkao Ragwang* being a new God never worshipped earlier and thus, not primordial. According to Max Mueller, the names of God exhibit an effort to express or represent 'an idea which could never find an adequate expression or representation' (1881: 420). The names of God were eloquent and convey ideas of majesty, authority, elegance, power, supremacy, awe, reverence, so on and so forth. According to Chaoba Kamson, *Tingkao Ragwang Chapriak* that worships *Tingkao Ragwang* already existed as a belief system even before the coming of Jadonang who claimed that the 'Kabuis' did not have a 'custom' of worshipping the 'God' (Kamei 2009). *Tingkao Ragwang* is another highly revered name to refer to the 'God' worshipped by the Rongmei people with no name of religion since time immemorial and thus the 'God' referred to even by Jadonang is primordial and not a creation of Jadonang. *Tingkao Ragwang Chapriak* is the name of a belief system given to the ancestral belief system. The name of their belief system, according to Chaoba Kamson, is *the only new reality* of *Tingkao Ragwang Chapriak*. The God which is the basic element of religion is the same as before and after naming the primordial ancestral religion.

Such a complex conception of the supreme power by a group across time and space certainly demands a more critical analysis of the variants of belief systems that are the results of these varied conceptions of the supreme power.

Pupou Chap

Pupou Chap is the ancestral primordial religion. Thuanbina Gangmei callously calls it 'Nuh Neihmei Chapriak' and qualifies it as 'the religion of taboo and prayer' (2014: 2). *Nuh-Neihmei* means taboo. Such conception of *Pupou Chap* is a fallout of superficial enquiry into the notion of taboo which is erroneously reserved for several ancestral belief systems.

It is believed that there has been no change in the belief and practices of *Pupou Chap*. The followers of *Pupou Chap* claim to be the devotees of the true religion of the Zeliangrong people. They do not welcome any incorporation of beliefs and practices from human agents. They believe that all their practices are the mandates of God and there is no incorporation of any feature as a result of social interactions or individual purported wisdom. For them, religion is a creation of God naturalised in their relationship with God, gods, goddesses and spirits.

Pupou Chap is marked by polytheism with a greater emphasis on one omnipotent God known as Apou Ragang. *Apou* is indicative of high reverence and *Ragang* means King of gods and goddesses (*Ra*- god/ goddess; *gang*/ *guang*- king). Rituals are performed to appease other lower gods, goddesses and spirits. The term *Pupou Chap* is used to identify the belief systems of their ancestors. The name *Pupou* refers to ancestors. Pu and Pou respectively mean 'father' and 'grandfather'. Pu is derived from 'Apu' meaning 'my father' and Pou is derived from 'Apou' meaning 'grandfather' or 'my grandfather'. The Apu and Apou here do not necessarily begin from one's own father and grandfather. They are symbolical terms for the ancestors beginning from the first human being. True, 'past is an explanation of the present, and it is recognized that the genesis of a social phenomenon is an important aspect of its present situation' (Aloysius 1998: 2-3). *Pupou Chap's* legitimacy dwells in the past and bears the legacies to be inherited by the present and future generations. Thus, religion here may be partly seen as a perennial relationship between the ancestors and the present generation with a continuous connection with the future progenies. Inheritance of legacies in the form of beliefs, customary laws and various practices become a part of their social, political and religious significance.

Among the *Pupou Chap* followers, the appeasements of the lesser gods, goddesses and spirits are found to be weighing more in their religious lives. Thus, according to their belief, even the creation of human beings is not done by *Apou Ragang*. *Apou Ragang* granted the divine sanction to Dampapu and Dampapui, god and goddess respectively, to create human beings and all the other works of creation were carried out by them. However, it was *Apou Ragang* who blessed human beings with a breath of life. Several gods, goddesses and spirits exist with specific roles believed to be performed by them. All the rites of passage are the same as in their other belief systems except for the instances of occasional animal sacrifice which is still extant among the followers of *Pupou Chap*. Other belief systems of the Zeliangrong people have abandoned most of the animal sacrifices and taboos.

Heraka

A note on the relevance of *Heraka* as a belief system of Rongmei people may be clarified at the outset here. *Heraka* followers are mostly Zeme people of Assam. *Heraka* followers from among

Liangmai, Rongmei and Inpui are hardly known now. At present, as in February 2020, a handful of followers of *Heraka* in Rani Gaidinliu's village at Luangkao in Manipur is an exception among the Rongmei. However, there is no *Heraka* follower in any of the Zeliangrong villages in Manipur valley. Some of its followers are found among the Zeme people of Nagaland.

According to Gangmumei Kamei, 'The Heraka does not worship smaller gods and goddess of the Zeliangrong pantheon; sacrifices to these gods are abolished. There is no worship of the village presiding deities or the worship of ancestors' (2006: 56). Interestingly, like TRC, *Heraka* also traces its origin to reformations under Jadonang Malangmei in the 1920s. However, *Heraka* is conventionally considered as monotheistic and TRC as polytheistic.

The labelling of *Heraka* as monotheism needs to be problematised. Pautanzan Newme refers to Banglagwang, son of Tingkao Ragwang (2011a: 2; 2011b: 23) as the first messenger sent to our world by Tingkao Ragwang to rule the world (Newme 2011a: 1). According to Chaoba Kamson, Banglagwang is one of the gods in the belief system of the Zeliangrong people (2012: 354). Chaoba Kamson contradicts Pautanzan Newme's claim of the Banglagwang being the son of Tingkao Ragwang. According to Chaoba Kamson, Tingkao Ragwang 'has no wife, no parents and no offspring' (2011a: 10). Thus, *Heraka* acknowledges the existence of Banglagwang as a god, probably without worshipping him. A sharp edge to cut the monotheistic claim of *Heraka* is the account of Chaoba Kamson[5] who was informed by the devotees of the *Heraka* belief system that they [followers of *Heraka*] were instructed by Gaidinliu Kamei to worship lord Bisnu of the Bhuvan cave.

The effort of *Heraka* to represent itself as monotheistic is vivid in the words of Arkotong Longkumer. Defining the term *Heraka* he says:

> '*Ka* is to fence, to obstruct, to avoid, to give up – all these words can be used in different contexts. "*Hera*" means 'small gods'. So all these neube [prohibitions] and sacrifices associated with the smaller gods must be fenced out, avoided, and only Tingwang must be worshipped. This is the meaning of Heraka' (2010: 8).

This fencing of the belief system to ward off other 'Hera' is a clear departure from their ancestral practice of worshipping supernatural power and other deities. This is something new to the Zeliangrong people. Gangmumei Kamei did not follow *Heraka* despite having followed Rani Gaidinliu tirelessly. He viewed *Heraka* as a 'reformed religion' (2004: 149). Also because of its claim of monotheism, he saw no element of originality in *Heraka* as it divested from the ancestral polytheism. This is despite Zeme, Liangmai and Rongmei all believing in the same God. Essentially, their belief systems are the same as they had the same origin. Until Jadonang's time the Zeme, Liangmai and Rongmei people were essentially one in terms of religion. It was with the reformation under Rani Gaidinliu in Zeme dominated areas that *Heraka* seemingly appeared more among the Zeme people. *Heraka* is hardly known among the Rongmei people in Manipur except in Rani Gaidinliu's village at Luangkao in the hill.

For Arkotong Longkumer, perhaps due to the narrowness of his field in Zeme areas of North Cachar (NC) Hills in Assam, *Heraka* is viewed as a consequence of miseries of 'scarcity of food' (2010: 47). Longkumer failed to see the side of Manipur post-independence. He did not discuss the conflict between the Naga National Council and Rani Gaidinliu's force, *Riphen*. The force of Naga armed groups operating with a cocktail of Naga nationalism and Christian evangelism was gradually becoming insurmountable for Rani Gaidinliu. The native belief systems were left at the mercy of Christian missionaries. It is this conflict with the Naga armed group that led Rani Gaidinliu to mobilise her people towards reforming the religion into *Heraka*. While Jadonang reformed the ancestral religion to mobilise the people to fight against the British, the Kukis and the Meiteis, Gaidinliu Kamei, after the death of Jadonang religiously mobilised her people to fight against primarily the Christian missionaries and the Naga National Council. She could do so primarily among the Zeme people in Assam and not with the Rongmei people to which she belonged because of the formidable strength of the Naga National Council in Manipur hills in the 1950s and 1960s.

Gaidinliu Kamei, through the inspiration from God, told the followers 'that offering of animals sacrificial worship to God

(Tingwang) is not required as such offerings are not accepted by Him (God) but those were eaten by demons' [sic] (Zeliangrong Heraka Association 2011: 4; also see Newme 2011b: 25). Zeliangrong Christians believe that *Heraka* was created by Gaidinliu Kamei and thus do not consider it a religion. Responding to such allegation N.C. Zeliang stated, '*Heraka* is not a departure from the traditional Zeliangrong Sansari religion but a *rational improvement* of it' [emphasis added to highlight the element of reformation and juxtapose it against the notion of primordiality] (2003: 23). And Pautanzan Newme, defending it, asserted that 'Heraka religion is not a man made' (2011b: 26). Such is the general trend witnessed among the Zeliangrong people: condemning and salvaging other religions and one's religion respectively. And this happens even among the non-Christian Zeliangrong religious groups. A negative categorisation of other religious groups is a stark daily phenomenon in many Zeliangrong villages.

It is said that Jadonang advocated a new religious cult called 'Charaa Rek' which was derived from the traditional Rongmei animism and influenced by Jadonang's informal interactions with Hinduism and Christianity (Roy 2013). However, Charaa Rek is now hardly known even among the Zeliangrong people. This is explained by the changes incorporated within Charaa Rek which completely evolved into *Heraka* with the compilation of *Heraka* scriptures in 1991 (Zeme 1991, cited in Roy 2013: 77). Arkotong Longkumer views *Heraka* as a reformed religion that has its genesis in 'the ancestral practice known as Paupaise' (2010: 1) or *Pupou Chap.* For Gangmumei Kamei, *Heraka* is a 'reformed religion' spread by Gaidinliu (2004: 149). However, consciously or unconsciously, Gangmumei Kamei is not known to have categorised his religious group Tingkao Ragwang Chapriak as reformed religion. Zeliangrong Christians believe that *Heraka* is a group of Hinduism as they are believed to use Hindu symbols *om* and *swastika*[6] (Kamei 2004). However, proponents of *Heraka* do not claim themselves to be Hindus in the sense of Hinduism and strongly assert a distinct religious identity despite calling themselves Hindus in the sense of Indian national identity.

There is a serious fallacy in the belief of *Heraka* concerning the Bhuvan cave. A work on *Heraka* by Pautanzan Newme (2011a) repeatedly mentions the Bhuvan cave as the source of inspiration that led to the beginning of *Heraka* under the leadership of Jadonang and Gaidinliu. However, the Bhuvan cave is the earthly abode of lord Bisnu and not that of Tingwang or Tingkao Ragwang. Jadonang himself claimed that it was lord Bisnu of Bhuvan cave who instructed him for religious reformations and a struggle for the Makam Gwangdi.[7] Jadonang did not interact with Tingkao Ragwang at Bhuvan cave, it was lord Bisnu.

Some believe that Jadonang was interacting with Tingkao Ragwang at Bhuvan cave in which Bisnu was acting as a messenger of Tingkao Ragwang. But this assessment would be an understatement of the indisputable importance of Bisnu within the context of Bhuvan cave and a display of desperateness for authenticity through Tingkao Ragwang. Thus, there is a relation between the *Heraka* and the god Bisnu. This relation with Bisnu, which is not explicitly revealed or acknowledged within *Heraka*, speaks volumes about its seemingly implicit polytheistic feature. Pautanzan Newme describes the Bhuvan cave as 'one of the godly pilgrimages for all human beings, for the reason that occasionally all heads of gods come together for meeting and the souls of all kings or rulers used to house here after their death' (2011b: 32). Chaoba Kamson specifically identified all the abodes of the eight godly brothers. According to him, Tingkao Ragwang dwells in a place called Ragwang Phaipa at Koubru in present Manipur and god Bisnu dwells in Bhuvan cave in Cachar in Assam (2014: 126). Koubru hill is called Ragwang Phaipa because Koubru hill is believed to be a place on earth where Tingkao Ragwang lays his feet while descending upon the earth. Phaipa means foot. Thus, the existence and the presence of god Bisnu here on earth is acknowledged in *Heraka* besides the worship of Tingkao Ragwang. Besides, as mentioned earlier by Chaoba Kamson, its worship is not alien within *Heraka*.

Tingkao Ragwang Kariak[8]

Champa is another religious group within Zeliangrong belief systems. In the Rongmei language, the term Champa is simply translated into 'chosen one'. The belief system of Champa is known as *Tingkao Ragwang Kariak* (TRK). While the Champa group got officially registered as a Society under the name Champa Society in 1968 under Societies Registration Act, 1860, it got its name as *Tingkao Ragwang Kariak* in 1972. Gangmumei Kamei assesses TRK to be monotheistic (2006). Champas acknowledge the existence of gods, goddesses and spirits. According to TRK, gods and goddesses were created by Didimpu and Didimpui while human beings were created by Dampapu and Dampapui as commanded by Tingkao Ragwang. Dampapu and Didimpu are gods while Dampapui and Didimpui are goddesses. They were all created by Tingkao Ragwang. TRK followers completely reject the belief in the appeasement of these gods, goddesses and other spirits.

It is believed by the Champas, like other Zeliangrong religious groups, that human beings lived with gods and goddesses in the earthly house of Tingpuringsuangnang, a god who was the owner of a male dormitory called *Khangchu* in the Rongmei language. When human beings, gods and goddesses lived together in the house of Tingpuringsuangnang there were regular conflicts between them. Human beings always fared better than the gods and goddesses in every walk of life and in all the feats and duels. Filled with jealousy and frustrations, the gods and goddesses began to plan to cause death among human beings. Human beings came to learn about the devious plan of the gods and goddesses and they also planned to do the same against the gods and goddesses. In this conflict, many gods, goddesses and human beings died. This is believed to be the beginning of death.

As the gods and goddesses could not subdue the human beings, they pleaded with Tingpuringsuangnang to separate the human beings from the gods and the goddesses. Then Tingpuringsuangnang commanded the gods and the goddesses not to enter wherever human beings are settled if the latter do not wish them to enter their habitat. The gods and goddesses may accept material offerings from human beings. The gods and goddesses are to be considered as friends of human beings and not to be worshipped. The soul of a human is the basic essence of life and belongs to Tingkao Ragwang. Therefore, the gods and goddesses are not required to be revered or worshipped. These arrangements or treaty between human beings and gods, goddesses and spirits were made by Tingkao Ragwang. This belief, according to Kambuirong Phaomei,[9] is the foundational difference between TRK and other belief systems of the Zeliangrong people. And for this reason, according to TRK belief, the gods and goddesses are not appeased or worshipped by human beings. In the context of TRK followers worshipping only God while merely acknowledging the existence of gods, goddesses and spirits, it becomes inappropriate to call it either monotheism or henotheism.[10] In monotheism, there is the worship of only God and there are no gods and goddesses. The existence of gods and goddesses are not acknowledged in monotheism. But TRK acknowledges their existence without worshipping them. For lack of an appropriate term to categorise TRK the author prefers to call it monotheistic in practice and polytheistic in belief. As the belief system of TRK is rooted in the treaty reached between human beings and gods and goddesses that led to the emergence of the worship of God without worshipping other gods and goddesses the belief system of TRK may be categorised into synthíkitheism. It is derived from the Greek words *sinthiki* meaning treaty and *theos* meaning god. In sinthikitheism, there is a worship of only one God but with an acknowledgement of other gods and goddesses without worshipping them. And the worship of God is made possible because of a treaty accepted by human beings and gods and goddesses.

The Champas celebrate the festival of *Nanuh*. Every newborn infant in a year is blessed and a ritualistic bath is given in which the infant is proclaimed as a member of the human group. *Nanuh dui* or Nanuh water is fetched only by old men and women from the village pond. Youths cannot fetch the water. The *Nanuh dui* is fetched early in the morning before animals come to drink water from the water body. The new infant has to be given a bath with the *Nanuh dui* only by the youths of the village. The bath is a ritualistic admission of the infant into the human world. This admission of the infant into a human group is to prevent the evil spirits from taking away the infant from the human group. It is ritualistic earmarking of the infant as an asset of God and making the infant a Champa or the chosen one, chosen by Tingkao Ragwang. The ritual of bathing to symbolise attainment of TRK membership is not restricted at infancy. The founder of TRK, Gaiganglung Phaomei, was given a ritualistic bath on 9 October 1969 despite having born in 1931 (Kambuilung 2011: 10). Thus, TRK allows for possible inevitable flexibility in its ritual or religious practice.

Note that *Nanuh* is celebrated not only by TRK. *Nanuh* is a festive ritual performed by all the Rongmei people. A child is also given a name on the occasion of *Nanuh*. The Rongmei people believe that if the newborn infant is not given its name very soon then the evil spirit will christen a name for the infant and it signals a bad omen for the infant (Tiba 2006: 174). *Nanuh* remains a very important festival for the Rongmei people. It is a crucial rite of passage for the Rongmei people.

The Champas believe that human beings were created by Dampapu and Dampapui who hid human beings for safety during the Parakin or the age of harmful deities. Human beings were emancipated at the beginning of Ragwang-kin, the age of God. The breath of life was blessed by Tingkao Ragwang who blew the air through fontanelle. It is for this reason that the death of a human being is customarily confirmed by a local priest after an examination of the beating on the fontanelle. They believe that the soul leaves from the fontanelle and the hair on the fontanelle is believed to be erect at the time of death indicating an outward movement of the human soul through the fontanelle. The soul leaving from the head signifies a journey of the soul to heaven. If a soul enters heaven it will not come back.

They worship on every full moon day like the *Tingkao Ragwang Chapriak* group and every Tuesday. Anyone can become a member of TRK after going through a ritualistic bath. The bath is given by using a leaf (locally called *Khaam Nui*) dipped in water and gliding the leaf up and down the body with a prayer. The bath has two aspects: *Loukeimei* and *Loukumei*. In *Loukeimei*, the leaf is moved down the body with the words *'Simei bumaeng goi lougan kandu tho'* (Let all the evil spirits be washed away). In *Loukumei*, the leaf is moved upward with the words *'Gaimei gun-ga ta lakulou dat thi de'* (All the good qualities are restored). Thus, TRK is prepared with a ritual to allow entry of any individual within their group.

Tingkao Ragwang Chapriak (TRC)

The emergence of TRC is also immensely hastened by the sense of exigency to salvage the remnants of Zeliangrong ancestral belief systems from the onslaught of the Christian missionaries and certain Naga armed groups violently flaunting the slogan 'Nagaland for Christ'. A crucial event that led to the formation of *Tingkao Ragwang Chapriak* was an unfortunate incident that happened in 1994 in some villages in the Khoupum area in Manipur in the Tamenglong district. The belief system of the villagers was still in the state of *Pupou Chap*. The villagers who were celebrating *Nanuh* were also consuming local wine. Such practice of drinking local wine was condemned and they were brutally attacked by a certain Naga armed group. The villagers were even told to be Christian if they want to be in Nagalim or the land of the Nagas. The villagers were forced to drink the wine at gunpoint more than they could and also made to dance the whole night in the rain. The fateful day also witnessed the death of a woman who had recently delivered a child. A violent entry of the Naga armed personnel into her house when she was in bed shocked her and she died instantly. This attack on the villagers on 22 February 1994 was an immediate cause of reformations in the 1990s under the leadership of Professor Gangmumei Kamei. These reformations ultimately led to the formation of *Tingkao Ragwang Chapriak.*

The followers of TRC believe in the existence of *Tingkao Ragwang* or the heavenly God. Besides *Tingkao Ragwang*, they also believe in and appease many other gods, goddesses and spirits. However, they abandoned many ritualistic sacrifices that were begun to be believed to be baseless and expensive. TRC, like *Heraka* and TRK, casts away many small powers believed to be tin gods and tin goddesses. TRC, like *Pupou Chap*, worships and appeases many gods and goddesses but it lays greater emphasis on the worship of *Tingkao Ragwang*. Its followers claim to follow their ancestral belief systems with some changes.

The name *Tingkao Ragwang Chapriak* was adopted at a Zeliangrong religious conference held on 14-15 April 1994 at Imphal in Manipur (Kamei 2006). The conference also led to the formation of the

Zeliangrong Religious Council as an authority of the Zeliangrong religion. *Tingkao Ragwang Chapriak* was declared the Zeliangrong religion. Besides casting away 'all taboo in the unnatural death' the adherents of TRC chose 'every full moon day and every Sunday' as the days for prayer (Kamei 2006: 77). While TRK chose Tuesday as a day of communal worship it is Sunday for TRC. This may be viewed as a strategy to address the issue of proselytisation by Christian missionaries. Communal worship on Sunday serves the purpose of diverting the children and youths away from the attractive Sunday affairs of the neighbouring Christians.

Comparison of the Belief Systems

It may be noted that the Zeme, Liangmai and Rongmei who constitute the Zeliangrong group do not have belief systems specific to their dialectical groups. No religion may be said to be exclusive to the Zeme or Liangmai or Rongmei. The Zeliangrong groups have a belief in the same God. The variants of belief systems found among the Zeliangrong people are the results of variations in the reformations. *Heraka* is more popular among the Zeme people but it was founded by Rani Gaidinliu who was a Rongmei lady. *Heraka* followers also identify Jadonang Malangmei as the leader of *Heraka* but Jadonang was also a Rongmei. There is a small number of Rongmei people following *Heraka*. Therefore, any of the belief systems of the Zeliangrong people are not specific to a dialectical group. They must be viewed as belief systems of the Zeliangrong people as a whole.

Heraka and *Tingkao Ragwang Chapriak* as they exist now are, theologically, poles apart. While the former claims to be monotheistic the latter preaches to be polytheistic. However, another dimension of theologies of both connects them in being worshippers of the same God. Both claim to be *pupou chap* in the sense of being ancestral religion. They both trace Jadonang to be the common leader of their belief systems. While *Heraka* dismisses other gods, goddesses and spirits *Tingkao Ragwang Chapriak* retain them to sustain the ancestral feature of their belief system. While they both worship the same God, *Heraka* does not make any animal sacrifices. The *Tingkao Ragwang Chapriak* group retains many of the animal sacrifices. This means that *Tingkao Ragwang Chapriak* with its continued belief in various rituals and cultural aspects of the past continue to celebrate many festivals. *Tingkao Ragwang Kariak* also celebrate only *Nanuh Ngai*. The *Tingkao Ragwang Kariak* group also shares similar belief with that of *Heraka*. They both worship only one God. Both have shunned various aspects of their ancestral culture. This renders them relatively less appealing to the Zeliangrong people whose ancestral ways of life were filled with diverse rituals, gods, goddesses and festivals. They seemed new and even strange to many Rongmei people. *Tingkao Ragwang Chapriak* with a certain degree of reformations and sustained lingering to most of their ancestral belief system and culture emerged to be a more popular belief system among the Zeliangrong people. This contributes immensely to its resilience.

Beginning from the reformations introduced by Jadonang Malangmei in the 1920s until the recent reformations of the *Tingkao Ragwang Chapriak* in the early 1990s the common thread is the worship of the common God, *Tingkao Ragwang*. Jadonang Malangmei did not give any name to the reformed belief system during his time. He continued with the tradition of not having any name for religion. However, the rest of the post-colonial reformations also gave names to the reformed belief systems. Interestingly, none of the belief systems claims to be dialectically specific. Rongmei belief systems may also be said to be Zeme belief systems and Liangmai belief systems. They are the same for all the groups.

Qualifying 'Ragwang' and 'Primordiality'

Names of the gods, according to Bousset, reflect the places the gods are believed to have come from (1907: 77). This is resonated in the use of the term Tingkao or heaven, the place where the Ragwang of *Heraka*, TRK and the TRC are believed to dwell. This concept of a heavenly dwelling of God is new to some Zeliangrong people who adhere to the nameless primordial belief system of their ancestors.

The probable genesis of the use of the term *Tingkao Ragwang* is Jadonang's experience during his childhood days. Jadonang experienced trances for several days and this was a reason for his mother's worry. Finding his mother worried and teary he told his mother, 'Mother, why do you cry when I was sleeping? I was going to house of Tingkao Ragwang and meeting Him' (Kamei 2009: 19). Jadonang was probably the first religious reformer to have used the term 'Tingkao Ragwang'. Traditionally, the Supreme God is known by different names: Apou Ragang, Pasupadam meipu, Apou Ragang Samtingphenmei and Haipou Ragang. With the complete absence of the use of the name *Tingkao Ragwang* among the *Pupou Chap* followers, the plausibility of tracing the origin of the idea and the usage of the term *Tingkao Ragwang* to Jadonang in the early twentieth century is indisputable. Jadonang did not create any God in identifying his ancestral *Apou Ragang* with the name *Tingkao Ragwang*. The concept of Tingkao or heaven used to qualify the God or Ragwang of *Heraka*, TRK and TRC are fiercely attacked by certain followers of *Pupou Chap*. This is also the basis of the argument of *Pupou Chap* that dismisses the primordiality claim of *Heraka*, TRK and TRC belief systems.

This book began with a conception of religion based on a position that the element of God is essential in it. Thus, the notion of God is crucial in religion. The conception of God is the basis of religion. The various belief systems and practices of Zeliangrong people evolve from the idea of God. The conception of God precedes all other beliefs and practices. All customary laws, traditions and moral questions are rooted in their idea of God who is believed to be the source of the universe and human life. The 'God-ward consciousness' (Case 1907: 5) in human conscience still forms the basis of religion. Thus, if the conception of God itself is new, here in terms of its position (heaven), then certain features of this religion are new and stand close to what may be termed as a reformed religion. Moreover, Gangmumei Kamei states that 'worship of these gods [gods of the pantheon including Bisnu] was started at a later period of the pre-historic time where the Zeliangrong people settled down in their habitat in the western hills of Manipur, southern Nagaland and eastern Cachar and north Cachar Hills' (2006: 71). Thus, worship of the seven other brother gods of Tingkao Ragwang itself is not a primordial feature of the belief system of the *Pupou*

Chap and the TRC as well. This does not mean the Zeliangrong people were without any of the features of religion before the pre-historic period. They were probably overwhelmed by the fear of innumerable natural forces and spirits and engrossed with the propitiation, appeasement and oblation of these forces. The very concept of the God as *Tingkao Ragwang* as understood among the aforesaid three groups is a new reality of the twentieth century during the colonial era and this concept is, according to *Pupou Chap* followers, borrowed from the Christianity where the spiritual father of Jesus is always referred to as 'Father in heaven'.

TRC stumbles into gross error in a ritualistic prayer of *Laangdai Mailak* (marriage ritual prayer) when a place Ramting Kabin was referred to as the origin of mankind (Kamson 2012: 194). Ramting Kabin was a transit camp of the Zeliangrong people during their migration from Makhel to Makuilongdi. According to Zeliangrong mythology, it was at Taobhei where the first human beings emerged and not at Ramting Kabin. The course of migration in succeeding order is as follows–Mahow Taobhei, Makhel, Ramting Kabin, Chawang Phungning and Makuilongdi. From Makuilongdi, Rongmei and Zeme migrated to other places leaving behind the Liangmai.

Festivals

A feature of Rongmei society that can further enhance an understanding of the concept of primordiality and the theoretical concept of social change is the festival. Festivals always stand as defining features of culture and also the belief system. The origin and the paraphernalia of a festival offer themselves as a lens to view and understand society. Festivals include rituals, *Kasoi-Kadam*, dances, songs, attires, legends, beliefs, world views, etc. Therefore, analysis of festivals certainly proves to be methodologically appropriate to draw an understanding of the notion of primordiality.

The concept of primordiality is vigorously sought after in any religious discourse. It is done either to claim and enhance respectability or to tarnish any belief system as man made, if not adjudged within the conventional understanding of the term as something in existence 'since the beginning of time'. Therefore, it is pertinent here to expound on this concept theoretically. To achieve this objective of theoretical understanding of primordiality and illuminate the sociological significance of the concept two festivals are examined here. *Gaan-Ngai* and *Tian-Ngai* are two important festivals of the Rongmei people. *Ngai* means festival; *Gaan* means light or brightness; *Tian* means bread.

Gaan-Ngai

According to Longphul Longmei (2010), mankind was blessed with cooked/ edible rice on rice plants. The rice of the paddy plants was cooked and ready to be consumed. Human beings ate the cooked rice from the paddy plant and they had surplus cooked rice. Unfortunately, the era of cooked rice on a paddy plant came to an end. Mankind began pleading with 'Tingkao Ragwang' to bless them with fire so that the uncooked rice could be cooked and consumed. Human beings continued pleading with their God unceasingly for a very long time. Later they saw smoke coming from underneath the earth. They found the smoke emanating from an earthen pot. As they lifted the earthen pot a flame came up and the fire began burning. They used the fire to cook the rice and ate the rice with sincere gratitude.

With the coming of fire through the blessing of God, there came light or brightness. It is because of this blessed incident that they celebrate *Gaan-Ngai* which translates into a festival of light. In the morning of the first day of *Gaan-Ngai* every family of the village must collect burning firewood from the Khangchu and with that fire, the hearth in every house must be lit.

Tian-Ngai

After the human beings settled on earth with the blessing of God they developed their social systems. They also began waging war against enemy groups. As they fought against their enemies they carried *Tian* or bread to eat during the days of the war. After they come back from the war with victory the whole village celebrates. This festival is known as *Tian-Ngai*.

Examining the two festivals we see that *Gaan-Ngai* is rooted in the relation between God and human beings. It originated in the days of God, gods, goddesses and spirits physically and spiritually interacting with human beings. These were the days their daily lives are marked by regular and direct interactions with the supernatural powers. In this context, the origin of *Gaan-Ngai* is appropriate to be termed as primordial. However, the origin of *Tian-Ngai* is not laced with any divine element. It is a result of social institutions. The village authorities such as the *Pei* and Khangchu are responsible for planning and waging a war. This festival emerged only after a war was fought. The fact that they fought a war against other groups also suggests that the days of God, gods, goddesses and spirits living together on earth with human beings had already elapsed. The days of common Khangchu in the house of Tingpuringsuangnang certainly had gone when *Tian-Ngai* was first celebrated. Therefore, in this sense, *Tian-Ngai* is not a primordial festival. Nevertheless, *Tian-Ngai* is an essential part of Rongmei culture.

Everything about a religion cannot be primordial. There are features of religion and culture that could not have been there when only the first two human beings were found on this earth. There are still many features of cultures and religions that could not have been there with only two original clans as believed by Zeliangrong people. Everything that began during the days of common Khangchu cannot also be viewed as primordial. The phrase 'since the beginning of time' is sometimes misleading for it is not clear with the notion of 'beginning'. What marks the beginning of this very 'beginning'? Therefore, sometimes, analytically, it is more appropriate to replace the term primordial with 'in the days of God' or *Rari-gan* to mean the era when human beings, gods, goddesses, spirits and God shared a common notion of spiritual dimension, physical space and time. Nevertheless, the claim of the primordial status of one's belief system remains a constant fact with significant sociological implications.

NOTES

1. Max Mueller used the term *Kathenotheism,* or simply *Henotheism* to mean 'a belief in single gods'. It is a *'consciousness that all the deities are but different names of one and the same godhead'* [emphasis added] (Mueller 1881: 137). It is a belief in the supremacy of each god in its specific domain. Max Mueller coined this term to conceptualise the absolute and supreme power of every god as presented in the 'numerous hymns of the Veda passages in which almost every important deity is represented as supreme and absolute' (ibid.: 137) and while the supremacy and absoluteness of a god is extant 'nothing is said to disparage the divine character of the other gods' (ibid.: 137). A lucid analysis of emergence of henotheism is stated as: 'Historically, henotheism assumes all gods are species equals and the elevation of one god is due to socio-political factors—not theological nuancing' (Heiser 2008: 28).
2. In TRK, Tingkao Ragwang is the only God worshipped. Other gods, goddesses and spirits are acknowledged in terms of their existence but they are not worshipped. This acknowledgement of the existence of other gods and goddesses in TRK renders it unqualified for monotheism.
3. He was the former Secretary of TRC Chabuan Phom of Assam, Nagaland and Manipur.
4. Chaoba Kamson responded to a question raised by the author to Dr Budha Kamei who was speaking as a resource person on the 'Concept of Tingkao Ragwang Chapriak' on the first day of TRC Chabuan Phom First Conference held at Ragailong, Imphal East, Manipur on 13 October 2018. Gangmumei Kamei's book *Jadonang: A Mystic Naga Rebel* narrates the account given by Jadonang on 3 March 1931 to Political Agent JC Higgins. Jadonang told Higgins that he was instructed by the 'God' to tell 'the Kabuis to worship the God, though I [Jadonang] know[s] it is not their custom to do so' (2009: 112). The 'God' referred to here is not qualified in the narration as *Tingkao Ragwang* but the fact that the God of the Zeliangrong belief systems is only one, which is accepted by all Zeliangrong traditionalists, the 'God' referred to by Jadonang in his account given to Higgins is, with the best possibility, the *Tingkao Ragwang* and, therefore, the 'God' of Jadonang is primordial and TRC is also a primordial religion. Nevertheless, a question that persists to be answered is: Why did Jadonang claim that the Kabui did not have the 'custom' of worshipping the 'God'? To

answer this question a perspective on worship and prayer on one side and *Kasoi-Kadam* on the other side needs to be juxtaposed. According to Khomeimacha Kamson, the Zeliangrong people lived a religious life of *Kasoi-Kadam* and not worship and prayer. *Kasoi-Kadam* has Kasoi and Kadam. Kasoi is the part of a ritual in which a priest seeks the blessings of God/ gods/ goddesses/ spirits. This is uttered by a priest. Kadam is the oblation. It is believed that Kasoi may be changed with omission and addition but Kadam can never be changed or mistaken. Therefore, the Zeliangrong or the Kabui people as Jadonang mentioned did not live a life of worship and prayer that may be done even by a child. They rather lived a life of *Kasoi-Kadam* that required a third party in the form of priest and expensive oblations and animal sacrifices offered to several gods, goddesses and spirits some of which are later considered to be baseless and superstitious. Jadonang is believed to have been sent by God to reform such a superstitious religious life of the people and prepare them to fight against the colonial rule for freedom. It was probably in this context that Jadonang told Higgins that it was not in the 'custom' of the Kabui to worship the 'God'. Apou Ragang, Apou Ragang Samtingphianmei, Haipou Sampraiguang, Pasumeipui Padammeipu, Tingkao Ragwang are the names used to identify the same God. Many rituals have reference to *Tingkao Ragwang* but the name *Tingkao Ragwang* was not used conventionally in the olden days. Note that some followers of *Pupou Chap* pointed out that *Tingkao Ragwang* cannot be the God as the name is locative and it is a skewed diversion from the traditionally known true nature of *Apou Ragang* who is timeless and unbounded by any place.

5. Chaoba Kamson gave this account of the followers of *Heraka* while he was speaking on the occasion of the first Conference of TRC Chabuan Phom (Assam, Manipur & Nagaland) organised at Ragailong in Imphal (Manipur) dated 13-14 October 2018.
6. During his visit in 2012 to Zalukie-B at Peren District of Nagaland the author visited a school, Heraka Vidya Bharati School, run by *Heraka* group. The metal gate of the school was embossed with symbols of *Om* and *Swastika* of the Hindu religion. Refer the unpublished doctoral thesis 'Zeliangrong Movement in North-East India: A study of perspectives from the past and the present' by Kamei Samson (2014).
7. Makam Gwangdi literally means kingdom of the Makam. Makam Gwangdi reflects the interconnectedness between religious reformations and political movement for external-right of self-determination

under the leadership of Jadonang Malangmei. Makam is conventionally interpreted as the Zeliangrong and the Nagas as well. Another narrow interpretation of Makam is the Kamei clan and its sub-clans. The connection between Makam and Kamei clan is the oral tradition of the Kamei clan that traces its root to a man named Kaamguang whose name is believed to be the origin of the name Makam. Kaamguang had seven sons who now constitute the seven sub-clans of Kamei clan. His descendants are now identified as Kaamguang Narian meaning Kaamguang's descendants. Jadonang's perspective of the kingdom was probably rooted in the village republic. The clan to which he belonged was Malangmei, a sub-clan of Kamei clan, a clan that occupied the Khullakpu position in his village, Puiluan. Among the Rongmei people the Kamei clan is known to have more number of people and consequently have more villages with Khullakpus who belong to Kamei clan. Jadonang probably thought the power of the Kamei clan or the Makam people will ultimately prevail over the kingdom of the Nagas he was fighting for.

8. The account of Tingkao Ragwang Kariak is based on an interview with Mr Kambuirong Phaomei. He is the leader of the Champa group. He was interviewed on 17 January 2018 at his residence at Langthabal Chingkha (near Manipur University campus), presently the only village in the world with TRK belief system.
9. In an interview in 2018.
10. This is based on the understanding of the notion of henotheism as discussed by Max Mueller (1878). According to Max Mueller, henotheism is characterised by worship of several gods whose powers and supremacies are nonoverlapping. The realities of the gods boil down to one reality of God.

CHAPTER 4

The Reformations

Mythology and Beliefs

Beliefs—no matter how mythical they may appear—are crucial in understanding the world view of the people. No religion is free from mythologies, myths, supernaturalism and even superstition. Those belief systems that establish closer relations with natural environments may seemingly appear to be more mystic and superstitious, and more mythical. However, being mythical and illogical may not be the exclusive characteristics of belief systems closer to nature. A Catholic Parish Priest at Imphal in Manipur once told me that if one approaches religion with reasoning it must be realised that religion is not the right field for any conversation around my pending rectification[1] and he closed the *Bible* trying to ensure that I submit to reason-free religion to avail rectification. Thus, lack of reason and logic in belief and practice is not something alien to any religion. Such suicide of reason is common in all religions.

N.K. Bose rightly captured the dynamics of religion in tribal ways of life in the words, '. . . religious experience of the tribal people depends, not so much upon everyday experiences and logical constructs based upon them as on dreams, visions and revelations which arise from the deeper springs of their being' (1971: 69). The phrase 'not so much' unambiguously points to something experiential and logical even in tribal religions. There is no complete abandonment of reason in the tribal world view as commonly perceived. N.K. Bose observed the endowment of living spirit to all beings as one of the universal features of the beliefs systems of the tribal people (ibid.: 61). Totemism which is sometimes viewed by Christians as superstition may be inculcated as a universal moral value system for a harmonious relationship with the surrounding environment. Totemism is called *gantheng* in Rongmei. *Gantheng* means food item to be avoided (gan= curry; theng= avoidance). The self-centred individualistic Christian evangelism that is concerned primarily with individual salvation cannot comprehend this theology of homeostasis inherent among the tribal people.

Belief in the dwelling of spirits in living and inanimate objects in the universe consequently leads to a highly revered position of the objects. Another reason for believing in the piousness of a totemic entity is the belief in it as a source of life or a boon to life. Ascribing divinity to certain elements of the universe is still extant. In the context of the harmonious functioning of the *Panch Tatvas – Prithvi* (Earth), *Vayu* (Air), *Jal* (Water), *Agni* (Fire) and *Akash* (Sky), Narendra Modi, the incumbent Prime Minister of India, states, 'The elements of nature are manifestations of divinity' (2018). It may be apt, in this context, to refer to an environmentalist Rosalyn Lapier of the Blackfeet community. According to the mythology of Blackfeet, mussel holds all the water in the world and mussel, according to their mythology, protects human life by securing the freshwater of the world and, therefore, mussels are revered as holy (Lapier 2017). The Native Americans, despite consuming it, consider salmon to be sacred; Mayans believe human beings were created out of corn and the Blackfeet consider turnip to be sent from the sky and thus sacred and staple food (Lapier 2018). Certain animals and plants are either avoided or one refrains even from hurting them because of beliefs surrounding them that connect them with the people sharing such beliefs. Thus, certain totemic plants and trees are never cut and totemic animals and birds are never killed. Realising the medicinal values of several herbs many forest dwellers take utmost care not to cut and burn the forest indiscriminately even for shifting cultivation.

Being superstitious and unmindful of animal sacrifices and even human sacrifices have been the traditional and even contemporary benchmark to qualify the belief systems of the tribal people. In this respect, the belief systems of the tribal people have always been relegated to evil practices and diabolical for human society. However, what is generally sidelined is the fact that,

A faith which establishes man's kinship with all that he sees around him, a faith which releases some of the creative forces within him, which burst forth in simple, loving ceremonies or occasionally in beautiful, lyrical poems or songs, or in art which is direct, and not trammelled by sophistication, can hardly be accused of being barren and destructive in its influence upon the human spirit. (Bose 1971: 62)

For fear of being relegated into a subjective assessment, I would merely say that the tribal belief systems are close to nature maintaining a relationship of spiritual symbiosis.

Zeliangrong Belief Systems

Zeliangrong people believe in the Supreme God and His seven brothers. The Supreme God is also known as Apou Ragang. The followers of *Heraka*, TRK and TRC call Him *Tingkao Ragwang*. He is the creator of the universe and destroyer of evil, source of life and justice. The seven younger brothers of the Supreme God, from higher to lower positions, according to Gangmumei Kamei in his work *Essays on Primordial Religion*, are (i) Bisnu also known as Munshnu, Manchanu, Bonchanu or Buisnu, (ii) Napsinmei, (iii) Kara-Ngong, (iv) Koklou, (v) Chonchai, (vi) Chara Kilongmei, (vii) Dimei (2006: 69). Later Gangmumei Kamei gave a self-contradictory account of God and His brothers elsewhere in his noted work *Jadonang: A Mystique Naga Rebel* (2009). In this work, while giving a note on the Bhuvan cave which is believed to be the holy earthly abode of Bisnu, Gangmumei Kamei describes Bisnu as 'the eldest of the eight brother gods of the Zeliangrong pantheon' (2009: xv). Gangmumei Kamei further contradicted his account of Bisnu being 'the eldest of the eight brother gods' in the same book elsewhere by identifying the position of Bisnu as 'second position to Ragwang in status' (ibid.: 24). Such an erroneous account of the Zeliangrong pantheon needs speedy rectification to ward off further battering of the TRC belief system as concocted and manmade.

The prayer and worship system is classified into *Neihmei, Ra-Kalummei* and *Ra-Khangmei*. *Neihmei* is a form of a short community and individual prayer offered to the Supreme God. In *Neihmei* abstinence from physical work is also mandated by the village authorities. Abstinence mandated during *Neihmei* (genna) must be observed strictly otherwise failure will incur misfortunes upon men. *Ra-Kalummei* includes, besides the worship and prayer to Tingkao Ragwang, the worship and prayer of *Na-Ragwang Chanaren*, the gods of the Zeliangrong pantheon, *Bambu* or the presiding village deities and *Kairao*—the ancestors. Thus, *Ra-Kalummei* is more elaborate as it includes appeasements of many gods and spirits. *Ra-Khangmei* is the appeasement of deities to avert their wrath and misfortunes upon them. Besides this, there is also a worship of the seven brother gods. This is called *Laren Roumei*. This is also done by those who desire to become a priest or priestess. These beliefs and practices of the Zeliangrong are found within TRC.

Background of Religious Reformations

The political movements in the 1920s and early part of the 1930s under the leadership of Jadonang Malangmei and Gaidinliu Kamei provide a good canvass to understand the religious reformations initiated by them. During the colonial days, the Zeliangrong people, especially the Rongmei, experienced forced labour (Yonuo 1982). The Zeliangrong people were coerced to pay a house tax of Rs. 3 (Mukherjee, Gupta and Das 1982). Compounding to the foreign money economy was the restrictions on 'customary hunting and fishing rights' (Rajkumari 2012: 41). The colonial authority had a propensity to declare the forest as a reserve to address their problem of fewer taxes and this disturbed the ancestral habitat and traditional livelihood of the dwellers of forests immensely (Rajkumari 2012). This induced resentment among the hill people, especially the Zeliangrong people (ibid.). When Jadonang began the movement the coloniser raised the house tax to Rs. 6 (Pamei 2001). This was becoming a crucial reason for collective action.

According to Namthiubuiyang Pamei, 'Zeliangrong people . . . suffered the most in the hands of the British imperialist, the Meitei rajas and later, in the hands of the Kukis who connived with the colonial powers. They were even harassed by their Naga brothers' (2006: 23). The Kuki invasion disturbed the 'well permanently settled villages' of the Nagas (Zehol 1998: 70). Sharing such a view

Gangmumei Kamei (2004) says that the loss of land as a consequence of the Kuki invasion ignited the Kuki-Zeliangrong tension during the colonial days. The Kukis, according to Naorem Joykumar Singh, are not indigenous people of Manipur (Singh 2005a: 46). They were brought by the British in the nineteenth century AD. According to R. Brown, the Kukis were made to settle in the 'Manipur Hill Territory' somewhere in the 1840s (1874). According to Jyotirmoy Roy, the first time the Kukis were heard of in Manipur was sometime between 1830 and 1840 (1973). Among the British authorities who played a crucial role in settling the Kukis in the colonial Manipur hills was the British Political Agent, McCulloch, who went to the extent of helping the Kukis with 'his own pocket' money (ibid.: 80). During 1851-2, the British and about 8000 Kukis invaded the lands of the Nagas in which the Kukis were supplied with firearms and ammunition (Pamei 2001; Yonuo 1982). The British had the objective of attacking the Nagas who used to raid the tax-paying British subjects in the valley. They were used fiercely by the British against the Nagas in the hills. In such punitive actions of the British, the socio-cultural, religious, political and economic lives of the Zeliangrong were immensely disturbed.

Gangmumei Kamei defined the movement under Jadonang Malangmei as 'the Naga Struggle against the British' (2004: 145). Asoso Yonuo views the Zeliangrong movement under Jadonang Malangmei as setting the stage for 'Naga nationalism' (1982: 80). It is interesting to note Asoso Yonuo's view despite the predominant religious elements in the mobilisation stage of the movement under Jadonang.

The Kukis, according to Gangmumei Kamei, had slaughtered the Nagas brutally and forcefully annexed their land (Kamei 2004: 146). A conflictual relationship between the Kukis and the Nagas during the colonial period is summed up in the words of T.S. Gangte as, 'The Maharajahs of Manipur were contented with periodical massacre and extension of their influence for specific purposes. The Kuki Chiefs were their allies' (2003: 10). It is in such context that Jadonang roared, 'The Meiteis have their king, Indians have also kings of their own. Why we should not have [our] own king? The Whiteman and we are all human beings. Why should we be afraid of them? All men are equal, we are blessed people' (Kamei 2009: 41). It is, therefore, in this context that Jadonang took the unity of the Zeliangrong people as the foremost mechanism to deal with the foreign forces. And, to do that he did not see any means to be better than religious reformations because religion was the closest element in the lives of the Zeliangrong people.

The Zeliangrong people during the colonial days were attacked from various sides. There was already a severe economic burden with the foreign taxation, this was compounded by the prevailing elaborate rituals involving expensive animal sacrifices, perhaps more in times of scarcity in an attempt to invoke the blessings of the supernatural power. Thus, the British, the Kukis, the Meiteis and the Christian missionaries harmed their economic, political, religious and cultural lives. A need for collective action against the alien forces was urgently felt. Religion was inseparable from their lives. There was no division between secular and religious lives. Religion was connected with every other aspect of their lives. This led to the emergence of religion as the proper basis for mobilisation of the people for political actions.

Reformations in Beliefs

To capture a holistic view of the various beliefs and practices of TRC a cursory glance over the overall reformations introduced by Jadonang Malangmei and Gaidinliu Kamei is a must. According to some TRC adherents, reformations began from the days of Jadonang and it continues even in the present days. However, such a view on the element of reformations is considered to be anathema within TRC by many of its prominent leaders. The desire for clinging to anything and everything that is primordial simply does not allow them to embrace the notion of reformation. Nothing about TRC is new to the leaders and many followers.

A strong sense of fraternity was instilled through Jadonang's religious reformations in the 1920s. In the presence of the colonial power, besides the oppressive Meetei rulers and infiltrating Kukis, Jadonang synthesised political movement and religious reformations towards achieving a political goal of Makam Gwangdi or kingdom of the Makam. The idea of national religion is grounded on the formation of a nation with the amalgamation of several tribes with their respective deities and temple worship is linked to the formation of a nation before which worship is done in the open (Bousset 1907: 71, 82). Jadonang's religious activities were also seen as part of an endeavour to consolidate the Makam people into a single kingdom, Makam Gwangdi. However, the name Makam remains incompletely understood sometimes referring to the whole Nagas and rarely referring to the Zeliangrong groups only. The term Makam stands ill-understood by the present Zeliangrong people. Makam is preferred to be used to mean the Nagas.

N.K. Bose underscores the significance of a holistic picture of religious aspects of tribal life. In presenting a picture of the belief systems and practices of the tribal people one has to present an account of '. . . the many-sided changes to which they have been subject through the contact and influence of the more prosperous neighbours' sometimes leaning towards Hinduism and sometimes towards 'westernism', and also an account of a 'new trend . . . of a new unification between Christian and non-Christian . . . so that their "tribal" identity may be reaffirmed, and in the process, a salvage takes place of as much of their tribal culture and religious faith as is consistent with the demands of modern life' (Bose 1971: 66). This holistic view also underscores a necessity for an interdisciplinary approach to the study of religion that can make such varied dynamics possible in the economic, political, social, cultural and religious realms of the tribal people to be brought to the masses.

The reformations heralded within the Zeliangrong religion were both in beliefs and practices. Moreover, the reformations were not accepted by all. Jadonang was the first to qualify the Supreme God as Tingkao Ragwang or Heavenly God who was earlier known as *Apou Ragang* and by other names. Compelled by the British backed intruders—Kukis and Meeteis—Jadonang was also the first to shape the religious-political dimension of Zeliangrong collective life in the form of mobilisation through religious activities for defence of their lands.

Jadonang, in his statement to the Political Agent of Manipur on 3 March 1931, clearly stated that it was not a customary practice among the Kabuis to worship the God (*Tingkao Ragwang*) although he had been asked in his dream to tell the Kabuis to worship the God (Kamei 2009: 112). One has to be certain here that Jadonang was referring to polytheism with an end to many baseless sacrifices without espousing a blanket ban on the worship of other gods and goddesses. Zeliangrong people were already worshipping several gods and goddesses and revering many spirits besides the worship of the Supreme God called *Apou Ragang*. In the subsequent section one sees that, from the two noted writers among Rongmei—Budha Kamei and Gangmumei Kamei, Jadonang was not endorsing any new religion but he was a mere reformer and his idea of the Supreme God, *Tingkao Ragwang* (heavenly God) itself is not a deviation from the ancestral conception of the Supreme God but a complementary religious vocabulary indicating heaven, which was already conceptualised, where all human beings supplicate for their souls to be after death. Jadonang certainly did not introduce the idea of worship of God because God was already worshipped even before Jadonang was born. Jadonang's contribution was the greater emphasis on the worship of God with the abolition of several sacrifices and appeasement of several gods, goddesses and spirits. This heralded reformation within the religious life of the Zeliangrong people.

Jadonang's maiden use of the term *Tingkao Ragwang* merits critical analysis here. Jadonang's activities were politically motivated towards achieving the kingdom of Makam. He was instructed by God to fight for the freedom of His people. Every religious activity carried out with immense reformations was aimed at facilitating wide mobilisation and mass participation in the political movement. He envisioned a state of freedom with no oppression and subjugation from foreign rule. Jadonang unequivocally roared,

> The Meiteis have their King, the Indian! (Tajongmei) have their rulers, why should we not have our own King? The White men and we are all human beings. Why should we be afraid of them? All men are equal. We are blessed people. Our days have come (Kamei 2004: 150).

Such a free state was akin to heaven or *Tingkao*. Such a state of freedom was promised to him by the god locally known as *Apou*

Ragang. So it was this *Apou Ragang* whom he identified to be the supreme ruler of the state of free or the land of free or *Tingkao* or heaven. So, He is none other than *Tingkao Ragwang* whom they have been worshipping as *Apou Ragang*. Heaven, according to Jadonang, is probably not the land of the blessed souls but heaven is a state of living. Every message from God was concerning daily lives and colonial rule. *Tingkao* is closely linked to worldly living and, therefore, Jadonang incorporated religious reformations within the political movement for Makam Gwangdi or *Tingkao*.

The knowledge of the other seven brothers of *Apou Ragang* was found among the *Pupou Chap*. However, before the reformation introduced by Jadonang, the *Pupou Chap* followers were not well organised in their belief system and, therefore, some adherents of *Pupou Chap*—driven by their needs and problems of lives—worshipped and gave greater emphasis on the younger brothers of *Apou Ragang*. The frequency of worship of *Apou Ragang* was diminishing as the people were engrossed more in appeasement of other spirits and deities. The younger brothers of *Apou Ragang* were never considered Gods, rather they were gods inferior to *Apou Ragang*. Drawing from this reformation of Jadonang TRC now worship *Tingkao Ragwang* (*Apou Ragang*) besides worshipping His seven younger brothers and appeasing several spirits. Therefore, it would be a historical fallacy to claim that Jadonang introduced the worship of *Tingkao Ragwang*. The colonial account of Jadonang's work needs to be scrutinised against the backdrop of the anti-colonial activities of Jadonang that even led to his hanging to death.

Budha Kamei,[2] in describing the background of the emergence of religious reformations under Jadonang said, 'The Universal God, pantheon gods, presiding deities of the villages and ancestors of the family or lineage are worshipped by them'. And Gangmumei Kamei while describing the background of the religious activities of Jadonang says, 'The people have an idea of a "Supreme God"' and he further observed that the people were 'so superstitious that the worship of the Almighty Universal God, Tingkao Ragwang, was submerged in the performance of innumerable sacrifices' and against this backdrop 'Jadonang was such a remarkable holy young man picked up by God to reform the superstition-filled religion of his people' [sic] (2009: 25-6). Thus, the Zeliangrong people were already worshipping the 'Supreme God' besides worshipping and appeasing the gods, goddesses and spirits that lead them to innumerable sacrifices and constricting superstitions. Therefore, Jadonang did not introduce any God but *emphasised* the worship of the 'Supreme God' by relinquishing certain baseless sacrifices. The fact that Jadonang visited the Bhuvan cave and preached about Bisnu and strengthened the worship of Bisnu through pilgrimage proves that monotheism, which *Tingkao Ragwang Kariak* and *Heraka* claim to be, was never a part of Jadonang's religious reformations.

Besides the notion of heavenly Supreme God, Arkotong Longkumer observed that in the days of reformation Jadonang used Hindu religious figures—'Bishnu and Mahadeo' intending to instil fear in the minds of the people (2010: 82). Longkumer further said that Gaidinliu invoked the sky god, *Soraren*, of the Meetei whom she claimed to have interacted with (ibid.: 82). To understand the 'Bishnu' and 'Mahadeo' of Longkumer we may examine the account given to J.C. Higgins by Jadonang himself after his arrest,

> The male god in my upper temple is Vishnu (God of Preservation), the female is his wife, but I do not know her name. The Mithun in the shrine is the bull of Mahadeo. I heard all about these things from the 'fukir' [fakir] at the Bhuban Hills temple—a foreigner, not a Manipuri. I first heard of this 'fukir' in a dream (School of Oriental and African Studies Archives, Higgins File, Ms 95022, 15: 11–18, cited in Longkumer 2007: 503).

This account tends to reflect tremendous changes in the belief systems of the people under the influence of Jadonang and Gaidinliu. Such account induces naïve minds into perceiving the religion of the Zeliangrong people as part of Hinduism. One must not miss the colonial undercurrents in such an account. One must not forfeit the privilege of accounting for the ulterior inclination of the colonial force. Such an account certainly debases the uniqueness of the people. It invariably projects the worldview of the tribal people inferior to the dominant groups. Therefore, it may be viewed as a part of the grand agenda of the colonial force to sustain colonialism (in the form of cultural colonialism) long after they have gone. This reflects what may be termed as intellectual imperialism—a tendency to sustain dominance over others in the intellectual domain even in a state of political freedom of others. The tribal people are never conceived of as a group capable of experiencing a higher level of cognitive abilities. The lived experiences and intellectual attainments of the marginalised groups are destined to be explained only within the context of the dominant groups' lived experiences. Arkotong Longkumer, unfortunately, missed the colonial motive of J.C. Higgins in his reading of the above account of Higgins. The colonial power simply could not accept that the people they oppress and subjugate could have a religious philosophy and pristine worldview of their own. For the colonisers, the colonised people, especially the forest or hill dwellers were close to savages and any fine element of human life such as religious philosophy is unthinkable with them. It was in the best interest of the colonial power to reduce everything about the tribal people in the context of the valley based tax-paying colonial subjects. Thus, the Bisnu of Jadonang is the popular Vishnu. For Higgins, nothing but Hinduism and Meitei people explain the revolting tribes in the hills. In taking Hinduism and religion of the tax-paying Meiteis in the valley J.C. Higgins ensure the cultural colonialism of the tribes in the hills by Hinduism and Meitei people. Such reading will not be missed by diligent scholars.

In the Zeliangrong context—notionally—polytheism probably preceded monotheism. Though monotheism is preached it is not rigidly practised. The concept of henotheism[3] appears out of context in any of the belief systems of the Zeliangrong people. This is because no representation of all the deities as 'as supreme and absolute' without disparaging the 'divine character of the other gods' (Muller 1881: 137) is seen in any of the belief systems of the Zeliangrong people. There is no belief in incarnation or *avatars*. Human beings probably knew many gods, goddesses and spirits whom they believe to be present in many places and objects. With many mysteries and varied needs and problems they probably related each mystery and each need with specific unseen formidable power. They probably identified and prioritised specific need and associated the fulfilment of that need to one particular power and that power is accorded the status of God as long as the specific need is of the highest value. Monotheism was certainly not known to be practised by the Zeliangrong people. The concept of monotheism is intriguing as it demands relinquishing all the gods and goddesses who serve specific purposes corresponding to the needs of human beings. Giving them up would come only with giving up their needs. This approach of studying religion may be termed as *need-religiology*[4] or study of religion based on the deities worshipped or appeased in the context of the needs of the people.

Scholars and contemporary believers of various Zeliangrong belief systems have succeeded in confusing the position of Jadonang between polytheism and monotheism. Did Jadonang advocate continuity of polytheism or reformation towards monotheism? Even Professor Gangmumei Kamei was not certain about the position of Jadonang between polytheism and monotheism. He says, 'The belief in the worship of the Supreme Being as practised by the *Heraka* is the introduction of the concept of monotheism[5] in the Zeliangrong religion which is traditionally polytheism' (2009: 99). However, Tingkao Ragwang Chapriak's adherents who were well consolidated in its present form under the able guidance of some personalities like Gangmumei Kamei since 14-15 April 1994, claim Jadonang to be its spiritual guide. They claim TRC to be rooted in the teachings and reformations of Jadonang. If Jadonang stood for monotheism as Gangmumei Kamei and *Heraka* group would like us to believe, how can TRC, which is essentially polytheistic, be rooted in the reformations under Jadonang? Another crucial question is: Why did Jadonang endorse the worship and appeasement of some gods, goddesses and spirits if he were propagating monotheism?

Gangmumei Kamei's claim on the monotheistic nature of *Heraka* is fallacious and contradictory. *Heraka* cannot be termed as monotheism because Gangmumei Kamei mentions elsewhere that 'the reformed Heraka cult has started the *worship of the Sun*' [emphasis added] (2006: 67). *Tingkao Ragwang* is not the Sun and the Sun is never assumed as an avatar or transfiguration of *Tingkao Ragwang*. *Heraka* would not embrace the humiliation of being categorised as animism with the worship of the sun. Therefore, worship of the sun must be understood as worship of another power besides *Tingkao Ragwang*. It is in this line of argument that *Heraka* does not qualify as monotheism. According to the belief of

Heraka, *Tingwang* is 'the creator of the universe, the Sun and the Moon and all living beings' (Newme 2011a: 4). This worship of an object, the Sun–as Gangmumei mentioned–created by *Tingwang* further pushes *Heraka* into the ambit of animism. Thus, Gangmumei Kamei analysis was restricted to only identifying the supreme being to adjudge a belief system as monotheism with disregard to other features of the belief system. Such intellectual provincialism poses a serious detrimental factor in the conceptualisation of the religious philosophies of Zeliangrong belief systems in totality.

The general secretary of *Tingkao Ragwang Chapriak Phom* (Assam, Nagaland and Manipur) claimed that TRC is polytheistic and a legacy of Jadonang's religious reformation. The general-secretary might want to re-examine his claim of TRC as a legacy of Jadonang given the assertion of Arkotong Longkumer who stated that 'Jadonang devised a set of new ritual practices based on traditional Kabui forms but closer to the Vaishnavite traditions of the dominant Meitei community of Manipur' (2010: 503). This assertion of Longkumer weakens the claim of primordiality of any belief system basing on Jadonang's legacy. According to the general secretary, TRC reclaimed the past cultural and religious legacies of their ancestors. This reflects Arkotong Longkumer's idea of 'reform' which is a 'more varied notion meaning an advancement, progress, a moving forward, but also reverting to older, more traditional ways' (2007: 500). This atavistic claim of the general secretary is widely shared by other adherents of TRC. He further claimed that if the past legacies are not reclaimed and new features are seen in religious beliefs and practices TRC will not be respected and accepted by the people. Thus, TRC is viewed by its members as a religious atavism.

According to the surveyed data, while 65.23 per cent of the respondents claim to treasure their ancestral belief systems only 33.44 per cent claim that they believe their religion is the true religion. A feeling of atavism is impressively high among the respondents. Such an affinity with their forefathers also caused the return of a few individuals from other religions.

There has been active conversion in the 1980s and 1990s in Manipur valley. The author personally witnessed this proselytisation. This period saw many Rongmei people in Manipur valley accepting

Christianity as their new faith. This was certainly not without animosity between the villagers. Some of the new Christians were excommunicated and some were even attacked physically by the villagers. In some villages where Christians were dominant the followers of *Pupou Chap* continued with their belief systems but with the cost of the stigma of *Jou Jangmei* (wine drinker). As TRC emerged with vigorous activities and with a sense of pride being instilled in the 1990s some of the converted Christians returned to their ancestors' belief systems. However, very few of the present adherents of TRC were in other religion earlier.

Table 4.1: Other Religion Followed Earlier

	Whether in other religion earlier?
	Per cent
Yes	1.3
No	97.3
Don't want to say	1.3
Total	100.0

Source: Author's survey.

According to Table 4.1 a mere 1.3 per cent of the respondents were not in other religions earlier. Though the size is small it nevertheless shows the presence of atavistic feelings among the adherents of TRC. Their reverence for their forefathers' legacies is commendable. Moreover, the fact that 97.3 per cent of the respondents were not in any other religions also reflects the strength and commitment of their faith in their religion. It also speaks volume about their efforts to ward off conversion. Nevertheless, there is a lingering perception of the threat of conversion. Because of historical accounts, past experiences and contemporary incidents, perception of the threat of conversion still runs in the minds of the adherents of TRC. According to the surveyed data, 34.1 per cent of the respondents still think there is a threat of conversion against which they need to keep vigil. Despite the fact that 97.3 per cent of the respondents were not in any other religion earlier, the threat expressed by 34.1 per cent of the respondents is critical.

TRC continued with polytheism. Accepting monotheism, which is a new thing for the Zeliangrong people, would tantamount to a destabilisation of the society and the teachings of TRC may even be termed as heresies. Reclaiming of the ancestral legacies was essential as Rongmei people are highly traditionalist (attachment to ancestors) in their outlook. But, in the context of nullifying many ancestral beliefs and practices and several other changes incorporated in beliefs and practices, 'even the modern ways of worship', how much of the past religious and cultural legacies are reclaimed will remain debatable among many academics of religion. Some are convinced of the changes within TRC while some adherents believe TRC to be in its primordial state in its entirety.

Despite the claim of inheriting the ancestral belief system some of its adherents still believe that it has changed even in terms of its belief which is most fundamental in any religion. 41.1 per cent of the respondents are not certain about the primordial state of beliefs of their religion, TRC. 14.4 per cent of the respondents think that the beliefs of their religion have changed and 26.8 per cent of them are not sure of the state of the beliefs of their religion. But in terms of changes in practices, interesting responses are seen. 74.6 per cent of the respondents claim that there are changes in religious practices. This leads to the inference that certain practices are not primordial. But 58.9 per cent of the respondents believe that their religion retains the primordial beliefs inherited from their ancestors. This strengthens the claim that TRC is a reformed religion with immense reformations seen in terms of its practices with the abolition of several gennas and taboos.

If a primordiality of a belief system is determined exclusively by a belief in an ever-existing God then every belief system is a primordial religion because the God of every religion exists with no beginning and with no end. However, if the primordiality of a religion depends on beliefs about God then many of the beliefs of the reformed religions are not primordial religions because some of the beliefs about God are new. Descriptions about God being worshipped in some belief systems are not the same as those of their ancestors. Thus, an indication of a change in a belief like God points to a detachment from primordiality. As the term primordial means an existence since the beginning of time any feature of belief in a religion claimed to be primordial must have been in existence since the beginning of time. It cannot have a reformed feature. Anything resulting from a reformation cannot essentially be primordial. The simplest understanding of something primordial is its existence since the beginning of time. And the existence of God has no beginning and no end. This is the primordial nature of God. However, religion cannot be entirely understood in the sense of the primordiality associated only with God. Religion has its meaning in social intercourse. Religion cannot exist without human beings. God may be primordial but religion is not necessarily entirely primordial. The social dimension of religion undermines the primordiality of religion. Much to the chagrin of devotees, primordiality must be sparingly and contextually used.

When the definition of religion is entirely based on a primordial God one may claim religion to be primordial just as the primordial characteristic of God who has no beginning. Time being timeless is the paradoxical nature of the primordiality of God. This seems to be the general understanding of religion being primordial. The origin of one's religion is invariably equated with that of the primordiality of God. TRC's claim of primordiality is an extension of this dimension of primordiality of God, *Tingkao Ragwang*. God being primordial and the religion being defined based on God the religion is inherently primordial.

The direction of the East is significant in religion. Jadonang said, 'Worshipping consists of facing east' (Kamei 2009: 31). According to E.E Evans-Pritchard, 'Nuer say that "the west is the side of death, the east the side of life"' (1956: 148). However, looking at many of the Kalum Kais (house of worship) of TRC, including the major one at Chingmeirong at Imphal in Manipur, the architectural positions of Kalum Kais do not facilitate the devotees to face east while worshipping. They face North. Some features within TRC that closely resemble those of Hinduism and Christianity have rendered TRC behind the eight ball in their claim of atavism.

Jadonang advocated reformation by ceasing to appease many gods and goddesses but he did not abandon appeasing all the gods and goddesses. After the death of Jadonang, the advocacy for the worship of *Tingkao Ragwang* was further strengthened and refined to the extent of warding off all gods and goddesses partly due to pressure on the economic and livelihood domain of their lives on account of innumerable expensive animal sacrifices and famine leading to 'scarcity of food' (Longkumer 2010: 47) in the course of their struggle against the colonial force and this resulted in an attempt[6] towards the reformations of Zeliangrong belief system. And religion being 'propositional' (Joppke 2018: 2) one cannot be uncertain about the position of Jadonang whose contributions towards Zeliagnrong belief systems must be accorded as an essential factor in an analysis of almost every aspect of Zeliangrong and the Rongmei in particular.

Gangmumei Kamei said, 'The religion of the Zeliangrong has the usual features of a primordial religion and it is definitely not animism' (2006: 66). And he further says that the gods in the elements of nature 'are worshipped as "presiding deity"' (ibid.: 67). His attempt to erase animism from Zeliangrong belief systems has not been fully appreciated. In the year of his demise an article that reflects on the political, academic and religious contributions of Professor Gangmumei Kamei one finds Rajesh Salam, a senior journalist of *The People's Chronicle* describing *Tingkao Ragwang Chapriak* as 'the worship of the elements of nature, interpreted through the supreme deity Tingkao Ragwang'. Salam remembers Gangmumei Kamei in the words: 'Nature was always close to him, and this was easily discerned when his eyes lit up with every discourse on the elements of nature, more focused on the intrinsic relationship that man shared with nature at all times' (2017: 4). Salam's reference to nature does not go deeper to acknowledge the spirits in nature. His assessment of Gangmumei Kamei reflects the proximity of the Zeliangrong belief system to nature.

In his attempt to erase a picture of animism from the Zeliangrong belief system and uplift the position of the Zeliangrong belief system to a higher echelon, Gangmumei Kamei resorted to what may be simply termed as incomplete analysis of literature. His reading of *The Golden Bough* by James Frazer (1922) is partial and deterministic towards disproving animism within Zeliangrong belief systems and granting higher status to Zeliangrong belief systems. Gangmumei Kamei concluded his reading of *The Golden Bough* in believing that polytheism evolved from animism after believers identified the animistic objects with specific names and functions. Gangmumei Kamei failed to recognise the limitation of James Frazer's analysis of animism evolving into polytheism. James Frazer while expounding on the shift from animism to polytheism cited an instance of 'The Worship of Trees' (the title of a Chapter in *The Golden Bough*) as animism (1922: 109-20). Frazer writes, 'When a tree comes to be viewed, no longer as the body of the tree-spirit, but simply as its abode which it can quit at pleasure, an important advance has been made in religious thought. Animism is passing into polytheism' (ibid.: 117). But it is not only trees that Frazer identified while expounding the transition of animism into polytheism. Frazer mentioned the expansion of animism from animals to trees in the writings of an ancient vegetarian, Porphyry (ibid.: 111). According to Frazer, several other objects are identified by animists. Trees were not the only objects identified as abodes of spirits. In this sense, when several spirits in many objects were recognised, human beings were already polytheistic in their state of animism. This *polytheistic animism* [italics mine] was missed by Gangmumei Kamei in his reading of *The Golden Bough*.

Polytheism was there even when human beings were animistic as they believed in many spirits dwelling in many objects and not just one or not just Frazer's animistic trees. Animism can be seen both in polytheism and monotheism if several spirits or only one spirit respectively is recognised in the objects. Animism is better understood as belief in the power of spirit in an object and not in the power of an object in itself which is the case in fetichism. Therefore, worship of the supreme being does not necessarily mean monotheism because, besides the worship of the supreme being several other gods, goddesses and spirits may be worshipped and appeased simultaneously. And if, according to Gangmumei Kamei, *Heraka*, which does not worship or appease gods, goddesses and spirits, is a 'legacy of Jadonang' how can TRC adherents claim Jadonang to be the proponent of TRC, which is polytheistic? Polytheism, according to Max Mueller, is defined as 'the worship of many deities which together form one divine polity, under the control of one supreme god' (1878: 289). Thus, polytheism is not merely the worship of many gods and goddesses. In polytheism, there is also an acknowledgement of the greatest or most powerful among all the entities worshipped. This is the case in TRC.

Gangmumei Kamei writes, 'Essentially, the Zeliangrong religion is a polytheism, there is an element of Henotheism as there is a belief and worship of one Supreme God out of many gods' (2006: 65). Henotheism seemingly applies to TRK which worship only the Supreme God while acknowledging the power and existence of many gods, goddesses and spirits but not worshipping or appeasing them. Here Gangmumei Kamei does not specify which religion he refers to. Is he referring to *Heraka* or TRC or *Tingkao Ragwang Kariak* or *Pupou Chap*. The very use of the term 'polytheism' explicitly refers to TRC or *Pupou Chap*. But henotheism is ambiguous. Nurturing further doubts Lanbilung Gonmei callously describes TRC with elements of 'Polytheism, Henotheism and Monotheism' existing simultaneously in it and further adds more uncertain elements into TRC with the phrase 'and so on' (2011: 54). Lanbilung Gonmei seems to be far removed from the simple knowledge that polytheism, henotheism and monotheism cannot be contemporaneous in one single faith if it has to be a legitimate belief system. Lanbilung Gonmei's claim is a serious contradiction with the claim of TRC General Secretary, Chaoba Kamson[7] who claimed that TRC adopted polytheism as polytheism is a primordial feature, and TRC avoided monotheism as monotheism, which is a recent religious philosophy among the Zeliangrong people, would destabilise the Zeliangrong community. Polytheism, monotheism and henotheism do not form simultaneous features of any of the belief system. Every progressive stage in a society witnesses certain elements of the preceding stage. And two or more forms of belief system may be seen within a community simultaneously. But different belief systems cannot be witnessed in one religion. A religious group must be either progressive or regressive in their belief.

It is with the understanding of this context of a paradoxical state of Jadonang's position and the murky claims on the forms of Zeliangrong belief systems that one can better analyse the various other reformations within various Zeliangrong belief systems introduced since the time of Jadonang and continued by Gaidinliu and which continues even to this day.

To avoid further confusion it is most appropriate to conclude by saying that TRC, because of worship of the Supreme Being, *Tingkao Ragwang*, besides many other gods and goddesses, is polytheistic. *Pupou Chap* is also polytheistic as it worships *Apou Ragang*, the Supreme God besides the worship and appeasement of several other gods and goddesses. *Tingkao Ragwang Kariak* of the Champa group is seemingly henotheistic as it worships only *Tingkao Ragwang* and merely recognises other gods, goddesses and spirits without appeasing or worshipping any of them. But it is not henotheistic. It claims to be monotheistic which is erroneous. *Heraka* fails to be categorised as monotheistic as it endorses worship of the Sun besides *Tingkao Ragwang*, as claimed by Gangmumei Kamei and also worship Bisnu, as accounted by Chaoba Kamson in a Conference of TRC Youths at Imphal in Manipur in 2018. The origin of the worship of the Sun could probably be due to the claim of Jadonang, 'if I destroy the *Hebuibang* (Semal tree) with one bullet, I will be a *heguang* and rule over the earth like the sun' (Longkumer 2010: 185). Arkotong Longkumer further observed that Gaidinliu also made a similar claim who also instituted the ritual of sunrise prayer known as *naimik kakelum* in Zeme term. This promise of assuming the figure of Sun by the two leaders could have been the driving force for the sustenance of *naimik kakelum* or worship of the Sun among *Heraka* adherents. It is, therefore, polytheistic as it is marked by worship of the Sun and lord Bisnu of Bhuvan cave besides worshipping the Supreme Being, *Tingkao Ragwang*. Therefore, a proper analysis of the various belief systems of Zeliangrong people leads to the conclusion that there is no monotheism, which is a belief in and worship of only one God without even acknowledging the existence of other gods and goddesses.

To understand TRC better in the context of a contest between polytheism, monotheism and henotheism, one may briefly expound on the relation between religion and culture. According to Ken Morrison, 'the separations and divisions they [human beings] make between the sacred and the profane, draws attention to the way religion is made manifest in the cultural world created by their acts'

(2008: 242). This is based on the analysis of Emile Durkheim's *The Elementary Forms of Religious Life*. For Morrison, culture is initially independent of religion and culture provided for the manifestation of religious beliefs and religious practices finds meaning in cultural expression of them. This also suggests religion being a part of culture as religion was imported within a culture. Thus, in accordance with Ken Morrison, one may claim that religion and culture had different origins but they interact and share a common platform to a certain degree. Culture is fertile soil for the germination of religious beliefs and practices.

It is in this context that one may understand the origin of TRC as a reformed religion which is sometimes allegedly traced to the formation of Zeliangrong Religious Council in 1994. Professor Gangmumei Kamei, though he followed Gaidinliu during the movement for Zeliangrong homeland under the banner of Zeliangrong People's Convention, was not an adherent of *Heraka*. *Heraka* was seen as a belief system in which Zeliangrong culture and identity cannot sustain for long. This is so because *Heraka* claims to be monotheistic and had relinquished the worship and appeasement of all gods and goddesses and many spirits. This also means that several age-old customary practices and festivals were shunned and this resulted in lesser cultural manifestations of religion under the *Heraka* belief system. Similar is the case with *Tingkao Ragwang Kariak* (TRK) that had ceased to worship and appease gods, goddesses and spirits though their power and existence is recognised. Certainly, *Heraka* and *Tingkao Ragwang Kariak* did not find many adherents. This is partly explained by the primordial polytheistic nature of the belief systems of the Zeliangrong people. Sudden preaching of monotheism or preaching against gods and goddesses was not very appealing to the masses. Therefore, *Heraka* is seen primarily among Zeme in Assam and *Tingkao Ragwang Kariak* is found only in one small village located at a foothill in Manipur near the Manipur University campus.

Professor Gangmumei Kamei was not in favour of losing the age old cultural identity. And TRC says, 'Loss of religion is loss of culture and loss of culture is loss of identity'. Therefore, one cannot forfeit the long treasured beliefs that they were all manifested in the cultural domain. This impelled the TRC to cherish the traditional belief systems with worship and appeasement of many gods and goddesses besides the worship of the Supreme God, *Tingkao Ragwang*.[8] This factually, logically and theologically puts TRC into polytheism.

Reformations in Religious Practices

In the days of head hunting, the villagers feared to move out of the village as their heads could be hunted. They feared the spirits in forests. Their saviours were worshipped and appeased within the frontiers of their village. The village authorities facilitated these spiritual needs of the villagers through the intercessory rituals of the village priests. This village confined belief and practice system was set to change with the dream journey of Jadonang Malangmei to the Bhuvan cave identified as the abode of god Bisnu. The religious pilgrimage to the Bhuvan cave was begun by Jadonang. Unlike the earlier days in which prayers and rituals were confined to one's village, identifying holy places and journeying to the holy places promoted inter-village gathering for prayers and rituals. This may be said to be facilitated by the presence of the British who also acted against head hunting. It is also believed that the emergence of temples as places of worship was an influence of both the neighbouring Hindus and Christians (Makuga 1994, cited in Roy 2013: 77; Yonuo 1982). Jadonang also tried to elicit a feeling of reverence among his people with an object of power. Jadonang is said to have used 'two sacred pythons' in his house which was purportedly intended 'to create faith in his supernatural powers' (Mukherjee, Gupta & Das 1982: 71) among the people. Tamphasana Rajkumari too believed that it was used to elicit reverence from the people (2012).

Jadonang also frequented Zeilad lakes in the Tamenglong district of Manipur. It is a popular myth that a divine sword (*'Khongchai bang'*) and a spear (*'Phentubui'*) (Kamei 2009: 43) are hidden in the lakes. It is also believed that after their retrieval, the Zeliangrong people will attain freedom from 'foreign rule' (ibid.: 43). These lakes are important historical and religious sites of the Zeliangrong people. Jadonang had to find a rationale and social environment for the operationalisation of the instructions he received from God through the divine dream amidst and against the economically taxing religious life and the bitter colonial situation of his time.

Jadonang abolished several religious practices considered superstitious. Relinquishing practices such as bride price and feasts came as a great relief to the poverty stricken people. But these practices are re-emerging in the contemporary times even among the tribal Christians. Taboos and associated rituals had consumed much of the resources and life of the Zeliangrong people. Jadonang, therefore, declared the following as no longer taboo: (i) birth of chicken, piglet, puppy, and child in the individual house or the village, (ii) climbing of roof of a house by a dog or sitting over its roof by a crow or kite, (iii) birth of stillborn child, (iv) death of a woman five days after delivery, (v) earthquake, (vi) falling of trees and landslides, (vii) injury from *dao* [sword] or spear, (viii) the first rains of the year (ix) the first hailstorm of the year (Kamei 2009: 35). When TRC was organised in 1994 the taboo associated with unnatural death was abolished (Kamei 2006: 58). It is in this sense that religious reformations do continue to prevail within TRC. And this makes TRC appealing even to the outsiders as it begins to appear rational.

Jadonang also introduced the construction of *Kalum Kai* or the house of worship. The Zeliangrong people never had a practice of praying in a group even inside a village even during the days of headhunting. According to Gangmumei Kamei, the idea of Kalum Kai introduced by Jadonang was probably drawn from other religions (2009: 30) as this was never witnessed earlier among the Zeliangrong people. Jadonang built two Kalum Kai during his lifetime. Kalum Kai, according to Gangmumei Kamei, is said to incorporate features of Hinduism and Christianity. From Hinduism, Kalum Kai incorporated the feature of idolatry[9] with the installation of the image of Bisnu (ibid.: 34). The practice of sitting on benches in rows while praying and worshipping inside Kalum Kai and preaching from a pulpit is believed to be extracted from Christian ways of communal worship (ibid.: 32). Jadonang emphasised the cleanliness of the mind and body of worshippers. Sinners have to cleanse their minds and souls of their sinful thoughts before entering the Kalum Kai. He built two bathrooms one each for boys and girls so that they can bathe before entering the Kalum Kai (ibid.: 32). Bathing before entering Kalum Kai imparts a strong sense of the need to be pure in mind and soul. Bathing symbolises the cleansing of one's soul from sins and it reinforces the need to be sinless and pure.

The emphasis on a bath before entering the Kalum Kai is an effort to ensure bodily cleanliness which can help keep the mind and the soul clean before the supreme power. It is to generate a psychological aura of purity that can help one to be absorbed into an ambience of spiritual intercourse with the supreme power without any temporal hindrances. Thus, advising married couples to bathe before entering the Kalum Kai carries both spiritual and hygienic significance. Note that TRC advises all believers including both husbands and wives to bathe before entering Kalum Kai. The advice is not only to married women or menstruating females. This point is of particular interest in the context of restriction on the right of females of menstruating age to enter a certain temple in India. The debate around the entry of women in Sabarimala temple stands out in this context. Members of the 'Thazhamon Illam' who are the tantris, or hereditary high priests, of the Sabarimala temple in Kerala, do not allow females between the ages of 10 and 50 years into temples due to menstruation.[10] In 1991, the Kerala High Court presented the various reasons for the ban on the entry of women of the aforesaid age group. The tantris are not willing to change this tradition despite the order of the Supreme Court to do away with the tradition of a restriction imposed on women of the aforesaid age group. In September 2018, the Supreme Court struck down such a ban on entry to the temple by women of the said age group. The Supreme Court said, 'One side we pray to goddesses; on the other, women of a certain age are considered "impure". This dualistic approach is nothing but patriarchy practised in religion. The ban "exacts" more purity from women than men'.[11] Such an uncomfortable phenomenon is alien within the Zeliangrong religious groups.

When TRC was formed in 1994 the group decided to pray every full moon day and every Sunday. They organised singing practices in villages and facilitated the active participation of youth and women in religious activities. However, the performances of rituals are still carried out by elderly men. They also adopted a symbol of *Tingkao*

Ragwang called *Boudan*. Citing the Report of TRC, Budha Kamei describes the *Boudan* as: 'The circle represents the universe/cosmos. Criss-cross lines within the circle represent the Zodiac in the sky. And the sun and moon represent the heavenly bodies which are the creation of *Tingkao Ragwang*' (2012). Such ways in the use of the religious symbol are new for the Zeliangrong people. A pictorial or material representation of *Boudan* were never used. The symbol *Boudan* must always be drawn on the surface of the ground using an iron axe. *Boudan* can never be represented except on the surface of the ground. A *Boudan* is never seen above the ground where it is drawn with an axe (*tan lougai*) as part of a ritual at a funeral.

The idea of religious conversion is not prominent in Zeliangrong belief systems. Every individual is a *Pupou Chap*/*Heraka*/TRK/TRC adherent by birth. Entry into *Pupou Chap* is made possible through entry into the Zeliangrong tribe itself by adopting any one of the several clans. However, if any individual wished to enter and accept the TRC belief system or a former TRC adherent wishes to come back a simple ritual is performed by using an iron axe and water only. The prayer recited in this ritual is as follow:

Tan chu kum chu	As cold as iron
Tan than kum than	As pure as iron
Tan tan kum tan	As strong as iron
Dui chu kum chu	As cold as water
Dui than kum than	As clean as water
Dui link kum link	As pure as water
Gutna bamdat tho	Come in and stay

Source: Chaoba Kamson, Gen. Sec. TRC (Assam, Nagaland and Manipur).

The above prayer is a part of sanctification and not conversion. It sanctifies the person from all the beliefs and practices of the past or other religions and accepts the person into the fold of TRC.

An important incident that could serve as a suitable example in understanding the reformation of religious practices among TRC is narrated by Khomeimacha Kamson.[12] According to him, the religious lives of Zeliangrong people are marked by Kasoi-Kadam and not by prayer and worship. While the Kasoi or a request for blessings may be changed the Kadam or the oblations can never be altered. Kamson mentioned that there was an incident in his village in which an elderly TRC adherent brought out some sweets *(laddu* and *jelibi*) as components of Kadam. 'This is taboo!', he exclaimed. The God or any other powers cannot be offered sweets as Kadam. Such is the extent of ignorance of some individuals including sexagenarians and octogenarians. TRC belief systems are yet to be rooted in conviction as it is still in a state of reformation and yet to jell.

TRC in Perspective

TRC may be viewed as an effort of the people to live with their evolving consciences. Giving up one's conscience to the effort of someone to proselytise is submitting one's self to others. TRC is a result of practical pressing problems. Many of the Zeliangrong people had to identify with 'Hindu' as their religious identity during Censuses as their belief systems or *Pupou Chap* had no names. TRC offers itself as a culture-based belief system of the Zeliangrong people, especially to the Rongmei people. It is a lifestyle-based belief system that reflects an effort of the people to organise life and give meanings to different aspects of their life. It is a reformed way of both secular and religious life legitimised in religion. This cultural resonance in religion in the form of TRC engendered a sense of intrusion by a body that stands as a guardian of Zeliangrong culture. The Zeliangrong Cultural Council is believed to have been perturbed by the feeling of their prerogative right over Zeliangrong culture being challenged by the reformers and leaders of TRC that espoused many reformations in the religious and cultural realms of their collective identity.

TRC and Village Institutions

TRC and village institutions are more into a cooperative relationship. TRC performs its religious activities for the welfare of the village.

TRC Phom acts more like a consultative body in matters concerning rituals and other religious activities. TRC, however, does not enjoy an exclusive authority over religious matters. Zeliangrong Union, the apex body of Zeliangrong people of Assam, Nagaland and Manipur also intervenes in issues of marriage and land disputes. It, despite being a non-religious body, even imposes customary laws upon the conflicting parties. According to the General-Secretary of TRC (Assam, Nagaland and Manipur), the elders of the village authority even consulted the TRC Phom executive members on religious matters. This is irrespective of the ages of the executive members of the Phom. This is a new trend that was never witnessed in a Zeliangrong society in which the knowledge and wisdom of the elders were regarded in high esteem and always equated with those of God.

With the growing influence of TRC across villages one may even probe into the possibility of a certain section of its adherents desiring to have the highest village authority under TRC. The fact that village authorities even consulted TRC on religious matters points to the occasional diffidence of the elders on religious matters. The younger generations with their ability to read and write enjoy the privilege of reading and understanding the significance of rituals from the many writings produced under TRC. TRC is no longer confined to the oral traditions of the elders. It is now engraved in the art of writing and electronic media and this provides ample opportunity to its adherents across different age groups to easily access the wealth of their religion. TRC even has a publication section.

The youth now understand the functioning of a village under their customary laws better. They are better equipped with mythologies and legends that form the foundations of their beliefs, rituals and village polity. They can now question the village authority with religious and moral authority.

A chi-square test of independence of the relation between the educational status of the respondents and the desire to have village authority under TRC is given below (see Table 4.2 and 4.3).

Null Hypothesis (H_0): The wish to have village Pei under TRC is independent of the educational status of the respondents.

Table 4.2: Crosstabulation of Educational Qualification and *Pei* to be under TRC

	Edu. Qual. of respondents and should Pei be under TRC		
	Should Pei be under TRC		*Total*
Educational Qualification of the Respondents	*Yes*	*No*	
No education	8.6%	6.8%	7.7%
Below HSLC	36.8%	36.7%	36.8%
HSLC	21.1%	14.3%	17.7%
HSSLC	10.5%	19.0%	14.7%
Graduate	13.8%	17.7%	15.7%
Post-graduate	7.9%	4.8%	6.4%
M. Phil.	.7%	.7%	.7%
Doctorate	.7%	.0%	.3%
Total	100%	100%	100%

Source: Author's survey.

Table 4.3: Chi-Square Tests (Educational Qualification and *Pei* under TRC)

	Chi-Square Tests		
	Value	*df*	*Asymp. Sig. (2-sided)*
Pearson Chi-Square	8.750[a]	7	.271
Likelihood Ratio	9.210	7	.238
N of Valid Cases	299		

a. 4 cells (25.0%) have expected count less than 5. The minimum expected count is .49.

Source: Author's survey.

Alternate Hypothesis (Ha): The wish to have village Pei under TRC is dependent on the educational status of the respondents.

The significance value is observed to be more than 0.05 and this gives reason to accept the Null Hypothesis which denies a relationship between the educational status of the respondents and their desire to have the village *Pei* under TRC. With a growing number of adherents of TRC in many villages in Manipur valley, it is evident even through casual observation that the village authorities are beginning to be influenced by TRC and certain sections wish to see village *Pei* under TRC. Some TRC elderly adherents do not see a difference between TRC as a religion and *Pei*, the highest village authority but this is independent of their educational status. Attachment to their traditional institutions is not deterred by their educational attainments.

The gender-based responses on the question concerning the desire to have village *Pei* under TRC need a deeper probe.

Table 4.4: Crosstabulation of Gender and *Pei* under TRC

	Gender of the respondents and should Pei be under TRC Crosstabulation		
	Should Pei be under TRC		*Total*
	Yes	*No*	
Male	52.4%	47.6%	100.0%
Female	48.9%	51.1%	100.0%
Total	50.8%	49.2%	100.0%

Source: Author's survey.

The above Table 4.4 shows more responses among males wanting to have village *Pei* under TRC. Only 48.9 per cent of the female respondents wish to see the village *Pei* under TRC. With no power and no role of women in village *Pei* and common practice of rebuking women who dare to talk within the premise of a village *Pei*, the embracing of *Pei* within TRC is not seen to be beneficial or meaningful to women. However, with no female in the highest decision making institution, *Pei*, the powers and roles of men are significant. There is invariably a greener pasture for men in seeing the village *Pei* under TRC where they already enjoy pre-dominance.

In an isolated case of allocation of community land of a village to a religious group, the pre-dominance of TRC is witnessed in one of the villages surveyed. The land was initially given to the devotees of Bisnu lead by Kaphun (name changed).[13] His relative was the village Khullakpu and this facilitated in acquiring of the land for a Bisnu temple. As there was no other belief system within *Pupou Chap* other than *Phuban Ra kalummei* (worship of Bhuvan god, i.e. Bisnu) which has a name the general understanding among the villagers and especially among the elders was that the belief system around Bisnu, the younger brother of Apou Ragang, was the belief system of the village. Until the year 1994, the villagers did not know *Tingkao Ragwang* as conceptualised among TRC. *Tingkao Ragwang* was called *Apou Ragang* by Bisnu worshippers who are also known as *Pupou Chap tatmei* (followers of *Pupou Chap*).

When TRC was formed the village Khullakpu did not like it as it was considered to be new and seen as a departure from the traditional belief system. However, true to its modern organisational skill, TRC members organised a signature campaign to gather support for Kalum Kai for TRC. As the support for TRC Kalum Kai was overwhelmingly immense, the village Khullakpu, reluctantly, agreed to earmark a portion of land earmarked initially only for Bisnu devotees. The Bisnu devotees could not build a temple as they could not mobilise resources for the construction of the temple. They even tried to get the support of Rishang Keishing, the then sitting Member of Parliament from the Outer Constituency of Manipur, but it did not materialise. The devotees of Bisnu had even acquired an architectural design of the proposed Bisnu temple so that they can get a loan from the state government. But it did not see success. Similar to Bisnu devotees the TRC devotees still could not mobilise fund for Kalum Kai. The land for Bisnu and TRC still lies vacant. The Christians opposed the allocation of village land on the ground that village land should be for the all villagers and not for a specific religious community. But they failed.

What we see in the aforesaid case of land for Kalum Kai is a reflection of the growing predominance of village institutions with TRC devotees and TRC belief systems. The decision-making process in the traditional village institution is begun to be influenced by the beliefs of TRC. It is pointed out that some younger elderly persons in the village *Pei* (court) rely on TRC literature and this partially brings the village authorities, especially the *Pei,* under the influence of

TRC. Moreover, the generation of elders who were actively engaged in the religious reformation period of TRC in the 1990s is now seen to be at the helm of village traditional institutions. This establishes a strong relationship between village traditional institutions and the reformed religion which sometimes appears as thick as thieves.

Religious persecutions have been regular in many Rongmei villages in Manipur valley. Persecutions continue even after many reformations within the belief systems of *Pupou Chap*. A Souvenir released on the occasion of the Silver Jubilee of Rongmei Naga Baptist Association (RNBA) gave a passing reference to persecutions of Christians in some Rongmei villages in Manipur valley (RNBA 2015: 3). This is vengeful persecution. The cause of a tenuous state of the traditionalists' belief systems has been often attributed to the activities of the Christians that sometimes included condemnation of the traditionalists' belief systems and practices. For some Christians, the fresh religious vigour elicited from the reformations of *Pupou Chap* was a reinvigorated destructive strength to avenge their forefathers' shame and pain inflicted by earlier Christians.

This growing influence of TRC over village traditional institutions has been perceived as one of the factors for persecution against Christians especially in the form of ex-communication or forceful participation of Christians in cultural festivals of the village. However, a former Secretary of Youth wing of TRC[14] dismissed such allegations. According to him, TRC does not impose any religious restriction or compulsion. Citing an instance from his village where the TRC central Kalum Kai is located he claimed that Christianity became more vibrant in his village at the same time when TRC also emerged vibrant and strong. The claim of the former secretary is partially substantiated with the fact that there lies a protestant Church in the village much to the chagrin of the village authorities. According to another TRC adherent[15] of the village, the village authorities were annoyed with the upcoming Christians as there is a written agreement by which the villagers agreed not to leave their ancestral belief systems to follow any other religions. The village authorities are not against any specific religion. Interestingly, the secretary of the village who was also a signatory to the agreement also converted to Christianity. Such allegations and counter-allegations have been a regular feature of the inter-religious relationship in Rongmei villages. Meanwhile, the growing influence of TRC on village traditional institutions is observed and with its reformations, its influence remains relevant amidst changing world around them.

NOTES

1. I eloped with my love who is also an Angami Catholic and, therefore, the Catholic doctrine condemned our union and it had to be rectified. A name given by the Church to such union, i.e. elopement is 'jungle marriage'. We had to make peace with the people of the Church to symbolise peace with God. If this rectification was not done my to-be-born child would be condemned, I was told by an elderly person of my Church. This is a manifestation of the social significance of religion in its function of social control with norms and values.
2. Budha Kamei. (2011). Haipou Jadonang: His Religious reform movement. *E-pao*. http://epao.net/epSubPageExtractor.asp?src=manipur.History_of_Manipur.Haipou_Jadonang_His_Religious_reform_movement_Part_2.
3. *Kathenotheism*, or simply *Henotheism* is 'a belief in single gods'. It is a 'consciousness that all the deities are but different names of one and the same godhead' (Muller 1881: 137). It is a belief in the supremacy of each god in its specific domain. Max Mueller coined this term to conceptualise the absolute and supreme power of every god as presented in the 'numerous hymns of the Veda passages in which almost every important deity is represented as supreme and absolute' (ibid.: 137) and while the supremacy and absoluteness of a god is extant 'nothing is said to disparage the divine character of the other gods' (ibid.: 137). A lucid analysis of emergence of henotheism is stated as: 'Historically, henotheism assumes all gods are species equals and the elevation of one god is due to socio-political factors—not theological nuancing' (Heiser 2008: 28).
4. The term religiology is taken from the work of Kishimoto (1967: 81), Religiology. *Numen, 14* (Fasc. 2), 8186. The needs to be identified here is invariably the collective needs of the community. This is because religion is more suitably defined in terms of shared feelings and not individualistic in nature.
5. This ascription of monotheistic position to *Heraka* is controversial.

6. It is an 'attempt' and there is not really indisputable monotheism within Zeliangrong people.
7. He was interviewed on 30 December 2017. He was kind enough to offer his valuable time to the author before the beginning of the prayer service in Kalum Kai at Chingmeirong. He is well versed in culture, beliefs and practices of the Zeliangrong people. His wide spectrum of interactions across age groups and social and religious groups immensely facilitated the interview.
8. This is still reflected in the recent First Chabuan Phom Conference in October 2018. The fear of losing the culture which is imminent with the adoption of monotheism is still a reality among the TRC adherents. Polytheism is probably the best means to sustain the rich cultural heritage of the Rongmei people. Worship of *Tingkao Ragwang* and appeasement of other gods and goddesses provides a plethora of opportunities to remain connected to their ancestral multitude cultural legacies.
9. This is an erroneous conclusion of Gangmumei Kamei on the use of idols inside Kalum Kai. Use of idol in Kalum Kai is a manifestation of neither fetichism nor idolatry. Idolatry means worship of idols which is absent among the Zeliangrong belief systems. Its significance is nothing different from the statue of Jesus inside a Catholic Church.
10. R. Krishnakumar. (13 May 2016). 'An issue of belief'. *Frontline*. Retrieved from https://www.frontline.in/cover-story/an-issue-of-belief/article 8523502.ece.
11. Krishnadas Rajagopal. (28 September 2018). Supreme Court opens Sabarimala temple to women of all ages. *The Hindu*. Retrieved from https://www.thehindu.com/news/national/sc-opens-sabarimala-temple-forwomenof-all-ages/article25068333.ece.
12. The identity of the person who brought out the sweets as parts of Kadam is concealed. What he did was not an accepted change in any ritual that can be endorsed by any group. The progenies will question the credibility of his authority in *Pei* as what he did was a taboo.
13. This issue concerning the giving of the land of the village is sensitive as there are voices raised against such a move of the village *Pei* to allocate village land to religious groups in the name of religions for religious purposes. The Christians of this village also raised their voices against it but subdued. This is a standing evidence of assimilation of village institutions into the systems of TRC. The political edge enjoyed by TRC by virtue of it being a majority religious group is indisputable in some villages. TRC group is not universally a minority group. They

are minority groups in some villages in Manipur valley. Wherever they are proved to be numerically stronger they display their political edge too through their influence over the village traditional institutions and through their religious views on customary practices and laws. Despite the presence of both *Pupou Chap* and TRK followers in Manipur valley, the authority of TRC over customary laws is conventionally, and for some grudgingly, taken to be final. All these are, in fact, facilitated by the presence of many TRC elderly men in the village traditional institutions who, according to customary practice are hardly questioned for they are traditionally believed to be divine representatives. Many villagers do not challenge or question them for fear of *gakku-pangu*. *Gakku-Pangu* is a customary fine in the form of a fully grown pig. The pig would be killed and its meat would be distributed compulsorily to every family of a village. The head, limbs and internal parts of the pig will be consumed by the elders of the *Pei*. Unless *gakku-pangu* is given, the family or the person remains excommunicated from the village. In a very severe case, the person or the family may even be thrown out of the village with no right even to claim the family's land in the village. And experiences have invariably proven that the state is helpless and, therefore, futile to raise their voices against the *Pei*.

14. The author interviewed him at his residence in 2018.
15. He was interviewed on the same day when the former secretary of youth wing was interviewed.

CHAPTER 5

The Resilience of *Tingkao Ragwang Chapriak*

Power and resistance are conventionally conceived as dialectical realities. Sometimes, in the absence of resistance, the excruciating dominance of power is perceived to be the sole reality. However, power becomes meaningful only in the context of its relation to resistance. Michel Foucault illuminates the relation between power and resistance and states that 'there are no relations of power without resistances; the latter are all the more real and effective because they are formed right at the point where relations of power are exercised' (1980: 142). Much later, Michel Foucault further contends that resistance is very much an expression of power just as dominance is (1990: 95, cited in Aloysius 1998: 24). Resistance is not to be misconceived as an act of the overpowered or morally subjugated or demoralised people. Resistance is an integral part of the power equation. Resistance is not necessarily an act directed against the power of dominance or oppression. It may be passive in terms of action but withstand any possibility of moral defeat. Here, resistance is extended to mean resilience when there is no actual reciprocal attack against the power of oppression or dominance. Resilience may be understood as the 'ability of an ideology and its proponents to continue to remain unchanged despite any tangible or intangible force acting against the ideology and the proponents' (Samson 2015b: 96). Thus, what is crucial in resistance is an ideology. It is the resilience of an ideology and the ability of the proponents of the ideology to resist any forces to assimilate and annihilate the ideology or belief. This resilience of resistance to the power of dominance is in existence with the onset of power of assimilation and annihilation which are integrals of power of dominance.

This chapter analyses the factors that contribute towards the resilience of *Tingkao Ragwang Chapriak* as a belief system. The following factors of the resilience of TRC constitute the major findings of the research.

Worship in *Kalum Kai*

It is Kalum Kai and not *Rakai*. Gonmei Lanbilung Kabui calls it 'Tingkao Ragwang Kalum Kai' and qualifies it as 'the house of worship' (2018: 78). Kalum Kai means house of prayer and worship. *Rakai* means house of God. The use of the term Kalum Kai facilitates the TRC to differentiate itself from the Christians who call the church *Rakai*.

TRC believes in the omnipresence of *Tingkao Ragwang* and sees meaninglessness in a structural abode of *Tingkao Ragwang*. Therefore, the concept of *Rakai* does not have a prayer of usage in TRC. This understanding substantiates the relevance of the Bhuvan cave when used only in the context of Bisnu. The cave which has become a place of pilgrim is not related to *Tingkao Ragwang* for He requires no abode. Emphasising Kalum Kai's physical position Gangmumei Kamei calls it 'Kao kai (High House or storeyed house as it was constructed on stilts)' [sic] (2009: 30). As their relation with *Tingkao Ragwang* is defined by worship and prayer Kalum Kai or house of prayer finds more relevance in the TRC belief system. The significance of the concept of Kalum is reflected in their utterance of the word 'Kalum' at the end of every prayer similar to that of 'Amen' among Christians.

The importance of Kalum Kai needs to be understood from a historical point of view. The practice of the construction of Kalum Kai which was pioneered by Jadonang Malangmei among the Zeliangrong people (Kamson 2011a: 9) is still not widespread. Kalum Kai is not a primordial feature of the belief system of the Zeliangrong people. Many followers of *Pupou Chap* do not subscribe to this Kalum Kai being part of their belief system. The only religious structures in *Pupou Chap* are the two *Bambu* or the shelters of the two village deities at the two ends of a village.

Besides subduing the political movement of Jadonang the colonial force went to the extent of destroying the Kalum Kai he had constructed. A deep-seated fear of the British was endemic among the Zeliangrong people after the death of Jadonang who was a messiah and the future king of the Makam Gwangdi. Even though his works were continued by Gaidinliu Kamei many of his former followers did not dare even to utter Jadonang's name in public and the religious activities were abandoned for a very long time even after India's independence. It was only from the early 1990s that the Zeliangrong people resumed their religious reformations. *Heraka* could not spread effectively in Manipur due to restriction imposed on Gaidinliu whose entry to Manipur was banned by the authorities. *Tingkao Ragwang Kariak* emerged as a reformed religion only in few villages and later confined to one village.

It was Mr Lingamlung of Keisamthong in Imphal West, Manipur who privately began, towards the end of the twentieth century, the practice of worshipping under a roof. Lingamlung's[1] children studied in Shillong and his children saw many Christians going to church every Sunday. They soon began to like the idea of going to a house of worship where a large number of devotees gather to worship God. They often spoke about it to their father, Lingamlung. They complained about the absence of a place of worship for the Rongmei people. Also, Lingamlung came to hear about discrimination committed by Meetei women against tribal women in a Hindu temple at Imphal in Manipur.

According to Lingamlung, some Rongmei women went to Govindaji temple in Imphal wearing their tribal attires. The Meetei women expressed displeasure with the multicolour striped tribal attires inside the Hindu temple. It is said that the Meetei did not ban the entry of those who wear a sari. Such stigmatisation of weaker groups by the dominant group that compels the discriminated groups to adopt religion other than those of the dominant group is widely observed among several other tribal groups (Baruah 2018). The conversion of Dr B.R. Ambedkar and several Dalits to Buddhism due to caste discrimination is classic in India. This incident at the temple engendered an uneasy feeling among the tribal devotees who visited the Govindaji temple. Lingamlung began to look for a solution.

According to him, he began worshipping *Tingkao Ragwang* in an unconventional structure beside the small shop he had in his village at Keisamthong in Imphal. Some of the fellow villagers soon joined him and he had to shift the place of worship inside his house that provided larger space for the growing number of devotees. However, that larger space of his house could not accommodate the ever-growing number of devotees and, therefore, he shifted the place of worship beside a village *bambu*. Soon he and the other devotees were joined by others from outside his village. He was approached by intellectuals like Professor Gangmumei Kamei, and other leaders of Zeliangrong. They initiated discussions and meetings delving into the need for a place of worship and soon resulted in Zeliangrong Religious Council in 1994. The discussions and meetings were further expedited and actualised in the form of the construction of Kalum Kai at Chingmeirong in Imphal East. The land for the construction of Kalum Kai was procured at a very cheap price as the owner wished to sell the land due to frequent flooding during the rainy season. Thus, the land offered itself as the germinating ground for several other Kalum Kais across Manipur. This was the contemporary trend in the construction of Kalum Kais of TRC.

Kalum Kai or house of prayer is crucial in the belief system of TRC. And it was during the struggle for Makam Gwangdi under Jadonang Malangmei that we witness for the first time the practice of construction of Kalum Kai. At present many villages are yet to have Kalum Kai. Fearing conversions of TRC followers to other religions Chaoba Kamson unequivocally stated, '. . . we should construct a place of worship in every village so that our people may not convert to other religion rather our people will concentrate to our religion' [sic] (2011a: 9). Despite the seemingly insurmountable force of conversion by Christians, the TRC community is seen to be resilient in maintaining its claimed primordial religious identity. And this is immensely facilitated by the process of the devotional congregation at Kalum Kais which is routinised every Sunday.

The construction of Kalum Kai has been a major religious endeavour immensely contributing towards the religiousness and credibility of TRC and thus the resilience of the beliefs and continuity of its practices. The structure of Kalum Kai bestows upon the devotees mental and spiritual gratifications with a strong sense of pride and credibility to TRC. The religious structures also serve as common platforms for philosophical and moral expositions with an aura of divinity and spirituality. TRC devotees now feel no lesser than the dominant Meitei Hindus and Tribal Christians.

Their religion is no longer worship of forest spirits or animism where rituals are performed only in open space. This is proven and shown by an organised and systematised way of worshipping inside a structure within a *structured liturgy*. The structure of Kalum Kai also infuses a sense of modernity in a belief system that otherwise was callously regarded as a primitive form of belief system and even animism. With the contemporary Kalum Kais in villages, religious entities are institutionalised and given wider social sanction to practice religious rituals across villages. This is also enhanced by the codification of the religious practices among the followers of TRC. With the dying of the condemned dormitory system in Khangchu where youths were imparted moral, ethical, spiritual knowledge and even livelihood skills, the re-emergence of Kalum Kais provides a suitable alternative platform for imparting not only religious doctrines but also moral and ethical tenets. It now remains as the edifice of institutions nurturing norms and values of Zeliangrong people.

The theory of social identity facilitates in understanding this phenomenon of a shift from village centric religious practices to inter-village religious activities with the emergence of Kalum Kai at Chingmeirong similar to that of a Parish Church that covers more than one village. The shared ancestral identity allows the TRC devotees to cross the barriers of village boundaries. The devotees overcame the difficulty of identifying with the larger Zeliangrong people outside their villages and embraced their religious identity as worshippers of *Tingkao Ragwang*. The Kalum Kai at Chingmeirong built after the formation of Zeliangrong Religious Council serves as a centre of the devotees of the three states of Assam, Manipur and Nagaland. Kalum Kai thus helps in infusing a sense of devotion with its spiritual ambience and also serves moral and ethical purposes. Kalum Kais facilitate the collective identification with the common religious identity as followers of TRC with codified religious beliefs and practices. The presence of Kalum Kais also enables the followers of TRC to differentiate themselves from the *Pupou Chap* who do not adhere to the reformed ways of religious life. Kalum Kais bind the village youths who could have been easily tempted by the glitters of Sunday affairs of the Christians. It gives the youth of TRC a tangible structure to religiously identify with and attach an individual's self to it.

Recognition of TRC

Recognition at state, regional, national and global fora of indigenous people and indigenous religious platforms infuses a sense of pride among the believers. It gives them an aesthetic experience of pride in their beliefs and practices. This feeling of importance acts as a strong consolidating factor. The strength and credibility of TRC as a belief system is enhanced with these recognitions. The experiences of a stigma attached to their belief system and humiliation are gradually withering away. The Christians' usual way of terming their belief system as Satan worship and animism immensely battered their pride. However, this diffidence or shyness concerning their belief system is fading away with growing global recognition of TRC as an indigenous religion. This indigeneity is the driving force of their growing pride.

Impressively, only 1.7 per cent of the respondents the author surveyed experience shyness while practising their faith (Table 5.1). The relation between perception of the strength of TRC and the feeling of shyness to practice one's faith is tested using chi-square.

Null Hypothesis (*Ho*): Shyness to practise one's faith in public is independent of the perception of the strength of TRC.

Alternative Hypothesis (*Ha*): Shyness to practise one's faith in public is dependent on the perception of the strength of TRC.

Looking at the value of significance in the Table 5.2 which is more than 0.005 the null hypothesis is accepted. Thus, shyness to practise one's faith in public is independent of the perception of the strength of the religion one follows. Shyness among few adherents is not a common feature anymore. The TRC adherents have realised

Table 5.1: Crosstabulation of Shyness to practice one's faith and TRC being strong

Shyness to practice and is TRC strong? Crosstabulation				
Shyness to Practise	Is TRC strong? Yes	No	Can't Say	Total
Yes	1.1%	4.2%	2.0%	1.7%
No	98.9%	95.8%	98%	98.3%
Total	100%	100%	100%	100%

Source: Author's survey.

Table 5.2: Chi-Square Tests (shyness to practise one's faith and TRC being strong)

Chi-Square Tests	*Value*	*df*	*Asymp. Sig. (2-sided)*
Pearson Chi-Square	1.306[a]	2	.521
Likelihood Ratio	1.077	2	.584
N of Valid Cases	299		

a. 3 cells (50.0%) have an expected count less than 5. The minimum expected count is .40.

Source: Author's survey.

the importance and credibility of their belief system. Realising the recognitions TRC enjoys the adherents shun shyness or any hesitation from practising their faith.

The recognitions bestow upon TRC credibility and respects from other religious groups. The adherents do not feel reluctant to speak about their belief systems and practises. They claim to speak about their religion with pride and conviction in their faith. Through their mass worship and various activities widely seen and acknowledged by other faiths, they speak about their religion on various platforms on various occasions. Based on the survey data a chi-square test of the relation between the variables, strength perception and talking about TRC is given in Tables 5.3 and 5.4.

Null Hypothesis (Ho): Talking about TRC with others is independent of strength perception.
Alternative Hypothesis (Ha): Talking about TRC with others is dependent on strength perception.

Table 5.3: Crosstabulation of Talking about TRC to others and is TRC strong?

	Talk about TRC to others and is TRC strong? Crosstabulation			
	Is TRC strong?			*Total*
Talk about TRC to others	*Yes*	*No*	*Can't Say*	
Yes	170	18	82	270
No	7	6	16	29
Total	177	24	98	299

Source: Author's survey.

Table 5.4: Chi-Square Tests (Talk about TRC to others and is TRC strong?)

	Chi-Square Tests		
	Value	*df*	*Asymp. Sig. (2-sided)*
Pearson Chi-Square	17.999[a]	2	.000
Likelihood Ratio	17.251	2	.000
N of Valid Cases	299		

a. 1 cells (16.7 per cent) have expected count less than 5. The minimum expected count is 2.33.

Source: Author's survey.

The significance value in the Table 5.4 is seen to be lesser than 0.005 and, therefore, the null hypothesis that states that talking about TRC religion are independent of strength perception is rejected. Thus, there is a relation between the practice of talking about TRC with others and their perception of the strength of their religion. With a growing sense of the strength of their religion, there is growing evidence of talking about TRC. Elders are often found talking about TRC informally at various gatherings of social, political or religious significance. The newfound strength perception in their religion provides the much needed fodder to proclaim their faith in public.

These recognitions also lend credibility to their beliefs, practices and leaders. The presence of a personality like Professor Gangmumei Kamei as one of the prominent believers of TRC facilitated the spread of TRC until the middle of the second decade of the twenty first century. The Professor enjoyed credence in the field of academic and public sphere at the state, regional and national levels. He played a crucial role in consolidating the belief systems and practices of TRC. His proximity with the freedom fighter Gaidinliu Kamei brought him closer to the national platforms. Being a historian and a close associate of Professor B.K. Roy Burman, the renowned anthropologist, the personality of Professor Gangmumei Kamei certainly blessed TRC towards its wider recognition.

According to the President of TRC Chabuan Phom (youth group),[2] with the recognition of TRC on a global platform, they do not feel the need to shift to any other religion. The global recognition infuses a sense of pride and strength into the members of TRC. The global recognition of Zeliangrong belief system came with the speech of Professor Gangmumei Kamei in the Twelfth Plenary Session of the United Nations Working Group on the Indigenous Population at Geneva during June in 1994 held as a part of the Year of the Indigenous Population (1992-3). Probably, enthused by this global recognition, TRC was formed in 1994. This fact is widely shared and cherished by TRC followers, especially the youths. TRC is now registered as a member of the United Religious Initiative which is based in San Francisco (Kamei 2006: 58). TRC is the belief system of the Zeliangrong people that has transcended the traditionally ritualised village boundary to be known and accepted by the highest international body as a religion of the indigenous people.

According to Amartya Sen, every individual or group has plural identities (2006: 29). And we are, Sen contends, constantly making choices between different identities to ascribe priority (ibid.: 30). Among the TRC adherents, religious identity is becoming a matter of judicious choice. Religious identity may be viewed as the fulcrum of all the other components of identity. The Rongmei people in Manipur valley have no political representatives from among them in the state assembly and the Indian parliament as well. Their voices are hardly reflected by the politicians. Their identity is hardly visible on public forums outside their villages. Crucial positions in the systems of the state are held by the Meeteis. With no conventional political power of assembly and parliament, the identity of TRC adherents of Manipur valley thrives primarily on their religious identity. It is by dint of their religious identity that they stand out. Religious identity certainly provides TRC adherents with a respectable niche both in social and cultural landscapes.

Organised Roles

Thuanbina Gangmei says, 'The Rongmeis indigenous religion which is practised since time immemorial has neither a founder nor a name like the other tribal societies of the world. It had no common religious authority or a common religious organisation' (2014: 2). The traditional village institutions were informal and not bureaucratised. The reformed TRC has a structure. Under its TRC Phom or TRC Organisation, it is moderately bureaucratic with designations such as president and secretary. It also has a youth wing. The religions of Zeliangrong people have been regulated by a religious authority named Zeliangrong Religious Council with its two organs: the Executive Council and the Ecclesiastical Council.

Among several activities of the youths of TRC, one that plays a crucial role in fomenting spiritual solidarity among the believers across age groups is the awareness programmes frequently conducted by the Chabuan Phom or Youth Organisation. Frequent visits to different villages and constant meaningful interactions nurture and sustain the spiritual lives of the believers. Youth being energetic and outgoing, drastically shed the inhibiting propensity of some believers and help believers to be more sociable. This makes the otherwise relatively isolated villages spiritually more communal. Such enthusiasm of the youth nurtured and propelled by a deep understanding of their beliefs and practices, continues to stand to propagate among the posterities. Such visits facilitate the relatively isolated villagers into the process of social identification and social categorisation within the context of TRC beliefs and doctrines.

The enthusiasm of the youth in religious realms remains manifested in various forums and different ways. The vibrancy of cultural activities in terms of songs and dances that add aesthetic beauty to their religious activities and propel their individual and collective spirit towards their belief is immensely contributed by the youth. Youth are also the carriers of religious significances such as symbols, artefacts, meanings, latent and manifest behaviour. A youth[3] from Ragailong village of Imphal East, Manipur was found having a tattooed religious symbol of TRC, Boudan, on the back of his neck. According to him, he wears the tattoo with a sense of pride.

The role of educated youths in enhancing the resilience of TRC is well acknowledged by its members. Education has been emphasised by the elders and youths. Education here refers to formal education. The traditional education that used to groom the youths in Khangchu and Luchu, for boys and girls respectively, seems to have withered away significantly. Felicitating the youths who passed in annual exams conducted by the Board of Secondary Education of Manipur and Council of Higher Secondary Education of Manipur and other successful candidates in various other examinations besides the fresh doctorates are regular activities of the youths. Such activities engender a sense of pride and confidence among believers. Such individual achievements are identified as their collective achievements. Such identification with the individual achievements in the academic field infuses a sense of pride in the self of other individuals. The changing lifestyles of the youths seen in the shift from drunkard state to intellectually stimulating facets are keenly observed by the younger generations. This allows the younger generation to emulate the intellectually cultured or cultivated lifestyles. These changes are witnessed primarily alongside the reformations of TRC marked by the incorporation of vibrant religious and secular activities assigned to the youths.

The achievements of youth in the field of education is also impressive. The basic level of education that can fetch a job now is commonly High School Leaving Certificate Examination. Based on the author's survey data, male respondents fair relatively better than female respondents. Among the surveyed respondents 45.2 per cent is female and 54.8 per cent is male. While only 5.50 per cent of the male respondents claim to have received no education, it is 10.40 per cent from among the female respondents. This highly skewed data on 'no education' is a matter of grave concern. Despite the significant changes in the roles of the female group in religious affairs they are yet to advance further along the path of gender equity in various aspects of their collective life.

The intellectuals among the TRC members play a crucial role through their writings and talks in dissipating the religious philosophies and practices and in clearing the misconceptions held against Zeliangrong belief systems. The occasional writings of Dr Budha Kamei on Zeliangrong belief systems, customary laws and traditional institutions in local newspapers in Manipur are highly valuable. Despite the high percentage of the female respondents who received education—89.6 per cent of the female respondents are at least matriculate—one still does not see any female among TRC believers writing on TRC or Zeliangrong culture in local papers. Therefore, the roles of females of the TRC group in other realms of life besides that of religion need to be examined in terms of diagnosis, prognosis and intervention. With no possibility even in the distant future to climb the higher echelons of religious hierarchical institutions. TRC needs serious introspection on the conditions of women.

A former Secretary of the Chabuan Phom of *Tingkao Ragwang Chapriak* (Assam, Nagaland and Manipur) contends that many youths are aware of TRC because of the vibrant activities of the youth. The youth are witnessed playing a crucial role in education and contributing immensely in spreading awareness about TRC among the villagers. They are also actively engaged in physical labour required in villages. The youth conducted door to door visits using postcards printed with information about TRC religion. The former secretary claimed that rituals were not taught in this awareness drive as rituals are earmarked for elderly married persons. The objective of the awareness programme is to create a sense of awareness about the present state of affairs of TRC. Conversion as an objective is ruled out in these awareness activities of the youth.

Equal enthusiasm is deeply rooted among the women's group traditionally known as Mathenmei Phom. Perception of gender equality is impressively high both among male and female respondents. The self-evident roles of women and girls in various religious activities tally with the survey data presented below in Table 5.5.

Table 5.5: Gender equality in TRC

	Is there gender equality in TRC			*Total*
	Yes	*No*	*Don't Know*	
Male	90.2%	3.7%	6.1%	100.0%
Female	86.7%	3.7%	9.6%	100.0%

Source: Author's survey.

Women participate actively in religious activities. They also represent the culture of the Rongmei people with their specific attire worn at a funeral, festivals and other social functions organised by secular organisations. They sing hymns as part of the ritual at a funeral. Youth and male elders are hardly seen singing hymns on such occasions. Women take a lead role in a marriage ceremony by singing wedding songs. Even in Kalum Kai, it is the women's group that is actively seen singing hymns standing before the rest of the devotees. Thus, unlike the traditional ways of life in which the role of women in religious affairs is almost negligible, the women of TRC is seen to be ecclesiastically indispensable.

Table 5.6: Frequency of visit at Kalum Kai

	Frequency of Visit at Kalum Kai				*Total*
	Never	*Monthly*	*Weekly*	*Daily*	
Male	0.6%	54.9%	41.5%	3.0%	100.0%
Female	3.7%	51.9%	39.3%	5.2%	100.0%
Total	2.0%	53.5%	40.5%	4.0%	100.0%

Source: Author's survey.

The Table 5.6 given above clearly shows the number of male adherents of TRC visiting Kalum Kai is relatively more than female respondents. Such a relatively higher frequency of male attendance at Kalum Kai may be explained partly by the traditional roles of females of a family who are commonly engaged with household chores which consequently prevent them from regularly visiting Kalum Kai. While only 39.3 per cent of the female respondents can attend Kalum Kai weekly, it is 41.5 per cent among male respondents. And while only 0.6 per cent of the male respondents claimed to have never visited Kalum Kai, it is 3.7 per cent among female respondents. Thus, in terms of praying daily and visiting Kalum Kai female devotees are relatively left far behind probably due to retention of certain gender based traditional roles at homes. The hope of emancipation from this is not nearby as the belief systems and the practices are still tied to the ancestral traditional conception of their belief systems. Such gender based division of roles is also partly tied to their beliefs.

Receptive to Changes

TRC is receptive to changes in the social, political and religious environments. The group makes itself relevant amidst various changes witnessed while adhering to the essence of their culture, morals, belief systems and practices. According to Harold Turner, many of the primal religions or religions that existed before the universal religions in the developing world, have collapsed under the proselytising influence of Christian missionaries but some continue to persist with their ability to adapt to various changes (1994, cited in Kamei 2006, 13-14). TRC, given the various changes, with 'modern ways of worship', as pointed out by an interviewee,[4] is conveniently viewed as a reformed religion. The octogenarian interviewee asserted that 'Pupou Chap is very near but TRC is primordial'. Change is the essence of TRC.

The idea of *Pupou* is conventionally used to refer to an extremely distanced era. It is often used to refer to the time that marked 'the beginning', the beginning of everything specifically the time of creation or close to it. Therefore, the idea of *Pupou* is not traced to one's near ancestors but the beginning of the moment of creation and thus primordial. Therefore, it is fallacious to claim that 'Pupou Chap is very near'. The other concept that expresses primordiality is *mei lungthao khourui* meaning when human beings came into existence. This traditional conception of primordiality or *Pupou* or *mei lungthao khourui* prevalent among the Rongmei people are the meanings of primordiality of TRC. Interestingly, one of its followers claimed that TRC is not a religion known to be primordial.[5] Such understanding is probably rooted in the contemporary reformations and several new features in TRC. Such observations are dismissed by staunch followers of TRC who claim reformations to be common features of all the belief systems in the world.

Changes have been witnessed since the early days of the twentieth century under the leadership and spiritual guidance of Jadonang Malangmei who necessitated religious and social reformations as a precursor to a political movement against the British, the Meiteis and the Kukis. Sometimes it might appear inappropriate to claim sweepingly that Jadonang was the proponent of TRC or TRK or *Heraka* as asserted by the adherents of these belief systems. He did not christen any of these belief systems. He was a part of *Pupou Chap* or ancestral belief system and he brought about several changes within *Pupou Chap.* As seen earlier, according to Gangmumei Kamei, Jadonang introduced the worship of the Supreme God without banning completely the worship of gods and goddesses. He reformed the *Pupou Chap* by banning the worship and appeasing of some gods and goddesses with their corresponding sacrifices and gennas. He introduced the system of worship in Kalum Kai or house of prayer and the use of idol inside Kalum Kai (see Kamei 2006: 107-8). Bathing before entering Kalum Kai introduces the notion of impurity and purity which never existed before (ibid.: 108). The idea and practice of pilgrimage among Zeliangrong introduced by Jadonang with his frequent visits to Bhuvan cave is a new phenomenon of the twentieth century. Many animal sacrifices were also accepted by Jadonang and he says, 'I sacrificed a mithun there which was provided by Kambiron' (ibid.: 110). Thus, even during the height of the days of reformations Jadonang endorsed some animal sacrifices which are now almost completely banned in TRK, TRC and *Heraka*. Two significant changes adopted by Jadonang within the Zeliangrong belief system are clear from the words of Gangmumei Kamei. Kamei says,

His [Jadonang's] construction of two temples; the earlier temple with a Church like a pulpit and articles in the central hall of the temple where he used to pray and preach, in the second temple he introduced a shrine with the temple, where he kept the clay idols of God Bisnu and his wife and a mithun- which were the influence of Hinduism as he saw them in Cachar plains of Assam (ibid.: 97).

Zeliangrong people can adapt to such major changes that they may continue with their belief systems with contemporary relevance without losing the essence of their indigenous religion. But it is also because of such changes in practices that resemble the practices of other religions that Zeliangrong belief systems suffer from scathing attacks.

Specific to the changes in Manipur valley one needs to analyse the historical trajectory of their settlement. The social intercourse between the Rongmei and the Meetei in Manipur valley presents an interesting ground for understanding the notion of change in the context of the religious life of the Rongmei people in the valley. The Rongmei people in the valley are known to have enjoyed immense royal patronage. Despite the realities of discrimination and subjugation experienced by the Rongmei people, it must also be sincerely acknowledged that the royal patronage and the patronage of other forces were unwavering.

According to Pouchalung,[6] Rongmei people in Manipur valley were well protected by the Meetei kings locally called *Tai-Gang* (in Rongmei language) or king of Tai. The Rongmei people in the valley were given land and ensured the security of their life and right over their gifted land. None of the tribal villages was evicted during the rule of the subsequent Meetei kings. However, there are grievances concerning the settlement of the Rongmei already simmering in Manipur valley. A deep sense of paralysed remorse is imminent in the article titled 'The Silent Demographic Influx of Imphal Valley' wherein the author, referring to the Rongmei in Manipur valley, unambiguously expressed a desire for the Rongmei people in the valley to be 'deported',

The influx by non-indigenous can be detected and deported, however, the influx by indigenous tribals [read especially Kabui] is permanent and cannot be deported. Considering the limited space available for Meitei/Meetei, this may perhaps be one of the driving forces to launch the movement of JCILPS.[7] However, the influx by tribals is not mentioned in any of the demands made so far (Kameshore: 2016).

Such fear expressed by the Meetei on the settlement of the Rongmei people in Manipur valley is new. However, such words are not yet taken very seriously by any intellectuals or public leaders from within the Meetei group. The fear of the majority is the womb of communalism.

Pouchalung contends that the Rongmei and even other tribal groups were advised by the kings to worship the Hindu deities and the Meetei deities as well. Thus, the Rongmei people in the valley were earlier known to have actively participated in Durga Puja, Kang, Diwali and even worshipped Sanamahi of the Meetei belief system. The tribals were very fond of Mahadev (Shiva). Pouchalung observed that the Rongmei people in the valley continue to enjoy patronage despite the political upheavals in the post-monarchist era. This is possible because of the intervention of the non-state armed groups who do not desire the tribals or the Rongmei people in the valley to be harmed. President of Kabui Mother Association (KAMA), Kakomlunglu, narrated several instances of Meetei non-state armed groups seeking her advice on matters about the relationship between Meetei and tribal people. According to her, the armed groups also intervened in some inter-village feuds caused by an occasional ban by Meetei women on the selling of wine in Rongmei villages.

Note that Ragailong, the largest Zeliangrong village in Manipur valley, established in 1891 and situated to the west of Khuman Lampak stadium has a temple of the Meeteis' deity Nongda Lairen Pakhangba. The temple is known in the Rongmei dialect as Pakhangpu Rakai. Pakhangpu or Pakhangba is one of 'the two most important gods of the Meitei pantheon' (Kamei 2015: 88). The Rongmei people in the valley actively or passively partook in the culture and belief systems of the neighbouring communities. They adapted to their social and cultural environment until they were re-organised into well-formulated religious beliefs, practices and structures. Such adaptability of the Rongmei never posed a threat to the neighbouring communities and their culture and identity enjoy a certain degree of admiration and respectability amongst friends and foes.

Religious Literature

Religious literature, especially in the form of prayer books and hymn books have been some new features within the Zeliangrong belief systems. Nothing was written or engraved on anything. Oral traditions and oral histories are foundations of the historicity of the Zeliangrong people. Even the script invented by Jadonang Malangmei in the early part of the twentieth century remains unintelligible and not even seen by many. However, TRC reformed itself to its advantage by using the Roman script to reduce their mythologies, cosmology, prayers, rituals, songs, gennas, taboos and doctrines in Rongmei and English languages. This is a sea change in the context of the religious life of the Zeliangrong people.

The popularity of religious literature, refer Table 5.7, is seen in 95.7 per cent of the respondents acknowledging the importance of the materials. The aesthetic role played by religious literature is immense with 83.9 per cent of the respondents according to religious literature as a factor of spiritual growth that engenders uniformity and elegance in prayer and worship as a group. Sometimes religious aura engendered within oneself is induced only in a group during a religious activity. Such religious feeling sometimes does not occur in isolation. The religious ambience evolving out of collective religious activities produces a spiritual gyration that pulls the mind and body of the individuals. Such an ambience enables the devotees to get mellowed in the spirituality of religious activities.

Table 5.7: Importance of Religious Literature

	Per Cent
Unite Believers	11.7
Promote Spiritual Growth	83.9
Don't Know	4.3
Total	100.0

Source: Author's survey.

Use of prayer books and hymn books enable youth, children and even women to engage in religious activities either in a group or as individuals any time and anywhere without the usual tradition of inviting a priest for religious activities. The religious texts, not holy scripture, also help them to pray more meaningfully and satisfactorily with a spiritual aura generated by the terms more closely associated with spiritual power. Note that according to the *Bible*, even the Apostles of Jesus were taught how to pray by Jesus himself. Therefore, praying with external preset words does not necessarily undermine a spiritual aura generated from within and from the surrounding. According to the General-Secretary[8] of the Phom, TRC is already in the process of completing its religious text.

Personal Spiritual Experience

Personal spiritual experiences affirm and reaffirm the religious meaning of one's life. The adherent enjoys a meaningful sense of religious life in being a worshipper of *Tingkao Ragwang*. This is sometimes shared verbally and the spiritual experience is transposed to another believer who may be affected spiritually. This promotes beliefs and shared meaning of their religious life. Such sharing is seen among the believers of TRC.

TRC members share their joy of experiencing *Tingkao Ragwang's* blessing. 97.7 per cent of the surveyed respondents proclaim the blessings of *Tingkao Ragwang* they enjoy. They believe that they are now able to earn better and live a better and more dignified life because of the blessings from *Tingkao Ragwang*. Their businesses prosper and their children are successful in examinations and job interviews after they became more devout in TRC belief systems and practices.

Such conviction consolidates their faith in *Tingkao Ragwang* and gives meaning to their life as adherents of TRC. They do not feel the need to look out for other 'Gods'. God answers their prayers and wishes. This is in contrast to the early period of proselytisation among the Zeliangrong people when Zeliangrong people felt that their ancestral God had failed to answer their prayers and solve their problems and thus turned towards the Christian God who sent the whites who were their rulers and who promised salvation and relief from temporal difficulties.

Zeliangrong Christians' Cultural Activities

The use of certain material and non-material cultures by Zeliangrong Christians is astounding against the backdrop of the sustained blitheness at every chance of scathing attack against ancestral belief system and practices. Therefore, the involvement of Zeliangrong Christians in cultural activities, despite severe criticism against traditionalists, allows for a wide acceptance of certain features of TRC even among the Christians who are otherwise traditionally known to be antagonistic towards every ancestral belief systems. The involvement of Christians in Zeliangrong festivals through the use of attires, songs and dances certainly help in animating further and sustaining the cultural aspects of the believers of TRC.

If one examines the students' bodies of tribal communities outside Manipur, one finds that the leaders and active activists are mostly Christians. The roles of student communities from traditional belief systems are rare perhaps due to their relatively lesser number. Despite this fact, traditional attires, dances and songs are still widely used by these student bodies in many of their annual programmes. Such participation in activities that requires the use of material cultures have already invited the fury of rigid elderly Christians. They fear that even the use of cultural materials signifies the triumph of evil over good. They view it as a loss of Christian faith. However, N.K. Bose, in the context of inter-religious participation in different festivals, maintained that 'Such participation was largely in common festivities, i.e. on social plane, and did not mean that one community had adopted the faith of another' (1971: 64). Such a position is also reflected by the Zeliangrong Christians in their participation in Zeliangrong cultural activities.

Thus, consuming *prasad* or ritually sanctified edible item, which many Christians strongly condemn, is neither an act of conversion to Hinduism nor an acceptance of the faith of Hinduism. Singing Christmas carol does not make Hindus Christians. Singing the national anthem of India does not make a Chinese or Pakistani

Indians. Mere participation in certain religious activities of a particular faith does not make any person of different faith a member of that particular faith.

A contradictory phenomenon of Christians involving actively in tribal cultural activities may be analysed within the context of the concept 'culturizing religion' (Joppke 2018). Often, the traditionalists express discomfort with the inappropriate use of material culture by the Christians. The traditionalists do not see the possibility of separation of religion and culture. Thus, Chaoba Kamson writes on the cover of his book (*Tingkao Ragwang Chapriak: Ra Pari*-Tingkao Ragwang Chapriak: Story of God) 'Loss of Religion is loss of culture. Culture and religion should go together. If culture and religion separate, it is just like a body without soul' [sic] (2009). Chaoba Kamson, the General Secretary of TRC Phom, is not very rigid in his conception of the relation between culture and religion. He does not espouse outright rejection or condemnation of a partial mingling of Zeliangrong culture and Christian elements. He and Dr Budha Kamei were among the important dignitaries at a function on 2 April 2018, when the youth of Taihu Baptist church performed choreography on a gospel song wearing traditional Rongmei attire on the occasion of Zeliangrong solidarity day commemoration. They were not known to have been agitated against such performance in which traditional attires were used and cultural dance steps being mellowed in a Christian gospel song with the word 'Halleluia'.

Narratives of the cosmology of the Zeliangrong people strongly points towards the religious basis of culture because the origin of creation is God. And T.S. Eliot agreed to such a conception in the words, 'No culture has appeared or developed except together with a religion' (1945: 15, cited in Joppke 2018: 2). T.S. Eliot was indecisive about according positions of predecessor and successor between religion and culture, and accepts the difficulty of ascertaining the cause and effect relation between the two (Eliot 1945: 15, cited in Joppke 2018: 2). If culture and religion invariably developed simultaneously can they be separated? Will the essence of culture be retained without religion? This is a question to which one probably cannot find a universally convincing answer. Thus, it becomes essential to contextualise a discourse on the relationship between culture and religion.

Joppke observed that when the state found difficulty in its attempt to separate religion and culture it has always tried to culturalise religion of a dominant group by privileging the status of majority religion while espousing neutrality towards religion. The state may not necessarily declare any religion to be the state religion. Doing so would lead to theocracy. And Joppke also observed that sometimes privileging of majority religion results in disadvantaging the minority religious groups. This is so because while the majority religion is culturalised the minority religious groups' belief and practices are viewed as politically unviable. Thus, while in 2011 the Italian state was permitted by the European Court of Human Rights (ECtHR) to put up crucifixes on public school walls, (*Lautsi and Others v. Italy*, the decision of 18 March 2011, cited in Joppke, 2018: 6) the same Court in 2001 had restricted the use of Islamic veils which was labelled as a 'powerful external symbols' that possess 'proselytising effect' (ECtHR *Dahlab v. Switzerland*, the decision of 15 February 2001, Joppke 2018: 7-8). To what extent is a culture, not religion? To what extent is culture secular? According to Joppke, T.S. Eliot's above contention suggests, to some extent, the sameness of culture and religion but Joppke clearly states that 'religion is propositional, while culture is dispositional' (2018: 2). Thus, the propositional and dispositional statuses of religion and culture respectively make religion more rigid as it concerns the judgement of one religion to be superior or the only truth. The dispositional nature of culture renders it more varied a subject to individuals or groups.

To some traditionalists both religion and culture have dispositional nature for they originated from the same source rooted in their belief in the creation narrative. Even to attempt to see them as separate is similar to squaring the circle. Though T.S. Eliot, even in his shrewdest intellect, could not ascertain the relation of causality between religion and culture the Zeliangrong people have not failed to continue to see culture through the prism of religion. However, among the Zeliangrong Christians, the element of ancestry persists and they continue to share a common belief in a common ancestor and the same origin. This shared belief in common ancestor allows for room for a shared culture which for Zeliangrong Christians are partially secular but completely religious for Zeliangrong traditionalists. But the patterns of use of cultures are different among the two groups. While Zeliangrong Christians emphasise the secularisation of culture the Zeliangrong traditionalists stress the religious essence of culture. As religion is dispositional, Zeliangrong Christians and Zeliangrong traditionalists are religiously set apart, sometimes even antagonistic, but culturally a certain degree of acquiescence is shared especially among the younger generations. This proffers an environment for the sustenance of Zeliangrong culture with cautiously chosen corresponding beliefs even among the Zeliangrong Christians. While the Zeliangrong Christians do not subscribe theologically to the beliefs associated with Zeliangrong culture, at least they acknowledge them to understand better the cultural practices to which they share a stronger sense of belonging.

The participation of Zeliangrong Christians in cultural activities is not seen to be extended to the realm of rituals and prayers. However, Chaoba Kamson claimed that 'All the festivals are related to the worship of Tingkao Ragwang, the Supreme God' (2011a: 17). Chaoba Kamson elsewhere illuminated on the origin of festivals rooted in the instruction of *Tingkao Ragwang* given to Tingpurengsonnang who was instructed to house the Khangchu (male dormitory) and teach the youth, songs, prayers, morality, ethics, food habits, drinks and avoid fighting among themselves (2014: 98). Kamson further contends that the instruction to nurture the youth with knowledge of dances, prayers and songs points to the element of festival in Zeliangrong culture. According to mythology, Tingpurengsonnang was made to be the first owner of Khangchu, a common Khangchu for gods and human beings, during *Rari Gan* or in the era when human beings and god, goddesses and spirits lived together.

Kamson here points implicitly to the meaninglessness of festivals without rites and rituals. But many Christians would like to view this aspect of culture as non-religious. Christians are beginning to be seen to be actively engaged in state endorsed festivals of the tribal people. The Christians thus occupy a crucial role in the interface between the state and ethnic cultures. According to the surveyed data, 95.7 per cent of the respondents subscribe to the view that loss of religion is a loss of culture and loss of culture is a loss of identity. Therefore, sometimes it is futile to initiate a discourse on culture sans religion or religion sans culture.

Attacks by Christians

Christians play contradictory roles towards the non-Christian neighbours—especially the tribal religious groups. While they attack the beliefs and practices of the tribal religions scathingly, they cherish the tribal cultural treasures with clear delineation and alienation of the ritualistic aspects.

The colonisers and the Christian missionaries were sometimes opposed to each other in terms of their objectives. While the colonisers endeavoured to allow the continuity of beliefs and practices of the tribal people so long as their colonial interests were served, the Christian missionaries were uncompromising in shattering the ancestral belief systems and traditional institutions of the tribal people to facilitate penetration and retention of Christian faith among the tribal people. Nirmal Kumar Bose says, 'It is only after Independence that Christianity has been swinging round to a point of view when allegiance to one's native culture is being encouraged' (1971: 63). This may probably be explained partly by the support extended by the Hindu organisations towards the tribal belief systems. The entry of Hindu organisations into the cultural domain of natives engendered a sense of exigency amidst the Christians with a need for a change in their strategy of proselytisation. The Christian missionaries began exhibiting empathy towards tribal cultural heritages. Had it not been for the Hindu organisations' partial support, the remnants of many tribal belief systems would have been reduced only on pages.

It is needless to reaffirm the state of antagonism between Christians and traditionalists even to these days. The village authorities of a Rongmei village at Chingmeirong at Imphal in Manipur once banned their children from studying in Don Bosco School (a Catholic school) located close to their village. Such a ban was imposed fearing the conversion of their children to Christianity. However, such a restriction was no longer seen in the late 1990s when some children from Chingmeirong village were even classmates of the author and some were together with the author in the Catholic school boarding where attending Eucharistic Mass, saying the Rosary prayer, attending Retreat programme besides the daily prayer programmes were compulsory for boarders. This village now has a Baptist Church and the village also hosts the Kalum Kai which is the centre of the TRC of Assam, Manipur and Nagaland. This stands as proof of the reformations within TRC, not just religiously but also psychologically and socially to be able to live together with all the religious groups.

Attacks by Christians may be claimed to have reverberating positive effects on Rongmei traditionalists in Manipur valley. The sense of complacence with which the early traditionalists lived was jolted by the incoming foreign beliefs. The tenuousness of their society and its institutions and structures was hardly realised until their belief systems were attacked by foreign belief systems. During the colonial days, the strong patronage of the Hindu Meetei kings immensely deterred the Christian missionaries from rapaciously intruding into the tribal villages in the valley to consume the 'lost sheep' or 'condemned souls' wandering in tribal villages. After independence with increasing migration of the Christian tribals into the valley, induced by skewed and valley centric welfare and development activities of the state, the proportion and influence of tribal Christians grew in valley tribal villages. Many tribal Christian missionaries found the valley tribals as the lambs of the Christ to be fed with Christian gospel and to be salvaged from the wilderness. Such perception of the tribal Christians engendered among the traditionalists a sense of utter disrespect to one's identity and meaning of existence and living. TRC may also be seen as a consequence of a collective effort to salvage ancestral belief systems and identity from the mindless onslaught against the belief systems and cultures of the tribal people.[9]

Unlike Christians, the TRC community is not known to be engaged in proselytising activities. Christian passion for conversion

Table 5.8: Source of a Threat to TRC

	Frequency	*Per cent*
Conversion	106	35.45
Condemnation of TRC	1	0.33
Changes among Younger Generations	3	1
Poverty	3	1
Outlived Practices	1	0.33
Ignorance	1	0.33
Poverty	2	0.66
Poor Education	2	0.66
Absence Of Burial Ground	1	0.33
Not Applicable	183	61.20

The above Table 5.8 gives counts out of a total of 299 responses with some respondents giving more than one response.

Source: Author's survey.

through baptism is one reality among many others that makes TRC asymmetrical with Christianity.

Table 5.8 shows a significant number of respondents, 35.45 per cent, claiming conversion to be a serious threat to the existence of TRC. It is also interesting to observe a significant size of respondents confident about the resilience of their religion and ruled out any threat perception. 61.20 per cent of the respondents felt no threat to their TRC. However, an important person from among the adherents of TRC pointed out an instance of monetary incentives for conversions to Christianity at Khoupum (Tamenglong District) in Manipur and Chingmeirong (Imphal East).[10] He even accused one of the Naga armed groups of physically assaulting the villagers at Khoupum to convert to Christianity. According to him, the Naga armed group cadres were Rongmei but their leader was not a Rongmei. So the interviewee analysed it as a perpetuation of colonisation and domination of the people by outsiders. He expressed deep anguish at the state of submission of the Rongmei Naga armed group cadres to the outside Nagas in the name of

'Nagaland for Christ'. He felt that the Rongmei cadres were merely used by other Nagas.

Among the Rongmei Christian community, the term that illuminates the idea of conversion is *puanthanmei*. The term puanthanmei may be understood as 'born again'. It is a popular term used by Rongmei Christians to advocate conversion. It means new birth (*puan* derived from *puanmei*- birth; *thanmei* derived from *kathan*- new). It is to become new or to be born again. The concept of *puanthanmei* conveys a sense of conversion as an indispensable criterion to achieve salvation. The old ways of life perceived to be typical of the traditionalists are considered to be evil or incompatible with the heavenly requirements. The term is used mostly for those who were not born in a Christian family. *Puanthanmei* was not just about new ways of life. However, the conventional understanding of *puanthanmei* emphasises religious conversion through the baptismal rite. A rigid *puanthanmei* required relinquishing the traditional belief system, festivals, rituals, traditional attires, folk songs, etc. This was the bone of contention between the traditionalists and the Christians but the ideal bedrock of *Puanthanmei*.

This requires putting the idea of conversion into perspective. The scriptural contexts in which conversion or baptism have been conceptualised differently in terms of rituals and their precedence are examined here. For this, Today's English Version of the *Good News Bible* is taken as a reference text. The Gospel of Matthew 28: 19-20 says, 'Go, then, to all peoples everywhere and make them my disciples: baptize them in the name of the Father, the Son, and the Holy Spirit, and teach them to obey everything I have commanded you.' Then comes the Gospel of Mark 16: 15-16: 'Go throughout the whole world and preach the gospel to all mankind. Whoever believes and is baptized will be saved; whoever does not believe will be condemned'. The following Gospel, i.e. Gospel of Luke does not have any reference to the final commandment of Christ to preach and to baptise. Such a final commandment is also not found in the Gospel of John. The Gospel of John 21: 15-17 nevertheless mentions Christ, after the resurrection, telling Simon Peter 'Take care of my lambs' three times. There is no reference to baptism. In the Gospel of Matthew, one finds Christ first referring to or emphasising baptism ('baptize them') or conversion. However, in the Gospel of Mark, one finds to 'preach the gospel to all mankind' as the first task. And baptism is only for those who believe. While the Gospel of Matthew sets baptism as a priority, the Gospel of Mark prioritises the 'gospel to all mankind'. Thus, of the four Gospels, one finds only one emphasising baptism or conversion. However, even this reference to baptism is still open to critical enquiry. Is it the conversion of ways of life to a pious one or change of religion?

A critical analysis of the period of 'the Enlightenment' is vividly given by Jim Ife who closely examined the interconnection between the general perceptions of a sense of superiority that prevailed among the people in the west with the period of Enlightenment. According to Ife, many in the west began to assume themselves to be intellectually superior to others in other parts of the globe and this impelled them to:

> '[A]ssume the role of bringing ... "enlightenment" to the "less enlightened" elsewhere, and this became the intellectual justification for the colonial domination of "less civilised" nations. It thus paved the way for traders, missionaries, soldiers, governors and "pioneers" to impose the more "enlightened" western ways on the remainder of the world, in the assured knowledge of their self-evident superiority.... Racism is a natural consequence of such a world-view' (2001: 64).

Those who were supposed to be converted by the missionaries were the 'less enlightened' and the 'less civilised' who were without the 'western ways' of life. Theology never allows examining all belief systems as equals. For Theologians of a particular religion, all other belief systems are not worthy of being called religions. There is one and only one religion and it is one's religion. Such a view invariably leads to viewing other religions as inferior ways of life. The cultures and traditions of the people who are outside one's belief system are consequently taken to be inferior and condemned. Conversion is assumed to be the answer to such a 'lowly life'. The supposedly 'inferior' belief systems of the colonised people are projected to be the cause of their state of colonisation. The 'lowly life' of the colonised people is best assumed to be possible of being salvaged only through the process of westernisation whose theological synonym is conversion. Therefore, the conversion is, historically and contemporarily speaking, best defined as a racist mission with an ethnocentric vision.

The vigour of a racist mission with an ethnocentric vision through conversion is gradually weakened with a growing number of stakeholders in missionary works from within the formerly colonised nations. Now the emphasis is on reconciliation and consolidation and not on conversion.

In a drastic departure from the tradition of evangelisation the Archbishop of Manipur, Dominic Lumon,[11] categorically said, 'We are not eager to baptise'. For him to preach the good news is a Christian duty commanded by Christ. Thus, the Archbishop draws himself close to the Gospel of Mark 16: 15-16, i.e. 'to preach the gospel to all mankind' and not to 'baptize' as in Matthew 28: 19-20. Religion, according to him, is a matter of an individual's belief and must not be enforced. However, certain Christian denominations still attack the traditionalists scathingly and speak of baptism or conversion as the only means to salvation.

My father often spoke of a neighbouring Christian group that records the names of individuals—to whom the group goes to preach the gospel—as members of their church even before baptism.[12] With an eagerness to increase members of a church some Christians spread their activities like wildfire to baptise or enrol new members into the church irrespective of the people's understanding of the gospel. *Puanthanmei* or conversion through baptism is set as an essential criterion to achieve salvation. This proves to be a serious threat to the existence of the belief systems of the forefathers. To counter these Christian activities TRC Phom educates their young minds and the elders as well to guard their beliefs and practices against conversion firmly.[13] Nevertheless, the attacks of Christians for conversion continue, but now it turns out to be a reason for TRC adherents to be on their toes.

Support from Hindu Organisations

Constant association with Hindu organisations such as Rashtriya Swayamsevak Sangh (RSS) and Kalyan Ashram energises the enthusiasm of the members of TRC. Unlike some Christians, the

Hindu organisations, without proselytisation, show respect to every ancestral belief systems of smaller groups. They also strive to protect and preserve the ancestral belief systems of the smaller and weaker groups by working with them to infuse a sense of greatness and uniqueness of their ancestral belief systems. Because of this non-proselytising but guardian role played by Hindu organisations, Zeliangrong traditionalists perceive the Hindu organisations to be non-threatening.

Some tribal people enjoy a sense of belonging with Hinduism. And 'The indigenous population of India', according to N.K. Bose, 'is supposed to have contributed in the past generously to the building up of what is known as Hinduism' (1971: 63). The propositional characteristic of religion should have not allowed any other belief systems to be parallel to Hinduism. But the non-proselytising nature of Hinduism allowed the acceptance and existence of non-threatening belief systems of the many smaller groups in India. This may be partly illuminated by the caste system that does not allow free entry of any group into the more privileged caste groups like the Brahmin and the Kshatriya. The admission of the tribal into the caste hierarchy is often restricted to the lowest. Certain exceptions like the absorption of some Kabui and Tangkhul people into the Kshatriya caste of the Meetei Hinduism under the Hinduised king Garibnawaz has already been discussed.

The presence of tribal belief systems as independent belief systems does not threaten the existing privileges of the more privileged caste groups. Even if the tribal people enter into the Hindu fold, they are invariably accorded very low status within the caste system. It poses no threat to the original caste groups. The religious and social privileges of the Hindus are secured within Hinduism and the tribal belief systems are never a threat to Hinduism. As they do not emphasise proselytisation they do not need to convert the tribals as Christians do. This makes cordial relationships between Hinduism and many tribal belief systems possible.

Based on an interaction with an active youth member[14] of TRC, the membership of Kalyan Ashram constitutes the locals who are not Christians. Using locals in the activities of Kalyan Ashram proved successful as the villagers identify easily with the locals and help is easily associated with Kalyan Ashram. In this process,

Hinduism is not viewed as a threat as Kalyan Ashram penetrates the lives of the locals through the locals and not through Hinduism. According to Lungaithao,[17] association with Kalyan Ashram gives him a boost. Kalyan Ashram, according to Lungaithao, is concerned with nationalism and not religion. Kalyan Ashram is concerned with salvaging the ancestral belief systems of the tribal people. According to him, being friendly with Kalyan Ashram does not result in conversion to Hinduism. The early Christians often intruded into the lives of the locals with a baggage of Christianity with western phenotypes and western cultures that were easily alienated by many traditionalists. The Hindu organisations despite not being local were warmly accepted as they came to strengthen the existing local belief systems. It was further pointed out that Kalyan Ashram members never speak of Hinduism while interacting with any of the ancestral religious group members. This enabled Hindu organisations to earn immense respect from among the ancestral religious group members and they humbly command indisputable respect among the traditionalists.

In Majuli island in Assam, despite the presence of twenty-two Vaishnavite satra (monastery) the Mising people of the island are converted to Christianity (Kashyap 2018). This is, according to Kashyap, explained by the concentrated effort of the Hindus only on preserving the traditional belief system of the Mising people while the Christians convert the Mising people. Such observation may also be witnessed among the Rongmei people of the TRC group who are closely settled with the Meetei Hindus in Manipur valley for centuries. The Hindu leaders are not known to have instigated the Meetei Hindus to destroy the belief systems of the Rongmei people in the hills and the valley. One may probably explain this with a reference to the practice of caste of Hinduism which could have, most likely, made the Hindus look at the Rongmei people to be ritualistically unclean and socially very low to be embraced wholly within Hinduism. And those Tangkhul and Rongmei who were converted to Hinduism in 1739 under the rule of Garibnawaz as discussed earlier are exceptions with a prime objective to serve the political interests and not religious interests. Thus, the Kukis are not known to have embraced Hinduism.

The practice of untouchability extended beyond the frontiers of Hindu groups to stigmatise and seclude the tribal people. Untouchability destroyed the social fabric of the Meetei society that was believed to have consolidated under the reign of king Pakhangba in AD 33. Untouchability enhanced the differences between the tribal people and the Meetei people. However, it certainly provides solace to realise that it served and continues to serve the purpose of preserving the ancestral belief systems of the tribal people as the tribal people are segregated and discriminated against by the belief and practices of Meetei Hinduism.

The Rongmei traditionalists find a support base in Hindu organisations to strengthen their pride in their unique ancestral belief system which is now revered by Hindu organisations. They are neither condemned nor stigmatised by the largest religious group of the nation. This support which is sometimes moral and financial proves to be crucial in building the resilience of ancestral belief systems and TRC is not an exception.

NOTES

1. The author met him at his residence in Keisamthong. He refused to speak with a voice recorder on and did not allow the author to take notes in a diary. He was referred to the author by Khomeimacha whom the author interviewed.
2. The author met him at Imphal. The author observed that he spoke with conviction and a sense of pride.
3. He wears the tattoo on the back of his neck displaying it for easy visibility.
4. An octogenarian in an interview on 23 June 2018.
5. The interviewee was interviewed on 11 March 2018. The interviewee associates the belief system of TRC to identity phenomenon. The interviewee opines that it is the search for identity by the youths who interact with several other ethnic groups that strengthens TRC that is still young and is in a reformative stage.
6. Name changed.
7. JCILPS stands for Joint Committee on Inner Line Permit System. It is an organisation spearheading a demand for the implementation of Inner Line Permit System popularly known as ILP in Manipur.

The objective of the implementation of ILP is the prevention of the entry of illegal immigrants and migrants as well. Their entry will be restricted with the issue of a permit known as Inner Line Permit. Note that even before the enactment of this Law by the Assembly the local organisations are already implementing it. The Bill concerning this provision has been unsuccessful in acquiring Presidential assent.

8. In one of the interviews held in the premise of Kalum Kai at Chingmeirong.
9. Ragongning Gangmei (name changed), in an interview expressed with a deep sense of anguish and a sense of complacence at the present state of TRC. According to him, non-state armed groups in the hills torture the non-Christians. According to him, cadres of a particular Naga armed group who do not belong to Rongmei community would beat the Rongmei villagers who are not Christians and point to their ancestral belief system as the reason for their poverty. Ragongning said that such tortures by Christians motivated the traditionalists to come together under a unified religious umbrella of Assam, Manipur and Nagaland. Common experiences of tortures by Christians made the youths to become more determined to adhere to their ancestral belief system. According to him, the threat is not only from the non-state armed groups but from the Christians as some Christians were also against the traditionalists and made attempt to harm the ancestral belief systems in collusion with the armed groups.
10. The interviewee was interviewed by the author for his Doctoral thesis in 2012. The author wanted to meet him again to get more information for the Post-doctoral work. Unfortunately he passed away due to illness.
11. The author met the Archbishop on 3 October 2018. The meeting with the author was not planned. The author went to meet the officials of the Archbishop Office along with an Intelligence Bureau Officer who was required to get information concerning funds received by the Archbishop's office. The author did not even anticipate that he would meet the Archbishop. However when the opportunity was presented, the author created an atmosphere conducive for retrieving such theological information. This must be reflected further by researchers who may be presented with opportunities for acquiring data unexpectedly at seemingly inappropriate places and time.
12. Registering a name in a Church record even before baptism seems to be common among the Baptist Church, at least in the Rongmei Baptist Church. Lungaithao is the President of Tingkao Ragwang Chapriak Chabuan Phom (Assam, Manipur and Nagaland). He was interviewed

on 22 March 2018. He shared his childhood experience of an attempt to be forcefully baptised by a Baptist Church. Attempts were made to convince him to accept baptism in a Baptist Church. One Saturday a member of a Baptist Church came to him and told him to become a Baptist and his name was entered as a member of the Baptist Church. Next day on Sunday some members of the Baptist Church came to take him to Church. He refused to oblige and threatened to shoot with a catapult the Baptist members if they forced him.

13. It is a contemporary fact that certain Catholic school authorities, the priests and nuns, in Manipur barter their school education with the faith of the local people. One evening the author received a phone call from his cousin sister who sounded very helpless. She wanted to admit her younger son in a Catholic School in Imphal as her elder son was already in that school. Sending them to different schools would be difficult for them as the boys were still very young. A priest of the Catholic school asked them to convert to Catholicism if they wanted their second son to be in the Catholic school. The author suggested that they should go for baptism and *use* the Catholic religion for the sake of education as the Catholic priests and nuns themselves have no respect for their religion. They prostitute their ordained religious position and English education to trap people into conversion. Note that this happens especially with the tribals and not with the Meeteis who are mostly Hindus. Many of the Catholic priests and nuns go to tribal lands with a pre-conceived notion that the tribals know nothing; they are simple, uncivilised, poor, weak and helpless. This perception guided their work and they found immense success as the systematic discrimination against the tribals by the dominant group nurtured an ideal ground for missionary exploitation. The pace of conversion of tribal boys and girls of Manipur valley villages such as Ragailong, Namdunlong, Sawombung, Kakhulong, Majorkhul, Sairem, Chingmeirong, etc., in exchange for school admission still remains unaccounted. Many of the Rongmei boys and girls left the Catholic church after schooling as the purpose of baptism came to an end with the end of schooling. However, the animosity and ill-feelings towards the Christians remain unchanged among some parents who were helpless because of their love for their children whom they wanted to give a quality education which remains a utopia in many government schools.
14. The youth was an active member of TRC Chabuan Phom. In an interview on 22 March 2018.

CHAPTER 6

Situating the Theories

Theorising enables one to visualise a pattern of operation of integrants of a society. It also opens a possibility to penetrate the eloquent meaning of seemingly mundane human interactions. A theory is a result of a meticulous and intimate examination and analysis of a social phenomenon that seemingly appears either too complex or very simple at a casual glance. If the social phenomenon appears to be complex a theory facilitates understanding and simplifying it. If it appears to be mundane the underlying factors are probed and holistic dynamics are presented in the theory. The complex intricacies are revealed. The purpose of a theory is to understand a world (Rootes 1990: 9). A theory provides a channel of thought to understand even the clandestine factors that actualise a social phenomenon. Words being the building blocks of thought concepts remain 'the cornerstone of any theorising' (Diani 1992: 2). Concepts build a theory and theory facilitates an understanding of a social phenomenon. This understanding of social phenomenon leads to more systematic and rational social intercourse.

Given the immense changes the TRC belief system has incorporated, the theory of social change is seen to be appealing as a theoretical framework to analyse TRC's beliefs and practices. Also because of its spread only among the Zeliangrong fraternities (Zeme, Liangmai, Rongmei and Inpui, though especially among Rongmei) with a sense of collective identity among TRC adherents social identity theory is taken as a theoretical lens to analyse TRC as a constituent of the larger identity movement. It is observed that TRC prevails only amongst the groups taken to be the descendants of the same ancestor.

Social Change

According to G. Aloysius, sociological studies of social change are found to be mere varieties of structural-functionalist approaches (1998). They are found to be ahistorical and independent of questions concerning 'change of power with respect to social structure' (ibid.: 21). Among the Marxists, studies of social change have been seen to be invariably adopting an economic-reductionist approach that viewed power and politics as functions of economic change. Aloysius contends that the political histories are found to be descriptive in their approach towards social change and present social change during the colonial era as the background of a political movement interpreted as a nationalist movement for freedom. In economic history, one finds a study of change focusing only on the question of whether India gained or lost economically from colonial rule.

The approach adopted in this study views social change as ongoing reformations as responses to various internal and external dynamics. The reformations are examined using a multi-dimensional approach. Social change is not merely economic or political. Political and economic factors are not the only factors contributing to social change. Religious reformations are not confined to questions of sacredness and profanity alone. Social change, being social, demands examining more than one factor while studying the change in any of the social dimensions. This theory of social change is analysed within the domain of social systems theory. The study agrees with the systems theory that 'person's development is profoundly affected by events occurring in settings in which the person is not even present' (Bronfenbrenner 1979: 3) to encompass the larger social group operating within even larger social systems. Reformations are initiated and incorporated until a certain level of social homeostasis is achieved within the group and stability in a relationship with other groups.

The conflict with the proselytising Christianity invariably put the position of TRC into near extinction. However, the surging global movement for indigenous people and the Hindu organisation activities for the Indian tribal people immensely helped TRC achieve stability and pride. The knowledge of the global movement for indigenous people is contributed immensely by the ongoing armed struggle movements in the state for sovereignty. These political movements are filtered to draw the strength for cultural rights of the indigenous people as envisaged in the discourse on indigenous rights across the globe. The role of the Hindu organisations that include helping the tribal people to protect their ancestral culture and ethnic identity too contributed towards raising the collective strength of the tribal people. It is in this context of the systems theory that social change is used analytically to understand the dynamics of reformation within TRC.

Social Change may be defined as the emergence or re-emergence of qualitative or quantitative features of a society. These features may be thoughts or ideologies shared widely in society. They may also be qualities of life improved or worsened due to the policies of the state or as a result of intragroup and intergroup dynamics. Social change is also seen to be qualitative as well as quantitative as 'it changes the values of individuals and classes by changing the situations in which they are placed' and there is a difference between the old and the new states which are 'incommensurable in any strictly quantitative sense' (Hamilton 1915: 576). A social change may also be conceptualised with a change in demography in terms of numbers or compositions of the people. Thus, to study social change demands an interdisciplinary approach that can analyse the social psychology, historical realities, the changing means and relations of productions, and the diverse beliefs of the people.

Theories on social change have been classified into global and specific (Hallinan 1997: 4). Global theories explain social change at an abstract level with a prediction of imminent results. However, it is observed that many of the social processes at micro and macro levels could not be accounted for by most of the global theories of social change. Specific theories are more intensive and present a more elaborate explanation of the social change.

It is an impossible task to quantify social change although it may be qualified in terms of its nature. It has not been measured quantitatively in terms of degree or intensity. Ascertaining the degree of 'shift' in society to claim a change in society is a hard task (Coser

1957: 201-2) to achieve. It is possible to identify areas of change but not in terms of measurable quantity or degree. New faiths may emerge thus contributing to what may be termed as religious demographic change. But one cannot ascertain the degree of faith of the people in their respective religion. One also cannot qualify a faith as better or worse than any other faith(s). The emergence of many new belief systems is certainly a social change but one cannot quantify the characteristics of the religions. However, a qualitative comparison of the tenets may be done.

MSA Rao (1984) categorises social change into structural and organisational. According to Rao, a total change of the social system through a revolution is envisaged in a structural change. Change seen at the level of norms, activities, and personnel in which one moves from one position to another is identified by Rao as an organisational change. The concept of change is not universal. There can be variation in degrees of change even in one kind of change conceptualised. Thus, organisational change, as presented by Rao, may still be of two kinds. There could be a positive organisational change when the change of position is towards a higher one. A negative organisational change could be seen when the positional change is negative or the position is a demoted one. Even a structural change could be without a revolution.

Revolution is a kind of change that is seen widely in the literature. It is, according to Samuel Huntington, 'a rapid, fundamental, and violent domestic change in the dominant values and myths of a society, in its political institutions, social structure, leadership, and government activity and policies' (1968: 264, cited in Tilly 1978: 193). While Rao sees revolution as a means to herald a complete change, Huntington suggests revolution as a kind of change in itself and not a mere means of change. And according to Lenin's book, *Collected Works*, vol. 33, 'Revolution is a change which breaks the older order to its new foundation' (1973: 110, cited in Singh 2005b: 3). What is indispensable in a conception of revolution is a total or complete change with all the features of society afresh. However, Tilly (1978) cautioned against a rapid social change because of its ability to herald disorder and even revolution while slow social change, according to Tilly, will be orderly. Another concept that is close to revolution is a transformative change that envisages a total change in a social structure that may be marked by violent change or revolution (Wilson 1973: 101). As in structural change discussed by M.S.A. Rao, transformative change also sees a change in the positions with lower status elevated to a higher position.

Reformation is a process of change that results in partial change without envisaging a complete change but seeking equity and justice within the system (ibid.: 24). How does one identify changes in reformation? Reformation looks forward to 'reorganize society in such a way that individuals and classes will come to occupy in the general scheme of things positions quite different from those which they now hold' (Hamilton 1915: 576). Here there is a need to qualify the term 'quite'. Quite is defined by the Oxford University Press dictionary as 'completely' or 'moderately'. As revolution or transformation envisage a complete change, the term 'quite' should be taken to mean 'moderately' and use the concept of reformation to mean a moderate or partial change. In religion, reformation may be sought in the context of practice without disturbing the beliefs. It may also be seen in the form of abandoning certain taboos and gennas without changing one's religion. Reformation is sometimes aimed at salvaging an existing system by seeking to rectify certain aspects believed to be detrimental to the continuance of the system.

Identifying the Changes in TRC

The qualitative and quantitative changes discussed earlier are identified within the context of reformations that nurture TRC. In terms of its beliefs, one has seen how followers of TRC naturalised a nomenclature *Tingkao Ragwang* which is locative. Unlike the followers of *Pupou Chap*, TRC popularised 'Tingkao' or heaven by its use as a qualifier for their God. While retaining some beliefs and practices, many other beliefs and practices were also incorporated within TRC. Reformations have been there since the colonial days. Reeling under colonial pressure and several expensive ritualistic sacrifices, the movement leaders opined to reform certain beliefs and practices. These partial changes continue even to these days.

Several abolitions of gennas and taboos facilitate in retaining the believers in TRC.

Tingkao Ragwang Chapriak falls within the domain of reformed religion. The practice of collective worship in Kalum Kai is one of the most spectacular reformations within their group. The practice of delivering a message to a congregation during worship with spiritual and moral flavours is still not found among the *Pupou Chap*. This is already a regular feature within the TRC worship system.

Institutionalisation through registration under the Societies Registration Act and formulation of structures of TRC are drastic changes for a traditionally village-confined belief system. It is not a revolution because TRC retains many age-old customary practices rooted in the primordial belief system of *Pupou Chap*. God remains the same and the pantheon gods stay stable. They also continue to appease other spirits and worship their ancestral souls like the followers of *Pupou Chap*. However, they incorporated fresh ideas about God their ancestors worshipped. The God remains the Supreme Power as in *Pupou Chap* but with the qualifier 'Tingkao' or heaven. This heralded a fresh debate on the divinity and omnipotence of the locative dimension of the God they worship.

Many of the features of the present TRC are, in fact, reformed features of the movement under Jadonang during the colonial days. While both *Heraka* and TRC draw immensely from the reformations of Jadonang, TRK claim to have its basis of beliefs and practices in mythology since the days of *Rari gan*.

Oral tradition and oral history are two major repositories of knowledge about their belief system and themselves. Prayers, songs, mythologies, and legends are part and parcel of their life. They are sacred. They reveal their world view. They guard their relationship with the supreme power and gods and goddesses. They are handed down from one generation to another generation. Their present and future progenies depend on oral traditions and oral histories to conceptualise their world view and cosmology. True, oral histories and oral traditions still occupy an important position in their religious and social life. However, with traditional village institutions gradually losing their lustre and with formal education overtaking the traditional learning system, oral histories and oral traditions are no longer as prominent as before. With cheap and fast printing technologies, oral histories and oral traditions are giving way to printed literature. The easy availability of religious resources has enabled even women, youth, and children to partake actively in religious activities that were conventionally dominated by elderly men or especially local priests. Religious literature has reformed the way people worship and pray. Prayers are reduced in printed form. Certain spiritual needs of the believers are served by the textual prayers instead of oral ritualistic prayer usually offered by the priests with occasional animal sacrifices. The religious literature also enabled a congregation with immense religious ambience and engender a strong collective feeling among the believers. This enhances mutual identification and social categorisation. Such features are still a far cry among the followers of *Pupou Chap.* The only congregation among *Pupou Chap* followers for collective prayer is during the prayer of *Hoi*. *Hoi* is a form of prayer which is offered only by male members of a village and the prayer is offered by repeatedly making the invocatory sound of '*Hoi*' with a beating of a drum. The *Hoi* prayer in TRC is still without females.

The importance of inter-village religious gathering is immense. Unlike the days of headhunting during which villagers were confined to the frontiers of their villages, reformations since the days of Jadonang allowed the villagers to come together even for a common political cause through the religious means of community worship. Such a congregation for religious practice is a spectacular reformed reality of present TRC. Religion is no longer the prerogative of the local priests. Many youth and even women engage in religious affairs at a personal level. They can engage in discussions related to their religion. Unlike the followers of *Pupou Chap* who are still confined to their villages for religious activities, TRC followers often have inter-village community prayer sessions. They organise religious conferences being attended by Zeliangrong believers of three different states of Assam, Nagaland, and Manipur. The notion of village republic is gradually being weaned away giving greater legitimacy to Zeliangrong nationalism with an ever growing sense of social identity. An individual's identity is finding deeper meaning in his or her social identity.

Such social identity emerging around religious phenomenon facilitates meaningful social comparison with the outsiders or other religious groups. The reformed religious identity acquired proves to be instrumental in the process of differentiating themselves from the *Pupou Chap*. With the name, *Tingkao Ragwang Chapriak* as a name of its religion the adherents of TRC are now able to identify themselves distinctly as people with religion. This identity of their religion gives them a formal religious identity. This facilitates its members to engage in the processes of social identification and social categorisation.

One of the most important changes that merit attention from a sociological point of view is the changes in the village polity. Unlike the earlier days in which religious affairs were under the strict supervision of the village authority, *Pei*, it is observed that TRC influences the village authorities immensely in religious affairs. The traditional institution of the priesthood is also partially diluted with the inter-village religious affairs which are supervised by the Zeliangrong Religious Council. A system of a religious council is a transformation because this tantamounts to submitting the religious authority of a village to younger generations. This is a shift in the power equation in a village polity. Through Zeliangrong Religious Council the officiating authority of the village priests in matters of religion is partly transferred to the modern institution of a council whose jurisdiction extends beyond the frontiers of a village. It is also seen that many TRC believers project a Rongmei village as a TRC village. TRC is invariably projected as 'the religion' of a Rongmei village.

To conclude a theoretical exposition on social change in the context of changes in the belief systems of Rongmei people it will be well to quote Max Mueller who established a strong relationship between change in religion and the need to remain relevant. According to him:

> . . . the history of religion also has been shown to exhibit a constant growth and development, its very life consisting in a discarding of decayed

elements, which is necessary in order to maintain all the better whatever is still sound and vigorous, and at the same time to admit new influences from that inexhaustible source from which all religion springs. A religion that cannot change is like a classical language, that rules supreme for a time, but is swept away violently in the end, by the undercurrent of popular dialects, by the voice of the people, which has often been called the voice of God (1878: 257).

TRC remains appealing among the Rongmei people across generations and different age groups. TRC's popularity outside of the Rongmei people is not significant. TRC has been able to positively respond to the changing temporal tastes of the younger generations. Change is a constant reality in TRC.

Social Identity

The notion of social identity illuminates 'individual's self-concept' (Tajfel 1978, cited in Greene 2004: 137) based on 'self-perceived membership' in an identified group (Greene 2004: 137). Social identity is understood as 'that part of an individual's self-concept which derives from his knowledge of his membership of a group (or groups) together with the value and emotional significance attached to the membership' (Tajfel 1978, cited in Greene 2004: 137). There is no formal membership in a group; it is a 'self-perceived membership' in a group.

Social identity theory propounded by Henri Tajfel and John C. Turner in *The Social Identity Theory of Intergroup Behaviour* (1986) outlined three cognitive processes associated with the concept of social identity. First, in the social categorisation process, one distinctly identifies the group to which one belongs and other groups to which others belong. And thus different groups are distinctly categorised. Then follows the social identification process where one identifies with the group members of the group categorised earlier. Here one enjoys a sense of belonging or being a part of the group identified. In the following process of social comparison, group members compare with out group and differentiate themselves from the members of the out group in terms of the characteristics perceived to be unique with the groups. In social identity, through the three processes, we see maximisation of differences between one's group or 'in-group (the group to which one psychologically belongs)' and other group or 'the out-group (psychologically relevant opposition group)' and develop a perception of 'greater differences' than actual differences with 'favouritism toward' one's group (Tajfel and Turner 1986, cited in Greene 2004: 137). Favouritism is done by implanting 'favourable qualities' to one's group and inflating the 'negative characteristics' of the other group (Brewer & Brown 1998, cited in Greene 2004: 138). In the process of favouritism of one's group and derogation of other groups, which need not occur simultaneously, a sense of superiority of one's group is also realised (Greene 2004: 138). According to Henri Tajfel and John C. Turner,

> mere perception of belonging to two distinct groups—that is, social categorization per se—is sufficient to trigger intergroup discrimination favoring the in-group. In other words, the mere awareness of the presence of an out-group is sufficient to provoke intergroup competitive or discriminatory responses on the part of the ingroup (1986: 281).

Social identity in which an individual acquires knowledge about 'self' based on knowledge about individual's membership in a group begins when the conception of the society about individual's membership in its group and the 'value and emotional significance attached to the membership' (Tajfel 1978, cited in Greene 2004: 137) is internalised by him or her as naturally given.

The theory of social identity in the context of TRC may be illuminated in the context of their belief system being ancestral religion and the Zeliangrong collective identity.

Ancestral Religion

Every member of TRC is believed to be its member since birth. There is no formal induction of any member into TRC from among the Rongmei people. The rites of passage are inherent parts of their worldly life. Even the first rite of passage performed at infancy is not interpreted into conversion. It is a part of their life blessed by *Tingkao Ragwang*. A child believer readily categorises the various religious groups and identifies with the religion to which it belongs.

This is facilitated by daily social intercourse with the social categories already present in the environment into which it is nurtured. The social categories of religions, cultures, language, places, etc., are infused into the child psyche to be naturalised. Systems theory holds good in explaining these social dynamics. The child readily accepts the already present realities of the society distinctly marked out from other social categories. The differences in the social categories are identified initially through their explicit differences. With this categorisation of the groups, the members in one's group are acknowledged as one's group members. A sense of belonging or collective feeling is developed while identifying those who are different or those who are in other clearly defined groups. Attempts are also made to enable believers to identify and understand the differences between one's groups and other groups. Such differences are also strengthened when the members emphasise the differences. There is also a widely shared favouritism towards one's group while debasing the features of other groups. This is social comparison. There is a 'sense of identity [that] can firmly exclude many people even as it warmly embraces others' (Sen 2006: 2) within one's group in social identity processes. Social comparison happens even with other belief systems of the Zeliangrong groups. Thus, TRC feels that *Pupou Chap*, Champa, and *Heraka* are different. It distinguishes itself from others in terms of beliefs and practices. This contributes to legitimacy as a result of differences. Sameness would have put TRC into a state of plagiarism.

TRC mythologies and beliefs, being rooted in the narrative of the Zeliangrong group, their worldview is rooted in the ancestral group. TRC origin is rooted in the proto-ancestors of the Zeliangrong. Their creation narrative excludes Meetei, Bodo, Punjabi, Maori or Chinese, etc. Their belief system is a reflection of their ancestral belief system and plausible only within their ancestral group. They identify their religious group only within their ancestral groups. Any other groups which are distinctly identified in terms of language, culture, or phenotype are still not identified as members of TRC. Thus, TRC is culture-specific. Its rituals are partly tied to their totemism. Their beliefs, prayers, and songs are language-specific. The rites of the passage concerning marriage are strictly bound to their practice of clan exogamy. Prohibition against the same clan marriage is rooted in their belief system. TRC cannot let loose all these to make it universal. Doing this will automatically render their belief system baseless. The basis of their social institutions and pattern of social intercourses are rooted in their beliefs. Like Christianity that precludes circumcision and makes Christianity more universal, TRC cannot risk embracing such a universalisation project. The beliefs and practices are rooted in the ancestral beliefs and practices that cannot be reformed to the extent of being labelled as 'western' and 'unconventional'. Its religious identity is, therefore, closely knit around its ancestral identity delineated from every other known culture. They are necessarily chained to social identification with their ancestral religion and ancestral identity that includes even the Rongmei Christians.

Zeliangrong Collective Identity

The process of social categorisation, social identification, and social comparison is also actualised in the context of their larger collective identity of Zeliangrong. The collective feeling is not confined to the respective constituent groups. The process of social categorisation of each group extends to encapsulate the larger Zeliangrong identity. Zeliangrong identity is unambiguously categorised as the ultimate reality of the identity of the constituent groups. Despite the variations in the dialects spoken by the constituent groups the group members of each group identify with the members of all the constituent groups. This social identification in which they identify with the members of the group categorised as theirs is facilitated by their narrative of common origin. Such a narrative of origin is an integral part of the TRC belief system. Their beliefs and practices are based on their origin narrative. Their ritualistic prayers and songs are also marked by tales of their common origin.

The shared origin narrative allows the Rongmei to identify with Zeme, Liangmai and Inpui as progenies of their common ancestor. Such a belief is more relevant in the domain of a belief system that accommodates the creation narrative. TRC believes that their proto-ancestor was the common ancestor of the constituent groups of Zeliangrong. Their proto-ancestor was a Hamai or God's child. It was *Tingkao Ragwang* who commanded Dampapu and Dampapui to create the first human beings who were called Hamai by *Tingkao Ragwang*. It is in the creation narrative of TRC or the traditionalist Zeliangrong people that the Hamai narrative is extant. TRC treasures the narrative of Hamai. The Christians subscribe to the Biblical narrative of human origin and their Biblical narrative of human origin undermines the Zeliangrong creation narrative that facilitates the continuity of collective Zeliangrong identity. It is in this sense that one may safely claim TRC and other ancestral belief systems of Zeliangrong people to be the crucial bearers of primordial Zeliangrong collective identity.

The promulgation of Zeliangrong Religious Council as the apex religious body of all the Zeliangrong belief systems remains an indisputable testimony to the indelible essence of the collective identity in the Zeliangrong belief systems despite their differences in beliefs and practices. It is this collective Zeliangrong identity that brings together all the diverse belief systems of the Zeliangrong people and sometimes even the Zeliangrong Christians. A complete essence of their identity with all its requisite paraphernalia comes from Zeliangrong traditional belief systems and TRC is one among them.

In casual or formal interactions, it is often observed that the Rongmei dialect is used more frequently as this dialect is usually spoken even by some elders of the other three groups. However, in most of the ritualistic prayers, even among the Rongmei, many of the Liangmai terms are used as the tongue spoken by Liangmai was the only means of communication among the Zeliangrong groups before they parted their ways from Makuilongdi and gradually developed their respective dialects. Thus, it is also in the ritualistic prayers of TRC that we find a strong element that binds the constituent groups of Zeliangrong. The ritualistic terms carry an inherent capacity to facilitate the Rongmei members to categorise their collective identity and easily identify with the Liangmai and other two groups as their ancestral brethren. The use of Liangmai terms in the holiest act of prayer by all the other three groups provides the authenticity and credibility of the narrative of their

Liangmai origin or their collective origin and thus binds them with a collective feeling. Liangmai language allows them to do meaningful social categorisation.

This whole processes of social change and social identity processes sustain the resilience and relevance of TRC within Zeliangrong identity discourse and maintain its prominence within the larger social canvass of religion. TRC cannot be dismissed from the identity discourse of the Rongmei in particular and the Zeliangrong in general. With its reformations, it can present itself as a relevant belief system appealing to the changing world views and catering to the emerging needs in diverse societies.

CHAPTER 7

A Concluding Note

Religion is concerned not only with the belief system. It is not a domain exclusively of a belief in the supreme power. It is also a promising ground for rigorous academic endeavour even by an atheist. Atheists, theists, agnostics and even fundamentalists are attracted to religious studies. While certain fields such as theology requires taking a position on the truth-validity of the existence of God in religious studies there is also scope for a more empirical engagement with religion contrary to subjective-cognitive religious experiences. The magical aspect of religion is ruled out in an empirical conception of religion. This, however, does not mean that every scientific discipline is purged from subjectivity. As discussed earlier, sometimes objectivity can be understood as a shared subjectivity of those who agree not to disagree with each other, and even over the differences. Chetan Singh conveys a sense of meaninglessness in what he calls a 'relentless search for an elusive "objective" truth' in history (2018: 10). Every discipline and field engaged with religious studies has its specific methodology, sometimes with shared methods. The complexities and intricacies associated with religious belief and practices sometimes render its interdisciplinary study essential. A parochial approach towards religion through methodological fundamentalism may be deciphered as akin to religious fundamentalism. Therefore, religious studies must allow for theoretical, methodical and analytical triangulation and not strangulation of other approaches.

Historical approaches often hinge on pieces of evidence such as a document. Theological approaches tend to exhibit a sense of complacency with the ontological position of existentialism of God. *A priori* conception of the existence of God of the theology and probing nature of history unambiguously stand as poles apart.

The historicity of the spread of good news of a divine entity may be plausible but its extension towards a meaningful magico-religious dimension may be a futile attempt. A platonic relationship with a divine entity in the form of formless spirits is impossible historicity. Such an effect of a platonic relationship with the entity worshipped may be crucial in a psychological approach towards religion. Religion being exclusively personal for some and social as well, one can fully endorse its systematic study in the disciplines of political science and sociology too. The historical antecedents of attempts to delineate religion and state have lowered the intensity of the study of religion in political science. However, the significance of religion in the ideological baggage of many political leaders is contemporaneous with the contemporary dynamics. Sociology by having a broad scope, naturally embraces religion as its domain of study. A study of religion is not limited to the aforesaid disciplines and field. Economics, geography and even genetic studies can wade through the realm of religion to provide a more holistic view of a subject of an enduring nature such as religion.

It is of particular observation that many of the significantly smaller cultural and linguistic groups are of great interest for many interested in religious studies. Often many of the belief systems of the smaller and weaker groups are taken as referent beliefs in understanding or theorising the various concepts in a study of religion or social institutions, customs and practices. Many of the belief systems of the smaller groups are believed to be in a pristine state and viewed as retaining a purer state of its origin and thus crucial for theorising in a larger context. Thus, an anthropologist may be relatively more interested in the belief systems of the tribal people or those settled in the forest or those settled closer to the natural environment, because of their interests in animism.

The *Tingkao Ragwang Chapriak* among the Rongmei people in Manipur valley presents a plethora of opportunities for a sociological study of religion. The social and political functions of religion, especially in the context of a high degree of pluralism in society, are illuminated in this study. The historical accounts of their settlement in the valley from the pre-colonial days to the post-independence days provide a holistic view of their relationships with the colonisers and their neighbours. Their relationships with their neighbours in the past proved to be the most enduring experience that shapes the course of their present state of affairs. They even internalise and naturalise a certain aspect of the oppressive reality of their relationships. This is well reflected in the institution of Khullak that has become so indispensable that Khullakpu is invariably and erroneously assumed to be the head of the pinnacle of village institutions. The social and religious legitimacy Khullak enjoys point to the importance of the social process of assimilation.

The historicity of the Rongmei people is deeply entrenched in the obtrusive narrative crafts of the neighbouring groups. As seen in the earlier sections the historicity of the traditional institutions sometimes depends on the historicity of the dominant Meetei groups. The historicity of the Rongmei people is seriously undermined by the absence of the art of writing. Despite the history of Manipur, accounted for by the dominant group, minimally recording the history of Zeliangrong people, the Rongmei people continued with their oral traditions and oral histories. This nurture the sense of their past. And this past contributes towards attachment to their ancestral belief systems. During an analysis of data generated from oral history and oral tradition, the primary emphasis is on the pattern observed in the data. This pattern developed coherently is what accounts for the credibility of the data. However, one must realise that pattern in data is nothing, but a higher degree of adherence to one idea on a certain theme. And this degree of adherence or conformity is a reflection of the higher number of respondents indicating the idea. Thus, the more the number of respondents ascribing to an idea, the higher is the degree of adherence and thus the credibility. It is, thus, on the frequency of respondents ascribing to an idea that determines the credibility of data based on oral history and oral tradition. Therefore, the oral history or oral tradition method may also be termed as a democratic method. In a democratic method, the outcome of research hinges on the pattern of the data which depends on the higher chance of conformity of ideas shared by many interviewees or respondents ascribing to the same idea.

The art of not writing among the Rongmei people is closely linked with the art of oral traditions rooted in their belief systems.

The art of oral traditions infuses a greater degree of legitimacy as writing is invariably the art of mankind and not divine. Nevertheless, contemporary accounts of the Rongmei people, including their belief systems are beginning to witness comfort with scripts. The Bengali script used by the neighbouring Meetei group proffers itself as a convenient means towards what may be called here textual belief. This journey from oral beliefs to textual beliefs is not without the narratives of conflict and assimilation at various levels of their interactions. The quantitative and qualitative changes across eras underwent by the Rongmei people in their beliefs and practices underscore the social, historical and political dimensions of religions. This raises a question on the issue of the pristine state of religion. For how long can religion be guarded against any external influence? Does change in belief system tantamount to dwindling credibility of its divinity?

The reformations within the belief systems of Rongmei people that impacted partially even the dynamics of the village polity are discussed. Customs and traditions are often intended to be retained in their pristine form. The strength of the claim of the elders to the originality of the traditional institutions and their associated practices reinforces the credibility of such institutions and practices. However, change is the only constant reality in society. And change is very much a reality of social systems. The impact of TRC's reformation upon the traditional village institutions especially in the realms of beliefs and practices are areas of continued sociological research. The believers of TRC wish to convey a message to their fellow believers and others who are not within TRC that every belief and practice of TRC is primordial. The atavistic impression is well managed among the TRC groups. There is a sense of pride among the followers of TRC for being able to continue with their ancestral beliefs and practices. Despite the contested and supposedly new name of even their God; obvious new ways of worship; disowning of certain old rituals; endeavour towards religious text; idols–not idolatry–and many other organised strategies of mobilisation that cut across the traditional villager frontiers, TRC continues to claim to be primordial in the sense of unchanging in their ancestral beliefs and practices.

The study examined the dynamics of the relation between TRC and village institutions within the framework of social change and also analysed the identity discourse within the theoretical framework of social identity. Social identity captures the interface between the individual experiences with religion and the social dimension of religion that influences the individual's conception of self within one's religion. With growing knowledge and understanding of the religious teachings, immensely facilitated by literature and interactions across ages, the conception of self among the believers of TRC is closely linked with the conception of their belief system maturing within a social context. A part of their self-conception is an integral component of their religion. The awareness programmes frequently conducted by the youth of the TRC groups of many villages within a well-structured institution of *Chabuan Phom* nurture and consolidate the collective sense of identity.

Wherever they can, it is also observed that TRC attempts to naturalise village institutions within the belief system of their religion. The traditional institutions are primarily viewed as offshoots of the religious institution, an institution under TRC. There is a natural identification of the traditional institutions with the belief system of TRC. This guides the conception of an idea of a village or a community among the TRC believers. This also facilitates easy identification with fellow villagers and sometimes allows comparison with other belief systems and institutions with foreign antecedents. This process of social comparison among the Rongmei groups belonging to different traditional belief systems is also witnessed. Thus, *Pupou Chap*, the followers of the ancestral belief system or traditionalists, does not identify with TRC. For *Pupou Chap*, being traditionalists means identifying with the ancestral belief systems without any element of reformation which is not so in the case of TRC. This remains one crucial challenge for the TRC to reckon with.

The debate of whether TRC is primordial or not remains a question to be further critically analysed. The theoretical approach, in which one may study religion with God as an essential component, or religion viewed as invariably associated with social dimension may be taken into account. If religion is viewed as essentially a God thing, then every religion is primordial. If God is the defining characteristic of religion, then God being primordial, a religion is primordial. The primordial nature of God naturally ascribes primordial feature to a religion. But if religion is essentially a social reality, then every religion, because of irrefutable changes in societies, has experienced a certain degree of changes or reformations and they are all best described as reformed systems. Incorporating new features and discarding certain old features are realities associated with religion. Religion here is a social reality and not an unaffected divinity. It is examined in this study that the conception of God among TRC is marked by certain new features. As seen earlier, one of the participants of the TRC *Chabuan Phom* conference pointed out the absence of the name *Tingkao Ragwang* in any of the rituals in the olden days. This locative feature of God as God of Heaven is a bone of contention in the debate concerning the primordiality of TRC.

The resilience of TRC, despite all the debates surrounding its origin and nature, continues to capture the inquisitive minds of social scientists interested in the sociological functions of religion. The factors that contributed towards the resilience of TRC affirm the social dimension of religion. Theological explanations that always start with the existence of God as its basis alone cannot explain the crucial social dimensions that are marked by ever-changing social realities. Religion is not only about theology or God. It is also about social institutions that are sometimes the results of secular interests and the political milieu of a place. Religion is not exclusively about magico-religious matters. Religion is intertwined with the dynamics of various psyche planes in diverse social environments. Social psychology with its social identity too proves to be a crucial theoretical tool towards the illumination of dynamics of religion. It is through the interdisciplinary approach adopted in this study that one can better glimpse into the little researched area as that of *Tingkao Ragwang Chapriak's* resilience.

Tingkao Ragwang Chapriak constantly makes attempts to represent itself as a distinct religious group both within the Zeliangrong group and outside of the Zeliangrong group. This has been a dilemma even for its members. While trying to be distinct from other faiths of the Zeliangrong group it identifies simultaneously with the same origin. Thus, social comparison and social identification happen at the same time. While challenging the forces of proselytisation of the Christian missionaries even from within the Zeliangrong group *Tingkao Ragwang Chapriak* identify with them in the context of the collective Zeliangrong identity. Nevertheless, these contradictory phenomena contribute towards its resilience.

The reformations incorporated within TRC is both a matter of progress and regression. It has been able to sustain the interests of the youths with new features into their religious life. It has instilled pride and self-esteem among its adherents. However, it suffers immensely from a lack of trust and confidence among many elders who reject reformations of their ancestral belief systems. TRC will continue to face these new internal strains from their neighbours who are not the traditional Christian foes. This is a greater challenge to TRC as the followers of *Pupou Chap* dismisses the claim of TRC being *Pupou Chap*. While it has gained immense respect and recognition with its reformations it has acquired new foes in *the Pupou Chap* group.

The propensity among TRC followers to represent the whole village or whole non-Christian villagers as followers of TRC is a potential element of conflict. It is also an element of subjugation. It suppresses the voices of the *Pupou Chap* followers who distance themselves from the TRC group. How will TRC Phom deal with the simmering element of dominance among some of its followers? Can TRC accommodate differences among non-Christian villagers?

It is their collective Zeliangrong identity that enables the TRC followers to identify even with the Zeliangrong Christians. The Zeliangrong Christians also celebrate the culture of the Zeliangrong. They fondly use the material and non-material cultures of the Zeliangrong. But in the context of Chaoba Kamson, the General-Secretary of TRC Phom, viewing every aspect of culture to be part of religion can Zeliangrong culture continue to provide a common platform to the Christian and non-Christian Zeliangrong people? While many followers of TRC do not feel comfortable with Zeliangrong Christians using the culture of the Zeliangrong even while being Christians, how will TRC respond to the allegations of the followers of *Pupou Chap* against TRC on their 'misuse' or reformations of their ancestral belief systems? The followers of

Pupou Chap do not identify with the TRC. But they identify with the members of TRC within the scope of ethnic identity as Zeliangrong. TRC stands in a very precarious position within the discourse on primordial religion due to invalidation by the *Pupou Chap* followers. However, it is the Zeliangrong identity that salvages them from this position.

Among the factors contributing towards the resilience of TRC, the attacks by the Christians is gradually wearing with growing atavistic feeling among Zeliangrong Christians since the problem of migration of the Nagas from Manipur valley in 2001. When the Government of India and the National Socialist Council of Nagaland (Isak-Muivah) agreed to extend a ceasefire agreement into the state of Manipur in 2001 violent protests erupted. Many Nagas settled in Manipur valley fled to the hills. Some villages in the periphery of Imphal received a direct verbal threat from certain valley organisations. There were incidents of stoning Naga villages at nights during the protests. This forced many Nagas to leave the valley. This also brought many of the valley Zeliangrong people into direct contact with their brethren in the hills. This infused a sense of love and fraternity. There was a resurgence of reverence for the ancestral culture and belief systems even among the Zeliangrong Christians. Therefore, animosity between Zeliangrong Christians and non-Christians are not as bitter as before until the 1990s. Many Zeliangrong Christian churches have begun incorporating cultural dances into their Christmas programmes and weddings. Many Christian girls and women wear traditional attire when they go to Church. With the active participation of youths in the religious affairs of TRC, a stronger bridge is also built between Zeliangrong Christians and non-Christians.

TRC also owes much to Rani Gaidinliu who opened the doors for the Hindu organisations to work among the Zeliangrong people since the 1970s. TRC's identification with both Jadonang and Rani Gaidinliu enable them to establish a closer relationship with the Hindu organisations who contribute significantly towards the preservation of the ancestral cultures of the Zeliangrong people. It is both the internal strength and external elements that contribute to the resilience of TRC. While the attacks of the Christians are antagonistic the other factors are benign. Thus, the benign factors are more than the antagonistic factor. TRC will gain much from the capitalisation of the benign factors while eliminating the propensity of dominance over *Pupou Chap.*

Appendices

Appendix A

Source: Photograph taken by the author.

Inside a newly inaugurated Kalum Kai at a Rongmei village Ramji in Imphal, Manipur. The golden colour circular metal is the religious symbol of TRC. Inside the circle, there is a replica of a Sun placed above and a Moon placed below with two horizontal lines crossing two vertical lines inside the circle.

Appendix B

Source: Photograph taken by the author.

A Mahadev temple with a trisul (trident) and a temple of Rongmei traditional religion with a spear on the same building of a Rongmei family at Keisamthong Kabui village in Imphal, Manipur. The waving flag is a Meetei flag with seven colours indicating the seven salais of Meetei community.

Appendix C

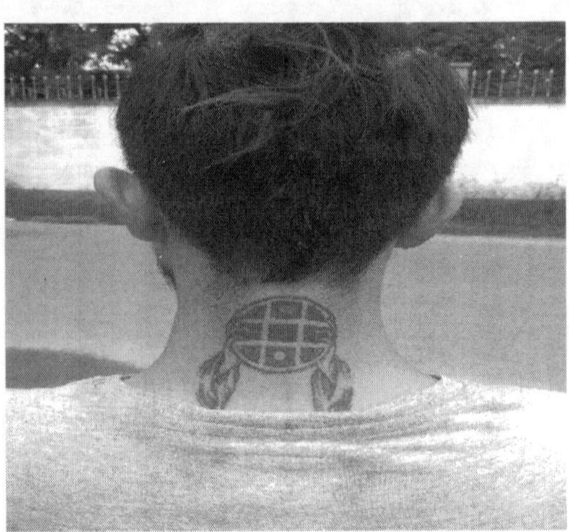

Source: Photograph taken by the author.

A Rongmei youth from Ragailong village in Imphal bearing a tattoo of the religious symbol of TRC.

Appendix D

Source: Photograph taken by the author.

A holy place in a Rongmei village. The deity was initially thought to be one of the Meetei deities and thus rituals were initially performed by Meetei priestess. Later it was realised by the villagers that the deity is of the Rongmei and now rituals are being performed by Rongmei priests.

Appendix E

Source: Photograph taken by the author.

A sacred place of Zeliangrong in Ramting Kabin at Senapati district of Manipur where Nepalese offered prayers. The Nepalese were stopped from continuing.

Appendix F

FELICITATION

A Felicitation and Blessing Programme for the TRC Students who stood 1st Division in HSLC Examination 2017 will be held on the 18th June (Sunday) 2017 at TRC Kalum kai, Chingmeirong.

Marksheet copy along with Contact No. may be submitted on or before 11th June (Sunday) 2017 for more detail information please Contact

Sd/- Organizing Secretary
Tingkao Ragwang Chapriak Chabon Phom (AMN)

Tse/2167-5,6

Source: Sangai Express.

A newspaper clipping of an announcement for felicitation programme for TRC students.

Appendix G

Source: Photograph taken by the author.

A programme conducted by TRC Youth wing to felicitate candidates successful in HSLC and HSSLC Exams.

Appendix H

Source: Photograph taken by the author.

Rongmei Christian children and youths singing and dancing in traditional Rongmei attires on Christmas at St. Peter Catholic Church, Ragailong and Namdunlong, Imphal.

Appendix I

Source: Photograph taken by the author.

Two noted personalities from TRC attend a solidarity day on 2 April 2018, organised by Zeliangrong Baudi at Chingmeirong. The second from the left is the General Secretary of TRC Phom and the person in the extreme right is Dr Budha Kamei, the noted scholar among TRC believers. Despite the fear of conversion these two noted personalities of TRC seemed to be comfortable associating with the Christians.

Appendix J

Source: Photograph taken by the author.

Chaoba Kamson, the General Secretary, TRC Phom and Dr Budha Kamei seated as dignitaries on the dais witness the youth of Taihu Baptist church performing choreography on a gospel song wearing Rongmei traditional attire on 2 April 2018. They did not agitate against such performance in which traditional attires were used and cultural dance steps being mellowed in a Christian gospel song.

Appendix K

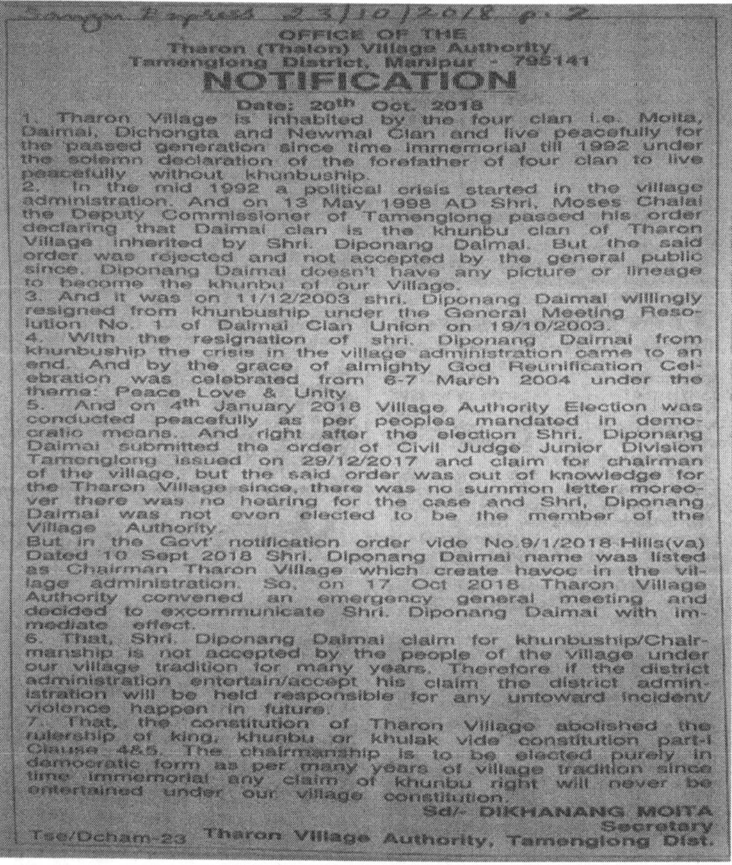

Sangai Express 23/10/2018 p. 2

OFFICE OF THE
Tharon (Thalon) Village Authority
Tamenglong District, Manipur - 795141

NOTIFICATION

Date: 20th Oct. 2018

1. Tharon Village is inhabited by the four clan i.e. Moita, Daimai, Dichongta and Newmai Clan and live peacefully for the passed generation since time immemorial till 1992 under the solemn declaration of the forefather of four clan to live peacefully without khunbuship.
2. In the mid 1992 a political crisis started in the village administration. And on 13 May 1998 AD Shri. Moses Chalai the Deputy Commissioner of Tamenglong passed his order declaring that Daimai clan is the khunbu clan of Tharon Village inherited by Shri. Diponang Daimai. But the said order was rejected and not accepted by the general public since. Diponang Daimai doesn't have any picture or lineage to become the khunbu of our Village.
3. And it was on 11/12/2003 shri. Diponang Daimai willingly resigned from khunbuship under the General Meeting Resolution No. 1 of Daimai Clan Union on 19/10/2003.
4. With the resignation of shri. Diponang Daimai from khunbuship the crisis in the village administration came to an end. And by the grace of almighty God Reunification Celebration was celebrated from 6-7 March 2004 under the theme: Peace Love & Unity
5. And on 4th January 2018 Village Authority Election was conducted peacefully as per peoples mandated in democratic means. And right after the election Shri. Diponang Daimai submitted the order of Civil Judge Junior Division Tamenglong issued on 29/12/2017 and claim for chairman of the village, but the said order was out of knowledge for the Tharon Village since, there was no summon letter moreover there was no hearing for the case and Shri, Diponang Daimai was not even elected to be the member of the Village Authority.

But in the Govt' notification order vide No.9/1/2018-Hills(va) Dated 10 Sept 2018 Shri. Diponang Daimai name was listed as Chairman Tharon Village which create havoc in the village administration. So, on 17 Oct 2018 Tharon Village Authority convened an emergency general meeting and decided to excommunicate Shri. Diponang Daimai with immediate effect.

6. That, Shri. Diponang Daimai claim for khunbuship/Chairmanship is not accepted by the people of the village under our village tradition for many years. Therefore if the district administration entertain/accept his claim the district administration will be held responsible for any untoward incident/violence happen in future.
7. That, the constitution of Tharon Village abolished the rulership of king, khunbu or khulak vide constitution part-I Clause 4&5. The chairmanship is to be elected purely in democratic form as per many years of village tradition since time immemorial any claim of khunbu right will never be entertained under our village constitution.

Sd/- DIKHANANG MOITA
Secretary
Tharon Village Authority, Tamenglong Dist.

Tse/Dcham-23

Source: Sangai Express.

Newspaper clipping from local daily paper Sangai Express dated 23 October 2018 on page number 2. This clipping includes a village authority erroneously claiming Charimanship as a part of traditional institution 'since time immemorial'.

Bibliography

Aich, T.K., (2013), 'Buddha Philosophy and Western Psychology', *Indian Journal of Psychiatry, 55* (Suppl 2): S165–S170. doi: 10.4103/0019-5545.105517.

Akoijam, I.S., (2004), *Manipurgee Cheengmee-Tammee* (A text in Meetei Language written in Bengali script), Thoubal (Manipur): Manipur Sahitya Samiti.

Aloysius, G., (1998), *Nationalism without a Nation in India*, New Delhi: University Press.

Antes, P., A.W. Geertz, and R.R. Warne, (2004), *Introduction*, in Peter Antes, Armin W. Geertz, Randi R.Warne (eds.), *New Approaches to the Study of Religion*, Berlin: Walter de Gruyter, pp. 1-9.

Aune, K., (29 March 2011), 'Why Feminists are Less Religious', *The Guardian*, pp. 1-3. Retrieved from https://www.theguardian.com/commentisfree/belief/2011/mar/29/whyfeminists-less-religious-survey.

Baruah, S., (20 July 2018), 'A Lesson from Arunachal Pradesh', *The Indian Express*. Available at https://indianexpress.com/article/opinion/columns/anti-conversion-law-arunachal-pradeshcm-pema-khandu-5266610/

Beteille, A., (1992), 'Religion as a Subject for Sociology', *Economic and Political Weekly, 27* (35), 1865-70.

Boedder, B., (1899), (2nd Ed.), *Natural Theology*, London: Longmans, Green, and Co.

Bois, H., (1916), 'A Sociological View of Religion', *The International Review of Missions (Geneva), 5* (3), 449-60.

Bosanquet, B., (1920), 'What Religion Is', London: Macmillan and Co.

Bose, N.K., (1971), *Tribal Life in India*, New Delhi: National Book Trust.

Bourdillon, M.F.C., (1986), 'Teaching the Anthropology of Religion', *Anthropology Today, 2* (4), pp. 11-14, http://www.jstor.org/stable/3032711.

Bousset, W., (1907), (2nd Ed.), *What Is Religion?*, (trans.) F.B. Low. London: T. Fisher Unwin.

Braude, A., (2004), 'A Religious Feminist—Who Can Find Her? Historiographical Challenges from the National Organization for Women', *The Journal of Religion*, 84 (4), pp. 555-72, http://www.jstor.org/stable/10.1086/422480.

Bronfenbrenner, U., (1979), *The Ecology of Human Development: Experiments by Nature and Design*, Cambridge, MA: Harvard University Press.

Brown, R., (1874), *Statistical Account of the Native State of Manipur, and the Hill Territory Under its Rule*, Calcutta: Office of the Superintendent of Government Press.

Cameron, D., (2001), *Working with Spoken Discourse*, London: Sage Publications.

Case, S.J., (1907), *The Historical Method in the Study of Religion*, Lewiston. Maine: Press of the Lewiston Journal.

______, (1921), 'The Historical Study of Religion', *The Journal of Religion*, 1 (1), p. 117.

Cheney, A.S., (1923), *A Definition of Social Work* (A Thesis in Sociology submitted to the University of Pennsylvania), Philadelphia: Alice S. Cheyney.

Coolingwood, R.G., (1916), *Religion and Philosophy*, London: Macmillan and Co.

Coser, Lewis A., (1957), 'Social Conflict and the Theory of Social Change', *The British Journal of Sociology*, 8 (3), pp. 197-207, http://links.jstor.org/sici?sici=0007-1315%28195709%298%3A3%3C197%3ASCATTO% 3E2.0.CO%3B2-H.

Dangmei, S., (2013), 'Cultural Positioning of Tribes in North-East India: Mapping the Evolving Heraka Identity', *Economic and Political Weekly*, 48 (1), pp. 27–30.

Diani, M., (1992), 'The Concept of Social Movement', *The Sociological Review*, 40, pp. 1-25.

Durkheim, Émile, (1965/1912), *The Elementary Forms of the Religious Life*, (trans.) Joseph Ward Swain, New York: Free Press.

Ecklund, E.H. and J.Z. Park, (2009), 'Conflict between Religion and Science among Academic Scientists?', *Journal for the Scientific Study of Religion*, 48 (2), pp. 276-92.

Editor, (1978), 'Zionism is Not Judaism', *The Campaigner*, 11 (10), pp. 1-3.

Einstein, A., (n.d.), *Einstein on Cosmic Religion and Other Opinions and Aphorisms*, with an appreciation by George Bernard Shaw, Retrieved from https://ia800402.us.archive.org/22/items/EinsteinOnCosmicReligion/cosmic-religioneinstein.pdf.

Elu, R. and Ndang, N.H. (2011), *Zeme Customary Laws (Zeme Paupai Sie)*, Nagaland: Zeme Council Nagaland.

Evans-Pritchard, E.E., (1956), *Nuer Religion*, London: Oxford University Press.

Farnell, L.R., (1905), *The Evolution of Religion: An Anthropological Study*, London: Williams and Norgate.

———, (1921), *Outline History of Greek Religion*, London: Duckworth and Co.

Foucault, M., (1980), *Power/Knowledge-Selected Interviews and Other Writings 1972-1977*, (ed.) Colin Gordon, (trans.) Colin Gordon, Leo Marshall, John Mepham and Kate Soper, New York: Pantheon Books.

Frazer, J., (1922), *The Golden Bough*, New York: The Macmillan Company.

Freud, S., (2004), *Totem and Taboo: Some Points of Agreement between the Mental Lives of Savages and Neurotics*, With an authorized translation by James Strachey. London: Routledge.

Gallaher, C., (2009), 'Researching repellent groups: some methodological considerations on how to represent militants, radicals, and other belligerents', in Chandra Lekha Sriram, John C. King, Julie A. Mertus, Olga Martin-Ortega, and Johanna Herman (eds.), *Surviving Field Research: Working in Violent and Difficult Situations*, London: Routledge, pp. 127-46.

Ganglaona, K., (2008), 'Ahui-Na: K.K.O Pamphlet', in *Silver Jubilee Celebration Souvenir (1983-2008)*, Imphal (Manipur): Ragailong Kamei Kaikhong Kariumei.

Gangmei, G., (2013), *The Customary Laws and Practices of the Ruangmei (Kabui) in Manipur*, Unpublished Doctoral Thesis, Manipur: Manipur University, Retrieved from http://hdl.handle.net/10603/26522.

Gangmei, T., (2014), 'Exploring the Rongmei Indigenous Religion: Tradition amidst Change', *Indian Streams Research Journal, 4* (6), pp. 1-10.

Gangte, T.S., (2003), *The Kukis of Manipur: A Historical Analysis*, New Delhi: Gyan Publishing House.

Ghurye, G.S. (1963), (3rd edition), *The Scheduled Tribes*, Bombay: Popular Prakashan.

Goldenweiser, A.A. (1917), 'Religion and Society: A Critique of Émile Durkheim's Theory of the Origin and Nature of Religion', *The Journal of Philosophy, Psychology and Scientific Methods*, 14(5), 113-124, https://www.jstor.org/stable/2940655.

Goldstein, W.S., R. King, and J. Boyarin, (2016), 'Critical Theory of Religion Vs. Critical Religion', *Critical Research on Religion, 4*(1), pp. 3-7.

Gonmei, L., (2011), 'God and Goddesses of the Zeliangrong Community', in Chaoba Kamson (ed.), *Socio-Cultural and Spiritual Traditions of Zeliangrongs (Manipur, Nagaland and Assam)*, Guwahati: Heritage Foundation, pp. 54-8.

Gordon, C. (ed.), (1980), *Power/ Knowledge: Selected Interviews and Other Writings* 1972-1977, (trans.) Colin Gordon, Leo Marshall, John Mepham and Kate Soper, New York: Pantheon Books.

Greene, S., (2004), 'Social Identity Theory and Party Identification', *Social Science Quarterly, 85* (1), pp. 136-53.

Hallinan, M.T., (1997), 'The Sociological Study of Social Change: 1996 Presidential address', *American Sociological Review, 62* (1), pp. 1-11.

Hamilton, W.H., (1915), 'Economic Theory and "Social Reform"', *Journal of Political Economy, 23* (6), pp. 562-84. https://www.jstor.org/stable/1820938.

Harris, H., (2001), 'Content Analysis of Secondary Data: A Study of Courage in Managerial Decision Making', *Journal of Business Ethics, 34 (3/4)*, pp. 191-208, http://www.jstor.org/stable/25074634.

Heiser, M.S., (2008), 'Monotheism, Polytheism, Monolatry, or Henotheism? Toward an Assessment of Divine Plurality in the Hebrew Bible', *Bulletin for Biblical Research*, 18 (1), pp. 1-30.

Higham, T., T. Compton, C. Stringer, R. Jacobi, B. Shapiro, E. Erik Trinkaus, B. Chandler, F. Groning, C. Collins, S. Hillson, P. O'Higgins, C. FitzGerald, and M. Fagan, (2011), 'The Earliest Evidence for Anatomically Modern Humans in Northwestern Europe', *Nature*, p. 479, doi:10.1038/nature10484.

Hodson, T.C., (1908), *The Meitheis* (With an Introduction by Sir Charles J. Lyall), London: David Nutt.

______, (1911), *The Naga Tribes of Manipur*, London: Macmillan and Co.

Hoover, D.R. (2006), 'Getting Religion', *The Review of Faith and International Affairs*, 4(1), 1-1, DOI: 10.1080/15570274.2006.9523231.

Hout, M., (2017), 'American Religion, All or Nothing at all', *Contexts, 16* (4), pp. 78-80.

Howerth, I.W. (1903), 'What is Religion?', *International Journal of Ethics*, 13(2), pp. 185-206, http://www.jstor.org/stable/2376451.

Ife, J., (2001), *Human Rights and Social Work: Towards Rights-Based Practice*, New York: Cambridge University Press.

Ingersoll, R.G. (1899), *What is Religion?*, Baltimore: Phoenix Publishing Co.

Iyer, V.R.K., (1994), 'Saga of the Nagas', *Economic and Political Weekly, 29 (12)*, pp. 674-8, http://www.jstor.org/stable/4400958.

Jakelić, S. and J. Starling, (2006), 'Religious Studies: A Bibliographic Essay',

Journal of the American Academy of Religion, 74 (1), pp. 194-211, http://www.jstor.org/stable/4094090?seq=1andcid=pdf-reference #references_tab_contents.

Joppke, C., (2018), 'Culturalizing Religion in Western Europe: Patterns and Puzzles', *Social Compass*, 65 (2), pp. 1-13, DOI: 10.1177/00377686 18767962.

Kabui, G., (1979), 'Social and Religious Reform Movements in Manipur', in S.P. Sen (ed.), *Social and Religious Movements in the Nineteenth and Twentieth Centuries*, Calcutta: Institute of Historical Studies, pp. 411-24.

Kabui, G.L., (2018), *The Zeliangrong Villages in the Valley of Manipur: A Historical Perspective*, Guwahati: Eastern Book House.

Kamei, B., (6 December 2012), *Tingkao Ragwang Chapriak: Part 1, E-pao*, Retrieved from http://www.epao.net/epSubPageExtractor.asp?src= manipur.Manipur_and_Religion.Tingkao_Ragwang_Chapriak_ Part_1.

——— (21 September 2018), 'Traditional Beliefs and Practices of the Zeliangrong: Constitution of a New Village', *Sangai Express*.

Kamei, G. (2004), *A History of the Zeliangrong Nagas: From Makhel to Rani Gaidinliu*, Guwahati: Spectrum Publications.

——— (2006), *Essays on Primordial Religion*, New Delhi: Akansha Publishing House.

——— (2009) [1997, 2002], *Jadonang: A Mystic Naga Rebel*. Imphal: Smt. G. Lanshailu Kamei.

——— (2015) (3rd revd. edn.), *History of Manipur: Pre-Colonial Period*, Delhi: Akansha Publishing House.

Kameshore, K., (24 May 2016), 'The Silent Demographic Influx of Imphal Valley', *Imphal Free Press*, retrieved from http://www.ifp.co.in/page/items/32239/the-silentdemographic-influx-of-imphal-valley.

Kamson, C., (2009), *Tingkao Ragwang Chapriak: Ra Pari*, Imphal: Jashillu Kamson.

———, (2011a), 'Proceedings of the workshop', in Chaoba Kamson (ed.), *Sociocultural and Spiritual Traditions of Zeliangrongs (Manipur, Nagaland and Assam)*, Guwahati: Heritage Foundation, pp. 7-22.

———, (2011b), 'Concept of Soul in Tingkao Ragwang Chapriak', in Chaoba Kamson (ed.), *Socio-Cultural and Spiritual Traditions of Zeliangrongs (Manipur, Nagaland and Assam)*, Guwahati: Heritage Foundation, pp. 45-53.

———, (2012), *Tingkao Ragwang Chapriak Thoushumei Kashoi Kadam*. N.p.: Tingkao Ragwang Chapriak Phom (Assam, Manipur and Nagaland).

______, (2014), *Maku Banru Khatni Taraang Laangpatmei*, Hiyangthang (Imphal): The Family Members of M. Ganglaona.

Kashyap, S.G., (2018), *Religion, Movement and Community Relationship: A Close Look at Majuli*. Abstract submitted for a two-day national seminar on 'Culturo-Religious Transition among the Native Communities of Northeast India' dated 9-10 September 2018, jointly organised by India Foundation, New Delhi, Department of Social Work (Indira Gandhi National Tribal University, Regional Campus, Manipur) and Centre for Manipur Studies, Manipur University at Imphal in Manipur.

Kishimoto, H., (1967), 'Religiology', *Numen, 14* (Fasc. 2), pp. 81-6, http://www.jstor.org/stable/3269522.

Kumar, P., (2004), 'A Survey of New Approaches to the Study of Religion in India', in Peter Antes, Armin W. Geertz, Randi R.Warne (eds.), *New Approaches to the Study of Religion*, Berlin: Walter de Gruyter, pp. 127-45.

Kumar, P.B.B., (1971), *Liangmai-Hindi-English Dictionary*, Kohima: Nagaland Bhasha Parishad.

Lapier, Rosalyn R., (2017), 'Montana Mussel: Mythology and Ecology', *Montana Naturalist*.

______, (15 June 2018), 'How Native American food is tied to important sacred stories', *The Conversation*, retrieved from https://theconversation.com/how-native-american-food-is-tiedto-important-sacred-stories-97770.

Leach, E.R., (2004), *Political Systems of Highland Burma: A Study of Kachin Social Structure*, Oxford: Berg.

Lindgren, T., (2014), 'Hjalmar Sunden's Impact on the Study of Religion in the Nordic Countries', *Temenos, 50* (1), pp. 39-61.

Longkumer, A., (2007), 'Religious and Economic Reform: The Gaidinliu Movement and the Heraka in the North Cachar Hills', *South Asia: Journal of South Asian Studies, 30* (3), pp. 499-515, http://dx.doi.org/10.1080/00856400701714096.

______, (2010), *Reform, Identity and Narratives of Belonging: The Heraka Movement of Northeast India*, London: Continuum International Publishing Group.

Longmei, L., (2010), *Kabuimei Khum-Ngai Lon*, Chinikon, Senapati District (Manipur): Kabui Literature Research Akademi (A text in Rongmei language written in Bengali script).

Macgowan, R. and C. Darrow, (1931), *Is Religion Necessary?*, Girard, Kansas: Haldeman-Julius Publications.

Malone, J. and A. Dadswell, (2018), 'The Role of Religion, Spirituality and/or Belief in Positive Ageing for Older Adults', *Geriatrics (Basel), 3* (2), p. 28, DOI: 10.3390/geriatrics3020028.

Maremmei, K. (ed.), (2015), *RNBA Centre Church, Imphal Silver Jubilee (1990-2015) Souvenir*, Imphal: Silver Jubilee Committee, RNBACCI.

Martineau, H., (1848), *Eastern Life: Present and Past*, Philadelphia: Lea and Blanchard.

Martineau, J., (1888), *A Study of Religion: Its Sources and Contents*, London: Oxford.

McCorkle, W.P., (n.d.), (revised edition), *Anti-Christian Sociology, As Taught in The Journal of Social Forces- Presenting a Question for North Carolina Christians*, Burlington, N.C.: A.D. Pate & Co. Printers.

Modi, N., (4 October 2018), 'In Harmony with Mother Nature', *The Hindu*, retrieved from https://www.thehindu.com/opinion/op-ed/inharmony-with-mothernature/article25115350.ece.

Morrison, K., (2008) [2006], *Marx, Durkheim, Weber: Formations of Modern Social Thought*, New Delhi: Sage Publications India Pvt. Ltd.

Mukherjee, D.P., P. Gupta, and N.K. Das (1982), 'The Zeliangrong or Haomei Movement', in K.S. Singh (ed.), *Tribal Movements in India* vol. I, New Delhi: Manohar, pp. 67-95.

Muller, F.M., (1878), *Origin and Growth of Religion: As Illustrated by the Religions of India*, London: Longmans Green and Co.

______, (1881), *Selected Essays on Language, Mythology and Religion*, vol. II, London: Longmans Green and Co.

______, (1898), *Theosophy or Psychological Religion*, London: Longmans Green and Co.

Newme, P., (2011a), *Heraka: The Primordial Religion and its Revitalization Movement*, Assam: Zeliangrong Heraka Association.

______, (2011b), 'Heraka: The Primordial Religion of Zeliangrongs', in Chaoba Kamson (ed.), *Socio-Cultural and Spiritual Traditions of Zeliangrongs (Manipur, Nagaland and Assam)*, Guwahati: Heritage Foundation, pp. 23-44.

Pamei, K., (2009), *Ruangmei Pary Khatni Chapriak*, Imphal (Manipur): Kalauna Pamei.

Pamei, N., (2001), *The Trail from Makuilungdi: The Continuing Saga of the Zeliangrong People*, Manipur: Gironta Charitable Foundation.

______, (2006), *Naga Crucible: Fifty Years of a Movement in Search of its People*, Tamenglong: Gironta Charitable Foundation.

Pamei, R. (1996), *The Zeliangrong Nagas: A Study of Tribal Christianity*, New Delhi: Uppal Publishing House.

Panikkar, K.N., (2013), *History as a Site of Struggle: Essays on History, Culture and Politics*, New Delhi: Three Essays Collective.

Parker, T., (1907), *A Discourse of Matters Pertaining to Religion*, Boston: American Unitarian Association.

Parsons, T., (1951), *The Social System,* New York: Free Press.

Peoples, H.C., P. Duda and F.W. Marlowe, (2016), 'Hunter-Gatherers and the Origins of Religion', *Human Nature, 27*, pp. 261-82, DOI 10.1007/ s12110-016-9260-0.

Petrovich, O., (2007), 'Key Psychological Issues in the Study of Religion', *Psihologija, 40* (3), pp. 351-63.

Phillips, N. and C. Hardy (2002), *Discourse Analysis: Investigating Processes of Social Construction*, Sage University papers series on Qualitative Research Methods, vol. 50, Thousand Oaks, CA: Sage.

Pisharoty, P.R., (1982), *C.V. Raman*, New Delhi: Ministry of Information and Broadcasting, Govt. of India.

Pratt, J.B., (1920), *The Religious Consciousness: A Psychological Study*, New York: The Macmillan Company.

Prest, L.A., R. Russel and H. D'Souza, (1999), 'Spirituality and Religion in Training, Practice and Personal Development', *Journal of Family Therapy, 21*, pp. 60-77.

Prins, G., (1992), 'Oral History', in Peter Burke (ed.), *New Perspectives on Historical Writing*, UK: Polity Press, pp. 114-39.

Pummer, R., (1975), 'Recent Publications on the Methodology of the Science of Religion', *Numen, 22* (3), pp. 161-82, http://www.jstor.org/stable/3269543.

Qi, X., (2017), 'Neo-traditional Child Surnaming in Contemporary China: Women's Rights as Veiled Patriarchy', *Sociology*, pp. 1-16, DOI: 10.1177/0038038516688613.

Rajukumari, T., (2012), *Ethnic Process in North-East India: A Study of the Sociopolitical Movement of the Zemis, Liangmeis and Rongmeis (Zeliangrongs) During the 20th Century*, New Delhi: Rajesh Publications.

Rao, M.S.A., (1984), 'Conceptual Problems in the Study of Social Movement', in M.S.A. Rao (ed.), *Social Movements in India: Studies in Peasant, Backward Classes, Sectarian, Tribal and Women's Movement*, New Delhi: Manohar Publishers, pp. 1-15.

Rashdall, H., (1910), *Philosophy and Religion*, New York: Charles Scribner's Sons.

Robinson, T.H., (1926), *An Outline Introduction to the History of Religions*, London: Oxford University Press.

Robinson, R. and S. Clarke, (2007), 'Introduction', in Rowena Robinson and Sathianathan Clarke (eds.), *Religious Conversion in India: Modes, Motivations, and Meanings,* New Delhi: Oxford University Press, pp. 1-21.

Rockmore, T., (2006), 'Before and After 9/11', *Ars Disputandi, 6* (1), pp. 115-27, http://dx.doi.org/10.1080/15665399.2006.10819913.

Rogers, D., (2005), 'Introductory Essay: The Anthropology of Religion after Socialism', *Religion, State* and *Society, 33* (1), pp. 5-18.

Rongmei, K.S. and S. Kapoor, (2005), 'Zeliangrong Today: A Naga Tribe of Manipur', *Studies of Tribes and Tribals, 3* (2), pp. 105-16.

Rootes, C.A., (1990), 'Theory of Social Movements: Theory *for* Social Movements?', *Philosophy and Social Action, 16* (4), pp. 5-17, retrieved from www.kent.ac.uk/sspssr/staff/rootes.htm.

Roy, B., (2013), 'Mapping the Heraka Identity: Are we Engaged Truly?', *Economic and Political Weekly, 48* (40), pp. 76-8.

Roy, J., (1973), *History of Manipur*, Imphal, Manipur: The Author.

Ruether, R.R., (1990), 'Prophets and Humanists: Types of Religious Feminism in Stuart England', *The Journal of Religion, 70* (1), pp. 1-18, http://www.jstor.org/stable/1203680.

Rush, G.B. and R.S. Denisoff, (1971), *Social and Political Movements*, New York: Meredith Corporation.

Salam, R., (8 January 2017), 'Gangmumei Kamei: Bridging the Ethnic Lines', *The People's Chronicle*.

Samson, Kamei (2015a), 'Identity Construction and Constitutional Recognition: An Experience of Zeliangrong', in Alex Akhup (ed.), *Tribal and Adivasi Studies: Lived and Shared Experience from Within* Kolkata: Adivaani Publication House, pp. 327-72.

———, (2015b), 'Resilience of Ideology as a Vanguard of Movement: A Study of North Eastern Turbulence', *Social Change*, 45 (1), pp. 95-106, DOI: 10.1177/0049085714561838.

Schmalzbauer, J. and K.A. Mahoney, (2008), 'American scholars return to studying religion', *Contexts, 7 (1)*, pp. 16-21, DOI: 10.1525/ctx.2008.7.1.16.

Seale, C., (1998), 'Introduction', in Clive Seale (ed.), *Researching Society and Culture,* London: Sage Publications, pp. 1-4.

Sen, A., (2006), *Identity and Violence: The Illusion of Destiny*, Great Britain: Penguin books.

Sen, S., (1987), *Tribes of Nagaland*, Delhi: Mittal Publications.

Singh, C., (2018), *Himalayan Histories: Economy, Polity, Religious Traditions*, Ranikhet, Uttarakhand: Permanent Black.

Singh, N.J. (2005a), *Social Movements in Manipur*, New Delhi: Mittal Publications.

——— (2005b), *Revolutionary Movements in Manipur*, New Delhi: Akansha Publishing House.

Singh, R.K.J., (1975), *States of Our Union: Manipur*, New Delhi: Ministry of Information and Broadcasting, Government of India.

Smith et al., (2013), 'Roundtable on the Sociology of Religion: Twenty-Three Theses on the Status of Religion in American Sociology—A MellonWorking-Group Reflection', *Journal of the American Academy of Religion*, pp. 1-36. DOI:10.1093/jaarel/lft052.

Srinivas, M.N., (1952), *Religion and Society Among the Coorgs of South India*, Bombay: Asia Publishing House.

Starr, L., (1996), 'Oral History', in David K. Dunaway and Willa K. Baum (eds.), *Oral History: An Interdisciplinary Anthology*, New Delhi: Alta Mira Press, pp. 39-61.

Tajfel, H. and J.C. Turner, (1979), 'An Integrative Theory of Intergroup Conflict', in W.G. Austin, and S. Worchel (eds.), *The Social Psychology of Intergroup Relations*, Monterey, CA: Brooks/Cole, pp. 33-7.

______, (1986), 'The Social Identity Theory of Intergroup Behavior', in Stephen Worchel and William G. Austin (eds.), *Psychology of Intergroup Relations*, Chicago: Nelson-Hall, pp. 276-93.

Tiba, Th. R., (2006), *History and Culture of the Maram Nagas: A Reconstruction from Oral and Folklore Traditions*, Unpublished Doctoral Thesis. Silchar (Assam): Assam University, retrieved from http://hdl.handle.net/10603/93525.

Tharoor, S., (2018), *Why I am a Hindu*, New Delhi: Aleph Book Company.

Tilly, C. (1978), *From Mobilization to Revolution*, New York: Random House.

Trueblood, D.E., (1957), *Philosophy of Religion*, New York: Harper and Row Publishers.

Tylor, E.B., (1871), *Primitive Culture: Researches into the Development of Mythology, Philosophy, Religion Language, Art, and Custom*, vol. I, London: John Murray.

______, (1958), *Origins of Culture*, New York: Evanston, Harper and Row Publishers.

Vansina, J., (1996), 'Oral Tradition and Historical Methodology', in David K. Dunaway, and Willa K. Baum (eds.), *Oral History: An Interdisciplinary Anthology*, New Delhi: Alta Mira Press, pp. 121-5.

Vijay, H., (2015), 'Apologetic Hinduism Sowed the Seeds for Aggressive Hindutva', *The Week*, p. 18.

Wald, K.D. and C. Wilcox, (2006), 'Getting Religion: Has Political Science Rediscovered the Faith Factor?', *American Political Science Review, 100* (4), pp. 522-9.

Ward, D.J.H., (1888), *How Religion Arises: A Psychological Study*, Geo. H. Ellis.: Boston.

Weber, M., (1930/1904), *The Protestant Ethic and the Spirit of Capitalism*, (trans.) Talcott Parsons, London: Unwin University Books.

——— (1978), *Economy and Society: An Outline of Interpretative Sociology*, vol. 1, ed. Guenther Roth and Claus Wittich, Berkeley: University of California Press.

Wilson, J., (1973), *Introduction to Social Movements*, New York: Basic Books, Inc. Publishers.

Xaxa, V., (2009), 'Tribes, Conversion and the Sangh Parivar', in Dharmendra Kumar and Yemuna Sunny (eds.), *Proselytization in India: The Process of Hinduisation in Tribal Societies,* Delhi: Aakar, pp. 19-36.

Yonuo, A., (1982), *Nagas Struggle Against the British Rule under Jadonang and Rani Gaidinliu 1925-1947*, Kohima: Leno Printing Press.

Zehol, L., (1998), *Ethnicity in Manipur: Experiences, Issues, and Perspectives*, New Delhi: Regency Publications.

Zeliang, N.C., (2003), 'Haipou Jadonang: The Great Freedom Fighter', in *Naga Dawn, Souvenir Zeliangrong Heraka Youth Organisation, Silver Jubilee 1978-2003*, Nagaland: Zeliangrong Heraka Youth Organisation.

Zeliangrong Heraka Association (Assam, Manipur and Nagaland), (2011), *Heraka: The Primordial Religion and its Revitalization Movement*, Assam: Zeliangrong Heraka Association.

Index